PERFORMING ARTS BROADCASTING

THE LIBRARY OF CONGRESS   WASHINGTON   2002

ISBN 0-8444-1007-1
ISSN 0887-8234

For sale by the U.S. Government Printing Office
Superintendent of Documents, Mail Stop: SSOP, Washington, DC 20402-9328

Cover
Jack Benny and Fred Allen, 1936

CONTENTS

Editor
Iris Newsom

Publisher
W. Ralph Eubanks

Designer
Stephen Kraft

Production Manager
Gloria Baskerville-Holmes

Production Assistant
Clarke Allen

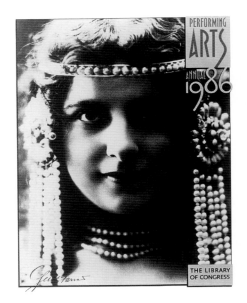

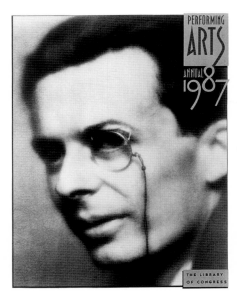

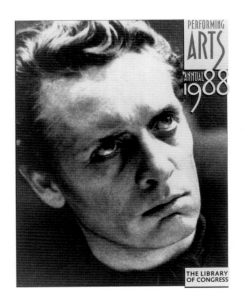

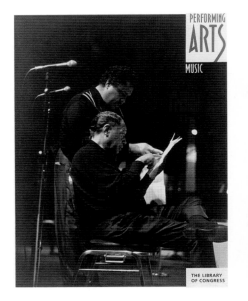

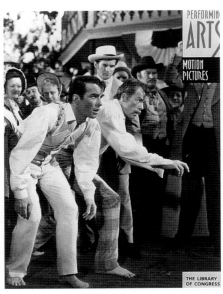

Editor's Note

In this final volume of the Performing Arts series, we concentrate on the Library's unsurpassed radio and television holdings.

Our overview of the Library's radio holdings begins with Karen Hanson's discussion of Mary Margaret McBride's radio interviews of accomplished and influential personalities that provides valuable insights into the pre- and post-World War II era. On a parallel though more proletarian track, Donald Kent's analysis of radio advice shows over the past fifty years reveals the dramatic behavioral and moral differences between past and present-day callers and advisors. Many fascinating tales of early radio emerge from Kathleen Miller's study of the Library's NBC Collection and Alan Gevinson's of the "documentaries" produced by the Radio Research Project of the Library of Congress. The story of Hollywood's influence upon early radio is told by Ross Care, and Peter Rohrbach describes how radio kept the American people vividly aware of the World War II conflict during the years before the United States entered into it.

Donald Kent describes how television producers in the fifties created audiences for arts-related programming by developing lively ways of presenting ballet, opera, and theater. He contends that *Omnibus* proved that culture and mass audiences could be compatible. Also in the fifties, the recorded works of television composers became part of huge recorded music libraries, and Paul Mandell traces the history and fate of this music–and of the people who composed and performed it. Krin Gabbard discusses early television's view of jazz performers as serious artists, a tradition which has helped create the image of jazz as being the artistic and creative equal of ballet, opera, and symphonic music. In our final televison article, Barbara Pruett follows the career of Groucho Marx from vaudeville, film, and radio, to his successful role as host of *You Bet Your Life*.

This editor's tribute to Gerry Mulligan traces his sixty-year career, which firmly established him as one of the great jazz innovators, and describes the opening of a permanent Library of Congress exhibition for the Gerry Mulligan Collection.

Since 1986, this series has presented articles on all aspects of performing arts in the Library's collections, and there have also been volumes specifically devoted to music and motion pictures, as this one has concentrated on radio and television. We hope you will visit the Library's Web site and continue to learn about the Library's impressive and constantly growing performing arts collections at <http://lcweb.loc.gov>.

As we cease publication of this series in book form, I would like particularly to thank our authors, who have produced articles of scholarly value in a manner comprehensible to the educated nonspecialist; the Library's reference staff and Publishing Office production staff, who have been so generous with their time and expertise, thereby assuring the accuracy of the articles and the high production values of the publication; Stephen Kraft, our designer, whose infinite patience and good taste have proved invaluable over the years; and our readers, whose informative and encouraging letters have assured us that this publication reached and has been disseminated by a varied audience of performing arts professionals, students, and devotees.

IRIS NEWSOM

Radio

"It's one o'clock and here is Mary Margaret McBride"

EARLY RADIO HOLDINGS
IN THE
COLLECTIONS OF
THE LIBRARY
OF CONGRESS

BY **KAREN HANSEN**

■ **Mary Margaret McBride and her associate, Vincent Connolly, celebrate an anniversary of the *Martha Deane Show* on WOR.**

Decades before a book endorsement from Oprah Winfrey emptied bookstores and library shelves or an hour of questions from Barbara Walters signaled a person's cultural weight, broadcaster Mary Margaret McBride delivered a unique mix of interviews with newsmakers and practical philosophy to a devoted audience of women that topped six million daily. From the 1930s through the 1950s, McBride created an unusual radio show composed of celebrity interviews, chatter, and shrewd advice, punctuated with rapturous pitches for her sponsors. This appealing, somewhat offbeat format managed to shatter the accepted format of women's programming and attract a loyal following who yearned for more than household cleaning tips and recipes for molded salads. Her ability to move effortlessly between a riveting discussion with an accomplished or influential person to an ecstatic promotion of a sponsor's product resulted in a captivating broadcast that proved both enormously popular and commercially successful. McBride should be regarded as the matriarch in the family of contemporary television and radio broadcasters for she pioneered the ad libbed, natural sounding interview, she filled her line-up with intriguing people, and she was an expert businesswoman. McBride's success allowed her to attract accomplished and influential guests, including people like Supreme Court Justice William O. Douglas, Langston Hughes, Gertrude Lawrence, Eleanor Roosevelt, and even news photographer Weegee. McBride's show is significant historically because her interviews and her dialogue open a window onto the cultural landscape of America from the 1930s through the 1950s.

When McBride died in 1976, her friend and fellow journalist, Cynthia Lowry, donated McBride's radio broadcasts and her papers to the Library of Congress. The collection consists of materials from the 1930s through the 1970s and includes radio transcriptions, photographs, newspaper clippings, awards, correspondence, and magazines. The Motion Picture, Broadcasting, and Recorded Sound Division is the primary repository of the Lowry Collection that includes over one thousand hours of radio programming. The division holds additional McBride materials in the NBC Radio Collection. The transcription discs include recordings from the 1930s when McBride hosted the *Martha Deane Show* over WOR, and recordings from her later radio career on CBS, NBC, and ABC. There are recordings of McBride covering both the Democratic and Republican political conventions in 1944 and 1948 and of

■ **McBride interviews Pres. Harry S Truman and one of her favorite guests, Eleanor Roosevelt.**

McBride's eyewitness account of Pres. Harry S Truman's 1949 inaugural ceremonies. The Library's collection also numbers broadcasts featuring Mary Margaret as a guest, and four 16 mm films, including a 1952 film of President Eisenhower's inauguration. The Manuscript Division is the repository of additional papers from McBride that include correspondence, notes on shows, publicity releases, and clippings. The scope and magnitude of the holdings constitute a collection that extensively documents the writing and broadcasting career of Mary Margaret McBride.

Mary Margaret McBride was born in Paris, Missouri, in 1899. She worked her way through the University of Missouri reporting for the *Times* of Columbia, Missouri. She graduated with a degree in journalism and worked for the *Cleveland Press* before landing a public relations job in 1920 with the New York-based Inter-Church World Movement. She left public relations to cover a city beat for the *New York Evening Mail*. McBride launched a successful freelance writing career as a sideline in 1924, penning articles for magazines, including *Cosmopolitan* and *Good Housekeeping*. McBride wrote several books, including *Jazz*, with Paul Whiteman and *Paris Is a Woman's Town*, with Helen Josephy.

McBride's radio career was born from her dwindling bank account. Her lucrative freelance writing career crashed with the stock market in 1929. McBride needed money, so her agent suggested she audition for a daytime radio program in development at WOR in New York City. McBride once told Bennett Cerf she landed the job "because I was the only one of fifty applicants who made no salary demands . . . I meant to but I just forgot. I think that's why they gave me the nod." McBride made her radio debut as Martha Deane, a sage midwestern grandmother, over WOR in 1933.

Radio was a relatively new medium when McBride embarked on her broadcasting career. The concept of a woman hosting a radio program was groundbreaking in the early 1930s. WOR envisioned the *Martha Deane Show* as a woman's program where a wise, experienced woman would share recipes, dispense child-raising tips and offer advice on home management. The producers created a fictitious background for Deane, complete with children and grandchildren. McBride acted the role of Martha Deane throughout the entire program. However, she found it troublesome to remain in character and stumbled over the grandchildren's names and mixed up the lives of the various children. After a few programs, McBride claimed she confessed on the air, "I can't do it! I'm not a grandmother! I'm not a mother. I'm not even married . . . I'm a reporter who would like to come here every day and tell you about places I go, people I meet." She then launched into a vivid description of a flea circus she witnessed the previous evening along 42nd Street in Manhattan. Her colorful words and dramatic narrative of the fleas and their behavior brought the event to life for listeners at home. WOR management decided not to fire her until they could gauge the audience reaction to McBride's confession. Listener response was overwhelmingly supportive of the change in the show's format, and McBride received permission to broadcast a show that allowed her to utilize her journalistic skills more fully. McBride gained editorial control, which was unusual for a radio personality or a woman at that time. Each day, McBride described the places she had been, restaurants where she had eaten, and what was happening in New York City. As a journalist and writer, she knew what elements made up a good story. She used her talent to create a radio show that made the sights and sounds of New York come alive for listeners. McBride said that she planned her program by imagining what she would like to learn about if she were a listener. The formula worked.

Estella Karn, her business manager, always looked for ways to keep McBride one step ahead of other daytime shows. She suggested that McBride interview celebrities. The first guest in 1934 was Eva Le Gallienne, who read Portia's "Quality of Mercy" speech from *The Merchant of Venice*. The performance proved so popular that McBride and Karn added the celebrity interview as a regular feature on the *Martha Deane* show.

McBride earned the reputation of being a skillful interviewer; she put her guests at ease and she had a talent for getting people to open up and talk about themselves. Celebrity interviews became an integral portion of the format on McBride's subsequent shows over CBS, NBC-WEAF, and ABC.

McBride developed her trademark "ad-lib" style of interviewing in her years as Martha Deane. She rejected the use of prewritten interview questions—they read like scripts—that were the norm at that time in radio. In the 1930s, network executives were too nervous about the potential loss of control and the editorial risks to allow unstructured interviews on the air. Radio interviews tended to follow a formula, with the broadcaster working from a script of questions. The result was an interview that sounded unnatural and stiff. Unscripted broadcasting was limited primarily to breaking news stories and sports coverage. McBride changed all that.

By dispensing with scripted questions, McBride moved the radio interview to a new, more conversational level. However, her interview questions were not tossed out randomly. She spent hours doing background research for each interview. She entered the studio armed with notes that she compiled after hours of study, often reading three books in one evening. She and her assistant, Janice Devine, managed to dig up obscure facts on guests, and McBride used this information to loosen up the interviewee. When McBride interviewed an author, she read his or her most recent book and any other publications written by the guest she could consume in one or two nights. "Sometimes I read three books in a single night, making rapid notes until 3:00 a.m. or after and memorizing details until I was able, when I opened my eyes next morning, to recite to myself more questions and answers than could ever be used in a single broadcast and this without reference to the notes," McBride commented. McBride was rumored to decline social invitations unless the host could convince her there was a potential story idea in the evening's activities. McBride's intensive preparation resulted in interviews with celebrities and guests that were both interesting and spiced with intimate details about the guest's personal life. Her research efforts paid off in the quality of her program. The interviews sound very relaxed and natural, almost like a chat with the next-door neighbor, but the dialogue remains highly informative.

During her years as Martha Deane, McBride assembled the four-person staff that would remain with her throughout most of her broadcasting career. Estella Karn, her business manager and producer, had known McBride since her days at the Inter-Church Center. In the 1920s, Karn and McBride had shared a Greenwich Village apartment with journalist Pauline Pfeiffer, later a wife of Ernest Hemingway. Estella functioned as a producer, making suggestions on ways to entertain the radio audience and developing strategies to increase audience loyalty. For example, Karn suggested that McBride cultivate her fans by personally answering their letters. The McBride staff maintained a file of fan letters and they filled the studio audience with listeners who had sent in letters. When McBride entered the studio, she shook hands with members of the audience, chatted with people, and often asked after someone's family. She remembered what people wrote to her and she used this information in her small talk. Her personal attention to a fan's life created a warm, almost homey atmosphere in the studio, and her concern helped build a large following of loyal listeners who felt they were friends of Mary Margaret McBride. Fans sent her samplers and dolls and gifts of food. Over the air, McBride read letters from fans, including advertising jingles they composed about her sponsors. An

■ Maine guide and expert fly tier Bert Quimby presents a streamer fly to Mary Margaret McBride on the *Martha Deane Show* in 1936. McBride interviewed ordinary people with unusual hobbies and occupations, as well as celebrities, on her show.

■ McBride talks with intelligent youngsters who field questions on the radio series, *The Quiz Kids*.

■ McBride's celebrity status made her a sought after panelist, spokesperson, and speaker. McBride prepares to baby-sit Melissa Montgomery, daughter of singer Dinah Shore and actor George Montgomery, to raise money for a charity.

example of this can be heard on a show from February 1939, where she seamlessly moves from the tetrahedral sails on Alexander Graham Bell's kites, to a description of sheathed mannequins in a shop window, to an exclamation that the clothed mannequins cause her to think of La France and Sateena (washing products from her advertisers), to the comments offered by a listener from Ohio on the value of La France and Sateena! She even received fan mail from celebrities and prominent listeners. John Farrar of the Farrar, Straus, and Young publishing house wrote, "I just can't help writing to someone . . . the fact that she doesn't

began working with McBride in 1935 on the *Martha Deane Show*. He was her timekeeper and her organization man, reminding her to move on to her commercials, nudging her to stick to the topic, and signaling when the hour was up. A bachelor, his personal life was often the topic of lively on-air discussions. These four people remained with McBride throughout her broadcasting career. Their talent, dedication, and exhaustive effort contributed to the success of the McBride programs.

McBride had a tendency to think out loud and share her feelings with the audience. She talked about her family and

■ Recipients of the Associated Press Poll's Outstanding Women of the Year award visit the Mary Margaret McBride show. Left to right, Dorothy Roe (Woman's Editor, Associated Press), Barnard college Dean Millicent McIntosh, author Pearl Buck, actress Gloria Swanson, Vivian Kellems, and McBride.

talk down to her public and that actually it becomes, to use a cliché, a magical education to anyone who listens regularly." For better or worse, the Library does not hold many of Mary Margaret's fan letters. When the government faced a paper shortage during World War II, she relinquished over three-and-a-half million fan letters she had in storage to support the war effort.

Another staffer, Janice Devine was a combination of researcher, producer, and booker. She checked leads for stories and she drafted show proposals for McBride. There are examples of Devine's proposals in the Manuscript Division at the Library. She preinterviewed prospective guests to make sure they were fairly articulate and unlikely to freeze up in a broadcast.

Hilda Deichler, her secretary, began working for McBride in her days as a freelance writer. Vincent Connolly was her announcer and straight man. Connolly

she shared details with listeners from the private lives of her staff members. She puzzled over trends in society, described meals in rapturous detail, and commented on her previous day's activity. What was most unusual was her degree of openness and self-criticism. For example, in a February 6, 1939, CBS broadcast centered on Norman Dine's sleep quotient theory, McBride laments, "I didn't call my mother last night at 10:00 because I was quarreling with Stella Karn. I couldn't sleep because I was sick with worry over the fight. . . ." By candidly discussing her own fears and human failing with the audience, she forged a bond with her listeners that caused the audience to view her as a friend. McBride's sincerity inspired trust in the listeners, and the dedication of the audience was a key element in the financial and editorial success of her program.

In 1941, NBC offered her forty-five minutes each weekday at 1 p.m. The *Mary Margaret McBride Show* broadcast over radio station WEAF(NBC) from 1941 to 1950. The *Mary Margaret McBride Show* devoted the first two-thirds of the program to talk and interviews and the remaining fifteen minutes were reserved for advertising plugs. During these years, her skill at interviewing, her talent for storytelling, her disarming style, and her shrewd salesmanship coalesced to produce a program unlike any other radio show. McBride's signature formula proved extremely popular with listeners, guests, and the program's sponsors.

McBride managed to interview the most influential people of her time and she discussed topics and issues that may have been foreign or even radical to the listeners at home. She discussed topics as wide ranging as theater, World War II, civil rights, psychology, and women's careers. She featured guests as disparate as the sixteen-year-old Dionne Quintuplets (who sang "East Side, West Side" in memory of Al Smith) and architect Frank Lloyd Wright. While McBride named Eleanor Roosevelt and Fiorello LaGuardia as her favorite guests, she once said explorers and authors were the best subjects for interviews. According to McBride, explorers relayed exciting and exotic tales, and authors were easy to research because she could just read their books.

McBride's show was one the first broadcasts to feature authors promoting their new books. Authors clamored to come on her show because an interview with McBride translated into a sales boost, and writers enjoyed being interviewed by her because she always read their work. Author and playwright Robert Sherwood wrote to a radio executive, "As her guest, you forget the mike and really enjoy yourself. When she asked me about my book she recited long passages from it, word for word." She made guests feel comfortable and they opened up to her. She was not interested in promoting herself and she made the guest feel as if he or she was the most important element of the show. The McBride Collection includes interviews with authors Vladimir Nabokov, William L. Shirer, Rachel Carson, Ralph Ellison, Edna Ferber, William Carlos Williams, Christopher Isherwood, and Erle Stanley Gardner. Guests ranged from playwrights Arthur Miller and Tennessee Williams to chefs and food writers like James Beard and Irma Rombauer, author of the classic *Joy of Cooking*. McBride talked with Laura Hobson, whose novel *Gentlemen's Agreement* addressed anti-Semitism, and southern writer Lillian Smith,

■ McBride features folk singer Woody Guthrie and a representative of the bulb association of the Netherlands.

whose haunting images of lynchings indicted racism in her book, *Strange Fruit*. On one broadcast, *New Yorker* writer and essayist Janet Flanner is interrupted by a news flash from the Pacific during World War II; on another, poet Langston Hughes gives a haunting and emotional reading of his poem, "A Negro Looks at Rivers" in 1945. McBride considered a 1952 broadcast featuring National Book Award winners Rachel Carson, Marianne Moore, and James Jones to be her literary coup. "I practically cut out the commercials that day," McBride remarked. When you listen to McBride interview authors, you gain new insight and perspective on why the writers wrote what they wrote. The writers tend to talk about the themes they made famous in their writing and they address the issues and ideas for which they became known.

Each day, Vincent Connolly opened the program with, "It's one o'clock and here is Mary Margaret McBride." McBride finished his announcement by introducing the topic of the day's show or by giving background information on the guest. For example, in a June 30, 1947, broadcast featuring Eleanor Roosevelt, McBride continues with "who just saw a wonderful movie last night. It was about the life of FDR." McBride sometimes led in with her own comments on herself or a current issue. In a broadcast dated July 4, 1952, before bringing on guest Edward Steichen, McBride muses, "I'm still scared and I hope you'll all be praying for me. I had a dream . . . I keep trying to do my broadcasts and someone keeps taking my mike. In a totalitarian country, this could happen. Maybe I've been reading too much about totalitarianism." She segued from this opening into a promotion for Amazo pudding. A few minutes later, she was talking to Edward Steichen about his reaction to witnessing the liberation of concentration camps at the end of World War II. This quirky contrast of seemingly unrelated ideas gives her show a quality that makes it distinct from all other radio program. But her stream-of-consciousness verbalization has a target. McBride knows exactly where she wants to take the guest. As Bennett Cerf commented in 1947, "Mary Margaret's thoughts, it develops, are about as scattered as a Times Square crowd on New Year's Eve, her approach as vague as a payoff punch by Joe Louis." McBride considered herself foremost a reporter. She viewed her role as that of an observer whose job it was to help the listeners learn more about the world. McBride interviewed celebrities, politicians, photographers, musicians, composers, and athletes. When she interviewed Frank Lloyd Wright, he articulated his major theme, the definition of culture in a democracy, and the interview reveals his thoughts and concerns. He explained to McBride that architecture in America must "be true to the principles that made this country . . . the principles of democracy. Democracy can't take the handrail down the stair, a democrat has to have courage . . . to keep his hand off the handrail and take the steps down the middle."

To the uninitiated, late-twentieth-century ear, the recorded sound of Mary Margaret McBride is discordant and troublesome. She had a high-pitched, singsong voice that sounds jarring at first and she seems to lack the authority we have come to expect from broadcast journalists. She punctuates her speech with "Oh, my gosh" and she often draws

■ McBride and business manager Estella Karn produced the show from different locations to keep audience interest high. McBride broadcasts from The Cloisters, the medieval collection of the Metropolitan Museum of Art in New York City.

out one or two words in a sentence for emphasis. The sound of her voice might lead people initially to dismiss her as a lightweight, capable only of dispensing cooking tips and household hints. Bob and Ray parodied her trilling voice in their "Mary Margaret McGoon" character who scolded the two with, "Oh, you silly, silly boys." Yet, once the listener moves beyond her homespun aphorisms and concentrates on the subject of her broadcast, the effect can be mesmerizing. Whether she is talking to James Thurber, Red Smith, or Secretary of Labor Frances Perkins, McBride concentrates on highlighting and emphasizing the words of the guest. Her on-air persona is warm, unassuming, almost understated. She does not overwhelm or overshadow her guest and she does not use any dramatic devices to detract from what the guest has to say. Her neighborly style and her gentle manner also contribute to her appeal to the listeners at home. She did not threaten her listeners or condescend to them. Her enthusiasm and respect for what her guest has to say are infectious and, as a listener, you find yourself eager to hear the next comment. McBride establishes a rapport with her guest that is infectious, and the listener becomes receptive to the messages the program sends.

McBride had a knack for getting guests to open up and

divulge little-known facts about themselves. She once said that people felt comfortable with her because when she was interviewing a guest, she was totally focused on the person.

She was warm and solicitous and she put guests at ease. Al Capp admitted that he was ashamed of his wooden leg when he was a child. The creator of L'il Abner explained he was a shy, withdrawn child who drew cartoons to fill up his lonely days. In a broadcast dated July 11, 1945, the news photographer Weegee recalled his impoverished childhood in what may be his only recorded radio interview. He described the crowded, squalid living conditions of the family's Pitt Street tenement and he reminisced about sleeping on the fire escape to breathe in fresh air on stifling, summer nights. During the Depression, Weegee was unemployed and penniless, so he was reduced to sleeping on a park bench in New York's Bryant Park. McBride and comedian Jimmy Durante literally wept together when he chronicled the bleak conditions of his childhood poverty. Gertrude Lawrence confessed that she and schoolmate Noël Coward were so poor they took turns riding the bike they shared back and forth to drama school during their adolescence in London. Coward was sensitive enough to saw off the bar on the frame so Lawrence could more easily mount and dismount from the bicycle. Listeners were not accustomed tot hearing the intimate details of famous people's lives. When the audience learned of the humble backgrounds of celebrities, it felt it was privy to secrets about a famous person. The interviews were like conversation at home and, as in a good chat, intimate details were revealed.

Eleanor Roosevelt was a frequent guest on McBride's programs. Mrs. Roosevelt once told McBride that Haile Selassie had terrible problems with his feet and he would shed his shoes after dinner at the White House. On June 30, 1947, Eleanor Roosevelt laughingly related the story of FDR's visit to a mental hospital when he was governor of New York. As his car drove by a patient mowing the lawn, the patient bowed and then made an obscene gesture toward Roosevelt. FDR quipped that his family could handle such disrespect, but the gesture offended his little dog, Fala, "because he is Scottish."

Actress Helen Hayes, a frequent guest, spoke with McBride about coming to terms with the death of her young daughter, Mary MacArthur. Hayes immersed herself in raising money for research on polio, the disease that had killed her child. Miss Hayes made several self-deprecating remarks, and McBride scolded her, "You don't value yourself enough." Hayes responds, "I'm one of the few people you know with a superiority complex."

Personal anecdotes and conversational interviews were the trademark of a McBride interview. McBride became the eyes and ears of Everywoman as she introduced her readers to new books, new ideas, and new people. She touched on topics as disparate as careers for women, psychology, and the plight of refugees.

In an interview with fellow journalist Cynthia Lowry, McBride said her goal was to help listeners make sense of the world. She admitted that when she first started her broadcasting career, she was primarily interested in her own success, and the main focus of her show was entertainment. When World War II broke out, McBride sensed her pro-

■ McBride discusses the voyage of the *Kon-Tiki* with Norwegian explorer Thor Heyerdahl, who sailed the balsa wood raft from Peru to Polynesia.

■ McBride interviews actress and radio personality Jinx Falkenburg (left) and New York socialite Vera Paley.

■ Gen. Omar Bradley selected the *McBride Show* for his first radio interview after his return from Europe at the close of World War II in 1945. Mrs. Bradley is on the general's right.

■ Bette Davis speaks with McBride. The *Mary Margaret McBride Show* broadcast a special from Davis's New Hampshire farm in 1941.

■ McBride greets her fans at one of her show's anniversary celebrations.

■ Eleanor Wilson McAdoo, Woodrow Wilson's daughter, discusses with McBride the 1945 United Nations Conference on International Organization in San Francisco, where the first United Nations charter was formally signed.

grams needed to take on a more serious tone. She felt more responsible toward educating her audience. She wanted to help people understand a confusing, frightening world and she wanted to tell people what they could do to help improve the situation. She became a window on the world for people who were coming out of the isolationism that had infected the United States after World War I. She saw the radio as a medium that could promote understanding and help listeners make sense of a changing world.

In the United States, segregated lunch counters, restricted neighborhoods, and limited job opportunities for women and other minorities punched holes in the tranquil fabric of American society. McBride used her program as a platform where women and people of different races and religions could showcase their talent, express their opinions, and, more basically, become familiar voices to the American public. McBride was guided by an almost zealous sense of duty to promote the rights and welfare of all Americans, regardless of race, ethnic background, religion, career, or sex.

McBride's guests included noted African Americans, successful career women, religious leaders, and people who overcame handicaps to lead successful lives. Her broadcast continually returned to the themes of the dangers of prejudice and limiting opportunities for people of different religions, races, and sexes. McBride liked to discuss the ramifications of prejudice and she addressed this issue with writers such as Pearl S. Buck and Zora Neale Hurston, luminaries such as Nobel Peace laureate Ralph Bunche and actress Ethel Waters, and politicians, such as Secretary of Labor Frances Perkins.

Accomplished African Americans, such as W. C. Handy, found a voice on McBride's program. Handy shared his hardscrabble life experiences that compelled him to write "St. Louis Blues." Cab Calloway revealed his humanity when he confessed that his signature lilt, "Hi de, hi de, hi de ho," was a nonsense phrase he injected into a performance one night when he forgot the lyrics. Poet Langston

Hughes explained that he wrote about "the backgrounds of the Negro people and [their] potentialities and [the hope that] this democracy will someday be a perfect democracy." Other notable African Americans McBride interviewed include dancer Pearl Primus, baritone William Warfield, and actor Avon Long.

McBride would not tolerate anyone making racial slurs or derogatory comments about a person's religious or ethnic background. Stage actress Laurette Taylor once used the word "nigger" to describe her character in the Broadway production of Tennessee Williams's *The Glass Menagerie*. McBride was horrified by Taylor's gaffe and she received a stinging memo from network executives demanding that she exert greater control over the behavior of her guests. In an attempt to make amends for Taylor's error, McBride

■ Anthropologist Margaret Mead shares her experiences with Mary Margaret McBride.

invited NAACP officer, Walter White, to address the danger and harm of racial stereotyping on her program. McBride wrote in her autobiography, *Out of the Air*, that White's articulate and intelligent explanation of how the subtle damage caused by using words that demean other races contributes to an environment permeated by racism provoked listeners to focus on their own attitudes and behavior towards people different from themselves. McBride viewed her program as an available platform that could be used to increase understanding between Americans of different races and backgrounds. She felt it was her duty as the host of a popular radio program to provide information that would positively impact on the everyday lives of all Americans.

Anti-Semitism was another cultural malady that McBride fervently wanted to eradicate. She questioned author and editor Bennett Cerf about the bigotry and prejudice he encountered when he toured America touting a book. Cerf related his experience on a book tour where organizers in two towns referred to a party that was gaudy because of the "shanty Irish" and begged him to excuse "those Jews" who were only allowed in the country club for the one evening of the author's tour. McBride was committed to social activism and she featured guests involved with foundations, politics, children's issues, and civil rights. When guests came on the show and talked about the charity fund-raising they were working on, the charity received increased donations from listeners.

McBride featured women writers, politicians, actresses, artists, journalists, and doctors. Journalists Enid Haupt, Helen Hiett, Dorothy Thompson, and Emma Bugbee chatted with McBride. Singers Jessica Dragonette, Patrice Munsel, and Dinah Shore, and comedian Beatrice Lillie, actress Mary Pickford, and choreographer Agnes De Mille faced McBride. McBride featured themes such as psychology and careers for women and she interviewed prominent women from these areas, such as India Edward, the executive director of the Women's Democratic National

McBride presented women celebrities and women in powerful, decisionmaking positions. She featured her share of mothers as well, including Amy Otis Earhart, Amelia Earhart's mom; and Ruth Dawson, the inventor of the Brownie. Just hearing women talk about the different activities they were engaged in caused women—and men and children, if they were listening—to think about the emerging and changing roles for women. McBride was trusted by her listeners, and an endorsement from McBride of an organization motivated her audience to support the cause.

Mary Margaret's gift for interviewing meshed seamlessly with the business acumen of Stella Karn. Karn guided the McBride show to editorial and commercial success. She understood that a successful radio program depended on the content of the broadcast.

■ **Mary Margaret McBride stages a breakfast fashion show featuring the latest spring bonnets to benefit the Associated Women Directors of the National Association of Broadcasters.**

Committee; psychiatrist Dr. Marynia Farnham; explorer Miriam McMillan, who made a trip to Baffin and Labrador; Florence Sabin and Lena L'Esperance on their careers in medicine; and author Fannie Hurst on how to develop an organization for women whose goal would be world peace.

Karn designed ways to keep the show interesting and appealing to the audience. She persuaded McBride to broadcast from remote locations, such as Haiti, the Virgin Islands, and Norway. McBride was the first civilian reporter allowed into Germany after the hostilities ended in 1945.

With a U.S. Army B-29 at her disposal, McBride filed a series of print and radio stories that captured the bleak, devastated lives of people enduring the war in England, France, and Germany. McBride took her listeners on a maple-sugaring expedition to Bette Davis's farmhouse in Vermont and she also gave them an audio tour of a Frank Lloyd Wright-designed chapel at Florida Southern College. When McBride was hospitalized following an appendectomy in 1947, she insisted on broadcasting the show from her bed at Doctor's Hospital in New York City.

In addition to promoting remotes, Karn produced anniversary programs that featured tributes from celebrities coupled with an opportunity for listeners to meet Mary Margaret in person. Twenty thousand fans packed Madison Square Garden for McBride's tenth anniversary program in 1944. Special guest Eleanor Roosevelt commented, "I am always happy when a woman succeeds . . . but when a woman succeeds superlatively, she is an inspiration to all other women." The celebration moved to Yankee Stadium for the program's fifteenth anniversary revels in 1949. Fifty thousand fans filled the ballpark to honor McBride and hear speeches by a star-studded cast, including Eva Le Gallienne, Fannie Hurst, Fred Waring, H. V. Kaltenborn, and radio personality Tex McCrary.

The unpredictable, quirky nature of the program was one of the major appeals to listeners. Celebrities dropped previously unknown facts about their private lives, and guests did not always behave as anticipated. McBride confronted unruly animals from the Bronx Zoo, author Marjorie Kinnan Rawlings admitted she broke Florida game laws, and actor Jimmy Stewart chastised Hollywood brass about their fear of television. In one memorable broadcast, McBride's attempts to interview actor Gary Cooper in her apartment were thwarted by the deafening hammering of two plumbers at work in an upstairs apartment. During the program, Karn appealed to the workers to suspend their job until the end of the broadcast. The men agreed to cooperate if she introduced them to Gary Cooper. Karn brought the men into McBride's apartment, and for the next ten minutes the show revolved around the meeting between the plumbers and Gary Cooper. This episode was enthusiastically received by the audience, which adored the spontaneity of many of McBride's shows.

■ **Mary Margaret McBride interviews Mike Wallace. McBride's notes from the program indicated that she wanted to ask him if he was a prude.**

usually carried twelve or thirteen sponsors, with many companies wait listed for a slot on the show. McBride would only accept sponsors whose products she or a member of her staff personally tested. If she could not attest to a product's value, she would not accept the sponsor. Her religious beliefs prevented her from accepting any alcohol or tobacco advertising.

McBride guaranteed that each advertiser received equal time and an enthusiastic product promotion. When she plugged a sponsor, McBride implored the audience to try a new brand of pudding or ice cream, begging listeners "Won't you please, oh please, just taste Dolly Madison ice cream?" Mary Margaret wove her pitches seamlessly into the lineup of the program. For example, she extolled the virtues of Dromedary Mix by citing the great success

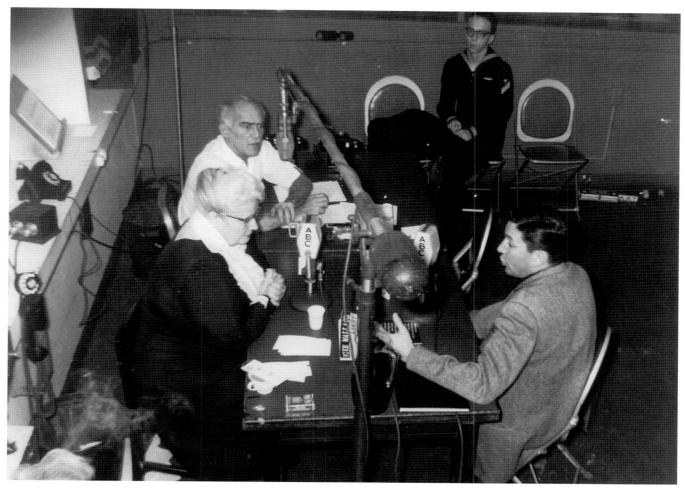

In addition to her contribution to the program's content, Karn acted as McBride's business manager, and her guidance was instrumental in steering McBride to financial success. One-third of McBride's daily program was devoted to selling the wares of her sponsors. McBride personally delivered the pitches for her "products" with the zeal and sincerity of a revivalist minister. Her astute salesmanship resulted in a surge in sales for her sponsors. McBride's program

Vincent's new sister-in-law achieved with a batch of muffins she made using the product. She was a master at combining descriptive words and emotional phrases so that listeners probably found themselves craving a Dromedary gingerbread cake as she rhapsodized about the pungent scent of the fresh baked muffins. When McBride offered promotionals or free samples over the airwaves, she was deluged by requests for the specials. McBride is fabled to be responsible

■ **Actress Mary Martin speaks with McBride the day after**
South Pacific **opened to favorable reviews in 1951.**

for emptying supermarket shelves of carrots after she reported grocery stores were overstocked with the vegetable.

McBride wrote her commercial copy with the same fastidiousness and attention to detail that she lavished upon her interviews. While she insisted on maintaining absolute control over both the content of the promotion and her method of delivery, advertisers did not balk at her restrictions because McBride was such a successful saleswoman. Her skill was rewarded with citations and awards including recognition in 1952 as one of "Twelve Master Salesmen" named by R. C. Forbes. McBride was the only radio personality and the only woman cited on the list.

McBride enlisted her guests to help with her sales pitches. She nudged Eleanor Roosevelt with, "You remember Sweetheart soap, don't you Mrs. Roosevelt?" McBride asked Langston Hughes if she should deliver her commercial in a poem. "I wouldn't mind," Hughes replied, "I like to hear other people rhyme, if they can." "If they can, " Margaret mused. Hughes composed an extemporaneous jingle about the baking mix that he recited, "Dromedary, help me carry, news of chocolate cake. Also, news of gingerbread for all the folks who bake."

As her radio program grew in popularity and more listeners responded positively to her unique personality, Mary Margaret McBride became something of a phenomenon. Jackson and Perkins named a rose after her in 1943, and she launched a line of clothing under her name at Montgomery Ward. Edward R. Murrow featured her on a segment of his television show, *Person to Person*, and the governor of her home state, Missouri, declared November 22, 1940, "Mary Margaret McBride Day." McBride was a sought-after panelist at special events and on radio forums. Her celebrity status was a result of the success of her program and the trust and admiration she inspired in her listeners.

Mary Margaret McBride tried unsuccessfully to make the leap to television in 1948. As the 1940s came to a close, her radio program lost segments of its audience to the increasingly popular "give-away" shows like ABC's *Stop the Music* (1949), created by Quiz Kids originator Louis G. Cowan. The success of these shows was due to an audience that had suffered years of consumer deprivation during the World War II mobilization. McBride's innovative radio program lost some of its originality and gloss by the early 1950s, and the time arrived for programming that appealed to Americans whose optimism and hope were sobered by the war and the threat of the atom bomb. McBride remained with NBC until 1950, switched briefly to ABC, and returned to NBC in 1954. The McBride network program ended in the mid 1950s, a victim of television. McBride continued writing, publishing books, and broadcasting on local radio in upstate New York until her death in 1976.

Mary Margaret McBride was a pioneer who explored and helped define the potential of radio from its early days. McBride's ad-lib interviews set a precedent and established a style commonly used in radio and television today, Her candid interviews, frank discussions, and book recommendations are typical features of contemporary radio and television programs. She extended the boundaries of women's programming, proving that American women would listen to more than recipes and tips on raising children. McBride introduced her listeners to people and places they had never visited and ideas they had never entertained. Furthermore, McBride's success as a salesperson demonstrated again the potential of radio as a vehicle for advertising. The commercial success of her program proved a woman could capably create and host a profitable radio show. McBride and her partner, Estella Karn, produced a creative one-of-a-kind radio show by combining their considerable journalistic and business talents and cultivating a devoted audience which promised to stay tuned.

The United States emerged from its postwar isolationism in the late 1930s because the world turmoil forced the country to confront events overseas. The failure of the League of Nations, the Depression, the rise of fascist and communist leaders abroad, and the growing crisis in Europe compelled Americans to question their fundamental assumptions about life. People in the United States were desperate to make sense of an increasingly unstable and ominous world situation. Mary Margaret McBride arrived in radio just when Americans needed a person they respected and trusted to guide them through the social, political, and international maelstrom that threatened to change their lives. McBride was the window on the world to a generation of listeners who yearned to understand changes that frightened them at home and in the world. Her unpretentious manner and her intelligent comments made the audience feel comfortable with her, and they trusted what she had to say.

McBride believed that she was obligated to communicate information that helped listeners reach a greater understanding of themselves and their place in the world. To McBride, radio was a medium for both education and entertainment. The McBride Collection is a worthy legacy of Mary Margaret's goal in that this aural history reflects the pulse of America in the 1930s through the 1950s. The hundreds of broadcasts and papers in the collection add a vibrant clue to what Americans were saying and thinking about in this era. The McBride Collection is a uniquely American gem that reflects our culture, our history, and what we were thinking about at the threshold of our modern world.

■ **McBride admires Colorado Gov. Daniel Thornton's boots when she interviews him at the Republican National Convention in 1952.**

KAREN HANSEN is a researcher and writer with a special interest in the history of broadcasting. A graduate of Barnard College, Ms. Hansen worked as a producer and researcher for CBS Network News. Her credits include features and documentaries for the CBS *Evening News, CBS Special Reports, CBS Weekend News* and *60 Minutes*. She helped to index the NBC Radio Collection at the Library of Congress and she has worked as a freelance researcher for authors, journalists, and academics utilizing the resources of the collection. Ms. Hansen coauthored the book, *Toward Understanding Children* and she has served as a judge for the News and Documentary Emmy Awards. Ms. Hansen currently works as a research coordinator for HIV/AIDS projects in the Washington, D.C., metropolitan area.

PROBLEMS ON THE
Radio Advice

BY DONALD KENT

"You have a friend and advisor in John J. Anthony, and thousands are happier and more successful today because of John J. Anthony," the radio announcer intoned. And then:

> Mr. Anthony, I have a problem. I'm thirty-two years old, my husband is two years younger than I am. The first night we were married he went out with an old girlfriend of his and came back at four o'clock in the morning and he was very abusive. Three years later he forged a check and he was sent away [to prison]. After that he went into the Army and I had trouble receiving my allotment. Mr. Anthony, now he writes me he wants to come back and he'll be coming home soon—and I don't want him anymore.
>
> So what are you doing?
>
> Well, Mr. Anthony, now I have another boyfriend that I'm living with, and he's very nice to me and he has given me the things my husband never gave me . . .
>
> Why did you remain with the man for that period of time under the circumstances?
>
> Well, Mr. Anthony, I thought maybe some time he would change.
>
> So you found yourself another boyfriend . . . And during the period of time you were with this boyfriend, did you get your Army allotment checks?
>
> Yes, I did.
>
> Did you feel you had any right to those checks in view of the fact that you had taken up residence with another man?
>
> Well, at the time, Mr. Anthony, I wasn't living with the man. And I do feel that I was entitled to the checks . . .
>
> All the things you've done—you tell me your husband drove you to those things. I don't follow that line of reasoning because if that is true, then you would have had a right to forge a check because your husband forged a check. Would you do that?

AIRWAVES

Shows–Then and Now

No, I wouldn't.

Your marriage never was any good. The marriage had no chance of being any good. You are agreeing with me. Your marriage should be dissolved. A divorce should take place. If this man in your life is really in love with you, marry him. But to continue to live with him under the circumstance you have outlined—and I don't say this from a moral standpoint, I'm not going to preach a sermon of morals to you—but I'm saying this because of its logic and because the community, too, has a right in the lives of individuals. What you are doing now is definitely wrong. And you have one great problem before you. And that is to straighten out your marriage, so you may continue your life in a manner of a dignified human being. That has not been done in the past ten years, either by you or your husband. And my advice to you is, if you can, get a divorce and straighten our your affair with this other man by a normal marriage, and good luck to you.

"Okay," she sighed. And John J. Anthony, one of America's earliest on-air advisors, passed the microphone to the next "guest," the next case.

"Mr. Anthony" was America's most popular on-air adviser on love, marriage, family, and other human relationships in the late 1930s and early 1940s. Each week twenty million radio listeners tuned in to his Sunday night *Goodwill Hour* when it was at its peak. His chief rivals on the airwaves, A. L. Alexander and *The Voice of Experience* (a male former social worker, Marion Sayle Taylor, who was usually addressed as "Dear Voice") also achieved popularity ratings that today's advice show hosts would envy.

Listening in today, it is a strangely dissonant experience to hear the voices of these on-air advisors and their troubled

■ As a an advisor on marriage problems, John J. Anthony ruled the airwaves in the late 1930s and early 1940s. At its peak his program had twenty million listeners. His academic background was murky, but he maintained he could learn more in five minutes than psychiatrists learn in ten years. The *New York Times* noted that his audiences were enthralled with "his speedy solutions to marital problems."

guests of more than a half century ago in the recordings of their programs preserved in the Recorded Sound Reference Center of the Library of Congress Motion Picture, Broadcasting, and Recorded Sound Division (MBRS).

The confusion and suffering of the callers rings true. The emotional outpourings, the sobbing, whining and muttering of guests on the early radio advice programs have little in common with the matter-of-fact tones of most persons who call in to advice programs today. Back then the persons at the microphone really seemed to feel they were in deep trouble, whereas today an increasing number of callers are asking *whether* they have a problem. The advice given on the early programs also seems often to be inadequate, incommensurate with the problems that people present.

For help in resolving the dissonance for today's listeners, I decided to enlist the help of several popular advice show hosts on the air today and a past president of the Association of Media Psychologists, Dr. Elaine Rodino. Each received the same set of printed excerpts from eight on-air dialogues with Mr. Anthony, A. L. Alexander, *The Voice of Experience*, and an English-language segment from an advice show conducted mainly in Yiddish. Each recipient was asked to review and evaluate two or three of the segments in terms of the problems that Americans faced in their lives in the 1930s and early 1940s and the problem-solving advice delivered over the airwaves in that era.

Commenting on the Mr. Anthony segment presented above, Dr. Rodino said, "This is the epitome of nonfeminist awareness, extremely moralistic and sexist. It's the wife's obligation to straighten things out. There doesn't seem to be any responsibility on the part of the husband, though he was the abusive one."

Dr. Judy Kuriansky, a clinical psychologist whose nightly show *LovePhones* originates in New York and is syndicated nationwide on rock-and-roll stations, commented, "If it's true that the woman with Mr. Anthony is expressing being abused, that would be trounced on by all the feminists in the world. The advice is totally unmodern. I think today there would be much more sympathy over her being abused. The focus would be much more on getting out of an abusive relationship, rather than doing what Mr. Anthony is doing. Although he denies it, he is moralizing to her about how she has a duty to the community to live the life of a dignified human being. Today we would take the point of view that her self-respect matters more. We would not focus so much on the fact that she was inappropriately taking her husband's money and living in sin with some other guy."

Dr. Judy, as she is known on the air, said she was astounded with another case where she found the advice "modern, clearly defined, as it would happen today." It was from a 1939 broadcast of A. L. Alexander's Board of Mediation that can be summarized as follows: A young woman has made marriage plans without letting her mother and father know that she intends to get married, because she believes they would disapprove. When the mother finds out, all four parties to the problem—mother, father, bride-to-be and boyfriend—have it out before A. L. Alexander and three board members chosen from the ranks of editors, professors, psychiatrists, and clergy. The young man is not securely

■ A panel of jurists gave legal and psychological advice to anonymous "guests" on A. L. Alexander's highly popular but short-lived *Goodwill Court*. The New York Supreme Court barred judges from participating in the show in November 1936, after it had run for two months. Alexander replaced the judges with professors and prominent citizens, renamed his program, and continued broadcasting until 1950.

employed, but it turns out that otherwise he is acceptable to the mother and father. The father explains that he doesn't want another mouth to feed and fears his daughter could go hungry if she married someone not financially secure. The parents want the couple to wait six months or a year, to become established financially, before giving their consent. After talking it over, everyone approves the plan to wait.

Dr. Judy agrees completely that "the best they could do is wait a year, so that he can get a good job and they can put a few dollars aside." She agrees with the arbitrator who tells them they don't have a problem: "The young man loves the daughter; the daughter loves the parents; the parents like the young man, and everyone is willing to wait a year." She adds, "I can hear myself saying it's not so easy to make it today with the salaries the way that they are out there, and that's just what this arbitrators are saying. And the parents are just like parents today—they have reasonable concerns, and they're not being vicious about anything."

Dr. Toni Grant, the first clinical psychologist to do call-ins on the air and who restarted her nationwide program in 1997 after a five-year break for marriage and work in the corporate world, focused on another case from A. L. Alexander's program. The key person in this family problem is a physically handicapped woman in her early twenties whose complaint is that her stepfather is intolerably hostile and rude to her. She comes to the microphone with her mother, who states that she remarried in hopes that her new husband would help finance better health care for her daughter. But the new family of three do not seem to be able to live together peacefully under the same roof.

Dr. Toni comments: "My first question would be why is this young lady unemployed or at least not doing something. She does sound spoiled and more concerned about her own happiness than anything else. I might have been a little more confrontational with her than Alexander's board has been. I'd have dealt with what her skills were and why she wasn't developing her skills. I might have dwelt on whether she was perhaps jealous of the new love in her mother's life and resented the stepfather. The board members suggest she might talk to him more cheerfully when he comes home from work, but the mother says that the young woman won't do that. So the mother is reinforcing the daughter's childish and immature self-centered behavior. It sounds as if the young woman has been indulged because of her handicap. The board members tiptoe around the central issue: You've got a spoiled, egocentric young woman here who is getting a lot of secondary gain or payoff from her handicap and who is refusing to grow up into a productive adult. She is resisting. When Alexander says, 'You've had the radio all day, let him get the baseball game on the radio when he comes home from work, and give him a nice kiss'—that's a little Pollyanna."

For Dr. Elaine Rodino, "this is an awful, awful case—a perfect example of Alexander and the panel telling the family just to try harder. To my sense they had already tried hard or they wouldn't have come to this show. But the panel basically tells them to go home and do more and try harder—and be more cheerful, putting sugar on something very toxic, a very unhappy situation. And this case shows how the whole handicapped issue was so nonunderstood in those days. The panel is going along with the feeling that this girl ought to be happy that this man is taking care of her. There is hardly any sensitivity to her pain or to the underlying issues of the stepfather who may resent taking care of her."

Dr. Toni found a "fascinating sense of sin" in the language of the thirties and forties programs. The word adultery comes up repeatedly. Atonement also, which is never heard of today, she said. One of the A. L. Alexander episodes focuses on a woman who says that the sickness and job loss that she and her husband have been experiencing are a result of her sin—she should have stayed with her former husband. Though she and her present husband love one another, she says they must atone for her sin by separating until the former husband dies. Her present husband disagrees.

> Alexander to the wife: It would be impossible for you to enter into a normal marital relationship with him [her present husband] in every respect, is that right? It would be sinful, inasmuch as you did a wrong and the way to atone for your sin is denial and suffering?
>
> She: (weakly) That's right.
>
> Protestant Minister on the board: Are you in love with your husband?
>
> She: I love him very much.
>
> Minister: Would you be happier if you violated that love,

as perhaps you did long ago to another man? Don't you think perhaps your way of salvation is to play true to this love? Let me ask if you believe in God ... Do you believe he is a God of love or vengeance?

> She: A God of love, but I do believe that we have to pay for our sins.
>
> Minister: . . . Well, of course sickness and unemployment come upon the finest people, don't they?
>
> Alexander: We realize there are some people who believe in salvation rather than self-realization—who believe that perhaps it's best that the flesh be humiliated so that the spirit will be exalted.
>
> Psychiatrist on the board: I'm not sure it's all religious belief. There were six years of happiness with no idea of sin or wrongdoing. The separation has been accepted by the [first] husband. The divorce was legal. They are at present in a state of affection for one another ... I wonder if a little care, and bringing up the physical vigor and helping to make life a little more cheerful, perhaps might relieve that sense of guilt.

"What struck me about the case was the language," Dr. Grant said. "Just because the woman uses the words sin and atonement easily it doesn't mean that she is a particularly moral or good person. It seems to me what we have here is a woman who does not like the reality she has created. Though there might be a sense of sin and atonement, there might also be a sense that she made a bad deal."

Dr. Toni added, "I keep wondering whatever became of sin, how the concept disappeared from the culture and from the language . . . It seems as if people believe that all bad behavior can be psychologically explained away. But the fact is that psychologically explaining doesn't make it right, or good, or healthy. It's just that you can psychologically explain it. . . . You can bemoan the disappearance of sin as a great loss in the culture, and in some respects it is. I certainly think that shame and guilt are two human emotions that have their place. When you do something bad you should feel guilty and ashamed."

Commenting on the atonement case, Dr. Rodino said, "What makes me bristle is that there's no sense of feminist psychology at all in this case. But I think the psychiatrist on the panel did give sound advice. He didn't just say stop being guilty, get over it, as the others were saying. He gave a real indication that it would take time to heal, and if the sense of guilt were relieved there would be no obstacle to their continuing their marriage—that would be the thing to build on."

Dr. Joy Browne, whose show is heard on about 260 talk show stations nationwide, also noted the moralizing tone of thirties and forties programs. "The stance is very different from mine—there is a sort of moral judgment inherent in many of the cases. That's not what I do. I am a practical problem solver. I look at the ramifications of behavior. People's morality is their own business, not mine. I'll try to help them understand why what they are doing is not going to work for them, help them see that it doesn't make any sense. But any time you put a minister on the radio with a psychiatrist, you are talking about a different kind of thing than what I do. It's a very different stance than the one I take."

As leading advisors on love, family, and other domains of

human relationships, John J. Anthony and A. L. Alexander both came to their roles with little if any of the academic preparation, clinical experience, or credentials expected of on-air advisors today.

Mr. Anthony claimed he had three academic degrees. He declined to identify alma maters, because he did not want to be "looked upon as an academician." At least once he said he studied under Sigmund Freud. His obituary in the *New York Times* in 1970[1] speaks only of his background as a textile manufacturer, taxi driver, writer, and teacher, while early radio critic John Dunning,[2] describes Mr. Anthony as a "Bronx hustler" and a "high school dropout" bored with the structured ways of formal education. Throughout his career he was attacked by judges, social organizations, and radio critics, many of whom openly branded him a charlatan, Dunning states.

Anthony, who was born Lester Kroll, shielded his personal past as much as he could. But he freely admitted that his first marriage, which ended in divorce and a prison stay for himself, spurred his search for solutions to marital problems and reform of divorce and alimony laws. His vocation came to him, he said, while serving a jail term for nonpayment of alimony.[3]

Anthony's expressed philosophy was based on marital fidelity and the Golden Rule. He frequently exhorted his studio guests and listeners to search their souls and come to the conclusion that life is basically full of loveliness and that love makes the world go round.[4] The *New York Times* found his radio audiences were enthralled with "his speedy solutions to martial problems." His answers to even the most difficult problems were brief and, some thought, profound. Others took him as a media oddity, and the expression "Tell it to Mr. Anthony" became the tag line of all sorts of household jokes, some of them not suitable for the ears of all household members.

Anthony attributed an important part of the improvements that came about in marriage and divorce laws during the 1930s to his own books, surveys, and radio programs. He also claimed that he was instrumental in inspiring Vassar College (Toni Grant's Alma Mater) and Columbia and Stanford universities to add special courses in marital relations to their curricula.

The Marital Relations Institute that he founded in the late 1920s as a site for individual marriage counseling continued for many years to publish surveys and reports that supported his positions and outlooks on love and marriage. One of its surveys found that 69 percent of the women who sent their husbands to jail for nonpayment of alimony were pathological cases.

Anthony's earnings in the late 1930s were reported as about $150,000 a year, approximately $3.5 million in today's dollars. This income was derived mainly from his radio show but also from the books he authored (for example, *Marriage and Family Problems and How to Solve Them*), lecture tours, and counseling he conducted at his Marital Relations Institute.

To critics who called him "Mr. Agony" and charged that he was making a rich living out of the miseries of others, he responded: "It's more money than any man is entitled to make. But after all, a man's value is judged by his social impact on the community." He said he was "essentially more experienced than most psychiatrists—I learn in five minutes what it takes them ten years to find out."

A. L. Alexander came to on-air advice radio from a career as a police reporter. On his beat he had seen the inequities of the legal system and wanted to do something to improve the situation. After one or two false starts on radio, he hit upon a winning strategy. He asked court defendants to air their problems over his program anonymously before a panel of judges. With some difficulty he persuaded two jurists to take part in the NBC show to give advice, both legal and psychological.[5]

The show that Alexander launched in September 1936, called the *Goodwill Court*, was an immediate sensation and ranked among the top ten radio shows in the nation. Caught up in the emotions of their personal troubles, the guests told the *Goodwill Court* of marital and other personal relationship problems, of troubles with loan sharks, of garnished wages, and other trials and tragedies shared by millions of listeners. But two months after the show's network premiere, the New York Supreme Court barred judges and lawyers from participating in it. Then Chase and Sanborn Coffee withdrew its sponsorship, and the program folded. It reemerged, however, as *A. L. Alexander's Mediation Board* and *A. L. Alexander's Arbitration Board*. The new programs, which ran until 1950, focused less on legal problems, more on human relations, using panels that included educators, psychiatrists, clergymen, and prominent citizens.

Mr. Anthony established his first major foothold in network radio in 1937 when he installed his *Goodwill Hour* in the Mutual Radio time slot vacated by Alexander's *Goodwill Court*. Once there, he encountered none of the troubles Alexander had experienced in finding panel members: he was a one-man show all by himself.

Anthony's and Alexander's only serious rival on the airwaves was the *Voice of Experience*, Marion Sayle Taylor, who read pathetic letters from people with problems with their family and marital relations, or poor health, drug addiction, and financial woes. By 1934, 1,000 people were writing to "Dear Voice" daily, and by 1939 the number was 6,000 daily. Radio audiences contributed hundreds of thousands of dollars, equivalent to more than ten million dollars today, to alleviate problems the baleful-voiced *Voice of Experience* aired on his program, which started on CBS in 1933, went to NBC in 1936, and to Mutual in 1937, running until 1940.

Taylor came to his role from social work in public health departments and a radio career that began in 1926. In a typical broadcast from 1936 in the Library's collection, the *Voice of Experience* stated:

> Now a nurse writes me and says, "Is it right for a mother to sacrifice her children to prolong the life of her husband who is insane? The husband and father is so unbalanced that he does not recognize the members of his own family. The doctor says that the only place the man should now be spending his days is in an institution. The mother is determined that he should not be taken away, and no amount of persuasion will alter her decision. The home is a wreck because of his viciousness. There are two daughters living at home. They have to deal with him at length, as he will not stay in

■ Dr. Joyce Brothers launched her career as a psychologist-sports expert by memorizing twenty volumes of a boxing encyclopedia, according to her account, and successfully answering the $64,000 question on the popular quiz show of that name. Here we see Dr. Brothers and her husband—Milton Brothers, who was a medical resident at the time—at breakfast reading press accounts of her winning the $64,000 jackpot.

bed unless under watch. Often the girls do not get more than two or three hours' sleep in the night, besides working harder and harder at home after office hours. And they contribute two to three times as much money as their room and board would cost elsewhere . . . I wish you could say something, *Voice of Experience*, to convince this mother that it is not fair for her to sacrifice these two girls, just because of her mistaken sense of duty towards this husband."

The *Voice of Experience* evaluated the situation presented in the letter as follows:

It seems to me completely obvious that this mother has completely lost her outlook on things and is subjecting herself as well as her family to a strain that they should not be asked to bear . . . The deprivation of the leisure and peace of mind that these girls are experiencing may have severe reverberations for them. They are still at that impressionable age when their personalities can show the reflection of their environment. Being cut off from all opportunities to do the things that young people do at that age and have the right to do is extremely unfair and as I say may have tragic and permanent consequences. It appears to me most important that this mother be persuaded to permit her husband to be confined in an institution. It may seem somewhat heartless to pass someone who is obviously in need of care to

strangers. But strangers, meaning the doctors in attendance in these institutions, are in a much better position to act in the best interest of the patient than is a troubled and unhappy family.

The immense success of Anthony, Alexander and the *Voice of Experience* gave rise to smaller, local, and sometimes ethnic variations of the on-air marital and family advisor. The Yiddish language programs of Rabbi Reuben Goldberg's Jewish-American Board of Peace and Justice on station WWRL, Queens, New York, provides a colorful example. One case before the board involves a husband and wife who want to separate but can't reach agreement on how to divide up the business they have run together for several years. She tells the rabbi and panel that she provided the start-up money and "Now I want to get it back." The "it" she wants is the entire business. But the husband does not want to give it up.

Both parties have agreed in advance to follow the "decision" of the rabbi and the board, which after due deliberation was spelled out in the following terms:

It is too easy to break up a home. And there is a situation such as seems to be presented here where the two parties apparently have not exhausted everything they could do,

■ Joyce Brothers went another seven rounds on the by-then renamed *$64,000 Challenge* program in September and October 1957, competing against seven boxing greats, and winning the jackpot again. Her winnings from the two shows included intermediate step prizes for a total of $134,000. With her, from left to right, are Sixto Escobar, Abe Attell, Paddy De Marco, Billy Graham, Ralph (Tiger) Jones, Tommy Loughran, and Tony Galento.

■ After winning her first $64,000 jackpot, Joyce Brothers remained on television as a cohost of *Sports Showcase*. In 1958, she launched her first psychological counseling show, offering advice on love, marriage, sex, and child rearing on NBC televison. She also was heard on radio shows on NBC and ABC stations. By the 1960s her beat extended to celebrities of the entertainment world, like the Beatles. Here we see Ringo taking her pulse.

■ Joyce Brothers's book, *Ten Days to a Successful Memory* (Prentice-Hall, 1957), offered help with everyday problems, such as remembering people's faces and names, based on the latest psychological research. It was coauthored with E. P. F. Egan.

■ Dr. Judy Kuriansky is the host of *LovePhones* on Z100 Radio in New York and other rock-and-roll stations in the United States and in Japan. Dr. Judy says she was once a rock musician and played bass in an all-woman band. Her call-in program runs four nights a week from 10 p.m. to midnight in New York with an "adults only" warning announcement. She targets the content to young adults aged eighteen to twenty-four.

■ Dr. Toni Grant, a clinical psychologist, launched America's first call-in psychology program on station KABC Los Angeles in 1975. Syndicated on ABC radio in 1981 and then by the Mutual Broadcasting System in 1986, it was carried by 180 stations. Over a million copies of her 1988 book, *Being a Woman: Fulfilling Your Femininity and Finding Love*, have been sold. In 1997, the *Dr. Toni Grant Program*

returned to the airwaves after a five-year lapse. The guiding purpose of the show, as she said, is to "demystify psychology and bring the field out of the consulting room and into the homes and cars and hearts of the American public." The *New York Times* magazine (November 17, 1966, p. 42) credits her with "putting media psychology on the

■ Dr. Joy Browne broadcasts for fifteen hours a week on the WOR radio network. More than 250 stations nationwide, mainly talk show stations, carry all or part of her program hours. She describes her program as Problem Solving 101, "psychology for the masses," designed to help callers see the ramifications of their actions.

■ Dr. Elaine Rodino was the 1997 President of the Association of Media Psychology, a division of the American Psychological Association, with approximately 450 members. The post is rotated annually.

Dr. Laura Schlessinger dispenses no-nonsense, straight-to-the-point advice about relationships, children, and life's crossroads on her syndicated radio show that receives more than nine thousand callers each day, according to *Radio Ink* (August 7-20, 1995). She received her Ph.D. from the Physiology Department of Columbia University Medical School and is licensed in California as a marriage, family, and child counselor.

and [therefore] they should not be permitted to go their separate ways. That is too easy. Now it is the board's advice that husband and wife do whatever they can to live a happy life. And more than that: The woman should have more understanding than possibly you can expect from a man. As a woman it's up to you, and you can find ways in which to satisfy and make your husband contented. We recommend that you go back home and that you try to live with your husband happily for a three-month period under the supervision of the board. That three-month period will be the thing that will make a happy home for you.

Both the wife and husband appear to give half-hearted acceptance to the recommendation and agree to give it a try.

Mr. Anthony's *Goodwill Hour* left the air in 1953. That also happened to be the year in which Joyce Brothers received her Ph.D. from Columbia University. It was a pivotal year for on-air advice programs. From the mid-1950s onward, the advisors on radio would no longer be exclusively male—in fact, males would become a distinct minority in the profession. And academic background and credentials would become a prerequisite. In a telephone conversation for this article, Dr. Brothers emphasized that she was the first doctoral level psychologist to have her own psychological advice radio program.

The well-known story of Joyce Brothers's emergence from academia and child-rearing to the world of radio and television has a certain fairy tale quality about it, true though it is.

In 1955 she tried for an appearance on the television quiz show, the *$64,000 Question*, presenting herself as an expert on boxing. The story has it that she memorized twenty volumes of a boxing encyclopedia to advance her preexisting knowledge base to the expert level. What is certain is that she became the second person and the only woman to carry off the $64,000 prize. Two years later she won another $64,000 prize in a contest against seven exboxers in a battle that the *New Yorker* called "one of the high points in the annals of boxing."[6]

In between those years, she was cohost on a television sports program in 1956, commenting on sports events and interviewing sports stars. And finally in 1958 she launched her own program on NBC television devoted to counseling and advice on love, marriage, sex, and child rearing. It was an instant success. In the 1960s and 1970s she also had programs on radio stations of the ABC and NBC networks, sometimes answering questions from on-the-air telephone callers.

The Library's recordings of Dr. Brothers's half-hour programs on NBC Radio reveal that they were solidly researched and constructed, and couched in easily understandable language, free of professional jargon. They have some characteristics of an excellent college class lecture. Dr. Brothers has said she often spent fourteen to sixteen hours of background work on a half-hour program.

As a pioneer in on-air counseling and advising, Dr. Brothers has often been the focus of the long-festering issue of whether on-air psychology is therapy, or mainly entertainment, or education, or something else instead—for example, voyeurism.

Dr. Brothers has repeatedly emphasized her view that she is not doing therapy on the air but merely trying to give her listeners information that will be of some service to them in everyday living.

Other on-air advisors largely appear to agree that what they do is not therapy, though it might be therapeutic.

Dr. Judy Kuriansky says her listeners often say they see her program as a vicarious learning experience. Research has shown that callers and listeners alike seek at least one of three things from advice programs, Dr. Judy says: "They want to know they are not the only ones with a certain type of problem, to know whether or not they are normal, and to know that there is some hope or help or something they can do to solve the problem."

The entertainment value of the advice shows cannot be overlooked, says Dr. Lilli Friedland, a past president of the Association of Media Psychologists.

But entertainment is anything that gets the ratings up. And that's sad, because it doesn't mean the program is education or has benefits of any kind—it just means the sponsors are happy because a lot of people are listening. But what we can do over the air is give advice or education. And the best way to do that is to take what the caller brings up and expand it to a generalized situation. We have to be clear about the fact that we can't know very much about the person calling in. But we might illuminate certain points that could help that person cope, or help people in general to cope. Then it's advice or education that may help not only the individual caller but some of the audience as well.

Dr. Rodino said:

There are the positives and negatives of advice-giving on the airwaves. Many of the listeners may generalize some of the advice to their own life, but it may not work with them, or with the caller either. And the caller isn't given much chance to go try it out, see how it works, and come back again next week. Also, both the caller and the listeners might get the sense that this momentary advice given by the radio therapist should be the answer or solution and resolve the issue. But it's very unlikely that this kind of quick advice could do that and be a major help over a long period of time. And can these persons be expected to follow through on the advice? In therapy there would be ongoing feedback with the therapist who can redirect the advice if it's not working, or alter it or reward the behavior. That can't happen in a five-minute time slot on the air.

Notes

1. *New York Times*, July 18, 1970, p. 25.

2. John Dunning, *Tune in Yesterday* (New York: Prentice Hall, 1967), p. 242.

3. Ibid.

4. Ibid., p. 243.

5. *Current Biography* (1942), p. 23.

6. *New Yorker*, September 13, 1958, cited in *Current Biography* (1971), p. 66.

DONALD KENT and his parents and siblings regularly listened to Mr. Anthony's Sunday-night programs in the thirties and forties. After a twenty-four-year career as a Foreign Service Information Officer, Kent joined the American Psychological Association in 1982 as Public Information Director. His first experiences with media psychologists date from his five years at that job. Currently, he is a reporter for the monthly membership publication of the American Psychological Society. He also writes on psychology, mental health, substance abuse, and behavioral medicine for university publications and participates in the peer review processes of research and development agencies of the Department of Health and Human Services. His foreign service career included ten years with the American Embassy in Paris and shorter periods in Ethiopia, Zaire, and as a State Department Press Officer

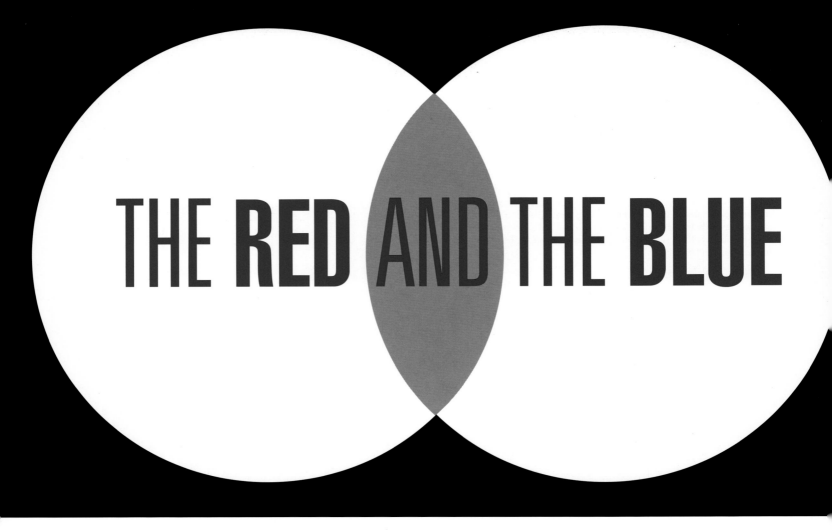

THE RED AND THE BLUE

THE NBC COLLECTION AT THE LIBRARY OF CONGRESS

BY KATHLEEN B. MILLER

Among the National Broadcasting Company archives, which the network called its "history files," is a rather ordinary letter, presumably saved in that location by mistake. Addressed to the network in 1984, the letter is from a man in St. Louis who wanted to know the call letters of the two radio stations in that city which were affiliated with NBC in 1940. One of the stations, he wrote, was on NBC's Red Network; the other on its Blue Network counterpart. Having tried unsuccessfully to obtain the information from local libraries and newspapers, he was turning to NBC for help.

The author of the letter knew something about NBC that most Americans either never knew or have forgotten: From 1927 until 1942, it was composed of two smaller networks, the Red and the Blue, which featured different programs. Thus, larger American cities, like St. Louis, had not one but two NBC affiliates essentially in competition with one another. Stapled to the inquiry is the first draft of a reply from a network employee stating that no sources had been found with the desired information. Yet the fact that correspondence was found in a file containing a 1939 network map identifying all NBC affiliates as of that year and that

the correct call letters of the St. Louis stations—KSD on the Red Network and KWK on the Blue—were scribbled at the bottom of her draft suggest that the gentleman finally did receive the information he had sought.

Although NBC must have received many inquiries about its past, it was not, of course, in the business of being a reference resource to the public and therefore inadequately staffed to handle such requests. Yet the network deserves much credit for saving its archives—CBS, it is believed, did not—and for eventually making them accessible to the public.

In 1992, the history files and a vast array of other archival materials (many relating to television) were donated by NBC to the Library of Congress, which was already in possession of the perfect complement to this bequest—approximately seventy-five thousand hours of NBC radio broadcast sound recordings. Housed in the Library's Motion Picture, Broadcasting, and Recorded Sound Division (MBRS), the NBC Collection constitutes not only the largest single repository of radio archives and broadcast sound recordings in America, but one that is also distinguished for its broad range of documentation.

Providing a context for our introduction to the NBC Collection, the story of the Red and Blue Networks follows and it focuses on their origins, as illuminated by some of the most important and entertaining materials in the collection. These include early documents from the history files; the pre-NBC logbooks of stations WEAF and WJZ (the future flagship stations of the Red and Blue Networks, respective-

ly), which list the daily programs; microfilmed copies of WEAF's early master books, containing program scripts and ad copy; and WEAF's pre-NBC press releases. (Evidently none of WJZ's early scripts was saved, and it is not known if the station even issued press releases before the formation of NBC.)

These sources not only explain the origins of NBC and commercial radio in general but, more importantly, comprise the best resource in America for reconstructing the

■ The technical superiority of WCAP's broadcasts was not the only reason Washington audiences preferred the AT&T station to RCA-owned WRC. Referring to the latter, a dissatisfied Washington listener wrote RCA president General James Harbord in 1923:

The artists in New York are so far in advance of any we have here in this city that your programs have met with criticism on every hand. Your service has to suffer until such time as you are able to arrange to broadcast the music of artists as good as WCAP. The Sunday evening program of WCAP broadcast from the studio of the Capitol Theatre, NYC, is eagerly looked forward to by all radio fans.

Shown here is the man who produced and directed that Sunday evening program—impresario Sam ("Roxy") Rothafel, manager of the Capitol Theatre, just north of Times Square. America's largest motion picture house at the time, the Capitol was also renowned for its live stage shows featuring primarily classical and semi-classical music. Eager to test the effectiveness of Western Electric's latest sound equipment from a remote (non-studio) setting, AT&T began broadcasting Roxy's Capitol Theatre artists in late 1922. It was probably no accident that the Western Electric microphone (shaped, appropriately, like a phone dial) is of equal stature in the photo to Roxy.

The program became known as *Roxy and His Gang*, a title that captures the folksy style in which Rothafel addressed his radio audience, but one which belies the high quality of the talent. Indeed, listed in WEAF's master books and press releases as concertmaster of the Capitol Theatre's orchestra is Eugene Ormandy.

content, and recapturing the flavor of early radio in the absence of broadcast sound recordings, few of which exist before the mid-1930s.

The Birth of Radio Broadcasting

In the early 1920s America entered the broadcasting age. No longer primarily an instrument for message transmission via wireless (as radio was then called), telegraphy, and telephony, radio was now a source of information and entertainment potentially available to everyone. As a result, radio was big business—in the hands of corporations that not only held patents on radio parts and equipment but were also station owners. As competitors in a young, essentially unregulated industry, these companies came into conflict. The resolution of their differences culminated in 1926 with the formation of NBC.

Facing off in the "radio wars" of the 1920s were the American Telephone and Telegraph Company (AT&T) and its subsidiary Western Electric—the so-called Telephone Group—and their Radio Group adversaries, composed of General Electric (GE), Westinghouse, and the Radio Corporation of America (RCA itself was partly owned by GE and Westinghouse). Between 1919 and 1921, the five companies had signed a set of agreements granting one another exclusive licenses in the field of radio based on the patents they had acquired previously. Problems arose from the fact that the patent-licensing agreements had been fashioned before the broadcasting boom, when radio was chiefly an instrument for point-to-point communication. When applied to broadcasting, the agreements became subject to differing interpretations by the Radio and Telephone Groups. Hostilities between AT&T and RCA were exacerbated by the fact that both owned rival radio stations in New York and Washington.

The New York stations owned by AT&T and RCA were WEAF and WJZ, respectively, the future flagship stations of the Red and Blue Networks. One of the oldest broadcasting stations in America, WJZ was founded by Westinghouse in 1921 and located in a company factory in Newark. To save New York performers a long commute across the Hudson, an additional studio, connected by Western Union wires to the Newark transmitters, was installed the following year in the old Waldorf-Astoria at Fifth Avenue and 34th Street, where the Empire State Building stands today.

In 1923 RCA took over the station and transferred the entire facility from Newark to New York, where it shared its quarters and staff with station WJY, already owned and operated by RCA. Assigned to the same frequency, the stations alternated their broadcasting hours. (Gradually, WJY became subordinate to WJZ, operating on a reduced schedule and disappearing altogether after the formation of NBC.) As station owner, RCA had much at stake: good broadcasting would result in the sale of receiver sets and parts, manufactured by GE and Westinghouse but distributed exclusively by RCA.

Meanwhile, with the opening of WEAF in the summer of 1922, AT&T had ventured into broadcasting for very different reasons. Since similar transmitting equipment was used for telephony and broadcasting, a radio station provided the phone company with a new venue for testing its latest technology. WEAF also operated as an experiment in "toll broadcasting"—Telephone Company parlance for radio advertising. Although hotels and department stores had already opened radio stations as publicity vehicles, AT&T was the first station owner actually to sell air time to outside sponsors, claiming, moreover, the exclusive right to do so on the basis of the patent-licensing agreements.[1] After a slow start, WEAF eventually surpassed WJZ in popularity and commercialism—a distinction that survived into the NBC years and broadly characterized the differences between the Red and Blue Networks.

Although there are no documents in the history files relating specifically to the early rivalry between WEAF and WJZ, the files do contain letters pertaining to WCAP and WRC, their respective sister stations in Washington.[2] There, as in New York, RCA continually faced an uphill battle against a formidable competitor. A self-described "Disappointed Invalid," whose sentiments were echoed by other Washington listeners, wrote WRC in August 1923: "Your broadcasting is pitifully poor while that of the Telephone Company is 100% efficient. . . . Go out and listen in on some of your work and then call on the Telephone people to start you right." (August 9, 1923)

The precise nature of WRC's "inefficiency" is not made clear, but we do know that the phone company stations were equipped with better transmitters than their RCA rivals. AT&T also, of course, owned the phone lines, which proved to be the most effective medium for relaying sound from a remote location back to the broadcasting studio as well as for hooking up two or more distant stations in a network for the purpose of shared programming. With few exceptions, however, AT&T refused to lease its wires to the Radio Group allies. To do so, the phone company argued, would be to jeopardize its valuable patent-licensing rights. Generally, only stations that paid AT&T a licensing fee had access to its superior equipment.

Perhaps this explains why David Sarnoff, then vice-president and general manager of RCA, admonished WRC's beleaguered station manager, F. E. Guthrie, not to "yield one inch to the Telephone Company in Washington because they have done nothing for us in the way of granting us facilities or making it possible for us to broadcast in Washington events in which the Washington public is interested." (October 9, 1923) Charles Popenoe, RCA's broadcasting manager, used even stronger language to vent his fury toward the phone company: "We have been trampled upon by these people time and again and now is the time to draw the line." (January 16, 1925)

AT&T's refusal to lease its phone lines to the Radio Group allies did not prevent them from broadcasting programs from remote locations, nor from frequently connecting two or more of their stations in a network. But it usually forced them to rely on inferior equipment—namely, the telegraph wires, which were never intended to transmit the human voice, much less music. Indeed, the early logbooks of WJZ and WJY, annotated by studio personnel, reveal that remote and network broadcasts were continually plagued by wire problems.

Commercial sponsorship served to increase AT&T's competitive edge. Many documents in the history files describe early advertising over WEAF, but none substitutes for the actual words themselves, recorded in the station master books. On August 28, 1922, "Mr. Blackwell" from the Queensboro Corporation stepped up to the microphone to deliver radio's first paid advertisement. He began:

It is fifty-eight years since Nathaniel Hawthorne, the greatest of American fictionists, passed away. To honor his memory the Queensboro Corporation, creator and operator of the tenant-owned system of apartment homes at Jackson Heights, New York City, has named its latest group of high-grade dwellings "Hawthorne Court."

Mr. Blackwell went on to describe a newly opened transit line that put Hawthorne Court within minutes of Manhattan and to lecture his audience on the salubrious effects of suburban living:

There should be more Hawthorne sermons preached about the utter inadequacy and the general hopelessness of the congested city home. The cry of the heart is for more living room, more chance to unfold, more opportunity to get near to Mother Earth, to play, to romp, to plant and to dig. . . . Let me enjoin you as you value your health and your hopes and your home happiness—get away from the solid masses of brick, where the meagre opening admitting a slant of sunlight is mockingly called a light shaft, and where children grow up starved for a run over a patch of grass and the sight of a tree.

Despite reports that the ten-minute ad resulted in several apartment sales, sponsors were slow to line up outside AT&T's "phone booth of the air" due to a strong aversion in those days to the very notion of advertising over the airwaves. Even David Sarnoff, who later built a network giant—NBC—on the advertising dollar was initially opposed. He favored the establishment of an independent corporation which would fund broadcasting through a tax on receiver sets, as the British Broadcasting Corporation is supported. Careful not to offend the public, nor to displease the government which had advised AT&T to ban "direct advertising," the phone company established strict guide-

WEAF and WJZ also aired radio plays, which are believed to have originated in 1922 at WGY, General Electric's station in Schenectady. Beginning in 1923, performances by The WGY Players (shown here in a 1926 publicity shot intended to illustrate the various ways in which sound effects were produced), were fed through the Western Union wires to WJZ, where they consistently garnered high praise from that sta- tion's often hard-to-please announcers. Like musical artists in radio's earliest days, the actors, including leading lady Rosaline Greene (pictured center), were not paid for their performances. A school teacher by training, Miss Greene went on to become a featured performer in numerous plays, serials, and variety shows over NBC.

lines for future sponsors. They could not describe the physical properties of their products, quote prices, or mention the location of their stores.

Intended to ensure discreet and tasteful radio advertising, AT&T's restrictions usually produced the opposite effect. Prohibited from simply pitching their products, advertisers often resorted to promotional gimmicks, as illustrated by the following commercial for the Happiness Candy Stores, sponsor of the popular song-and-patter team of Billy Jones and Ernie Hare—the so-called Happiness Boys.

> "The Home That Happiness Built" in Forest Hills, Long Island and that was given away free by the Happiness Candy Stores to emphasize the fact that Home, Happiness and Happiness Candy are closely connected was delivered to its winner, Traffic Officer, Oscar Hettler of the New York Police Force, and Mr. And Mrs. Hettler and their five little children moved into "The Home That Happiness Built" today. With the thought of home at this time comes the thought of Mother for Sunday, May 11th, is Mother's Day and sons and daughters everywhere will think of sending some remembrance to their mothers. You can make mother happy on Mother's Day by sending Happiness to her. (May 9, 1924)

All of WEAF's early commercial programs, even those which appealed to the most educated audiences, ended with a plea for fan mail: "Make the Happiness Boys happy by sending friendly letters to them," their announcer exhorted listeners. Not solely a means of gauging a show's popularity, fan mail was sometimes a way of luring customers into the stores. The A&P stocked its grocery chain not only with produce, but with "applause cards," which audiences were urged to fill out in support of the A&P Gypsy String Ensemble. Equally clever was the use of fan mail as a conduit for direct advertising. In return for letters of appreciation to the black face Gold Dust Twins, the manufacturers of Gold Dust cleansing powder rewarded listeners with a booklet entitled "The Accomplished Housewife," which, to be sure, did not endorse Ajax.

Advertising agencies also required performers to make live appearances, where, away from the studio, they could talk with impunity about the location of the nearest A&P or the price of Gold Dust powder. As a result, radio artists, who had previously worked for free, now demanded pay. To defray these additional expenses, RCA redoubled efforts already in place to find sponsors willing to underwrite the cost of programs which were commercial-free but which carried their names, like *The Royal Typewriter Salon Orchestra*. AT&T protested this practice as violating the spirit, if not the letter, of the patent-licensing agreements.[3] The radio wars continued to rage.

Meanwhile, America was in the throes of a radio craze. Sales of receiver sets soared, to the benefit of RCA, while the phone company's already ample coffers began to overflow as the resistance to radio advertising showed signs of abating. A few of WEAF's sponsored programs—both lighter fare and distinguished classical music programs— were being fed to distant stations licensed by AT&T. By late 1925, a network of phone wires, specially equipped for the purpose of broadcasting, stretched as far west as St. Louis— coincidentally, to aforementioned station KSD. This was

■ **Widespread opposition to ether advertising made it difficult for WEAF to attract a steady advertising clientele in its first year of operation. So AT&T decided to start producing programs of its own, which by virtue of their popularity sponsors would want to adopt. Recruited as a sustaining (non-commercial) feature in August 1923, the song-and-patter team of Billy Jones (left) and Ernie Hare had found a sponsor in the Happiness Candy Stores by the year's end. More importantly, they experienced no diminution in popularity as a result of commercial sponsorship. Almost single-handedly, the program reversed WEAF's fortunes, as other musical acts soon obtained sponsors.**

"You remember Rosie's chow / He's living in the mustard now . . ." sang The Happiness Boys in a spirited rendition of a tune called *Pretty Puppy*, preserved in an unusually early broadcast sound recording (probably dating from July 31, 1925) in the Library's collection. Surviving the transition to NBC and spawning a host of imitators, Jones and Hare remained on the network until 1932, when elaborate variety shows were starting to supplant more modest programs like theirs. In the meantime, they had acquired a new sponsor, the Interwoven Stocking Company, and thus a new name—The Interwoven Pair.

the origin of network broadcasting and, more specifically, the genesis of NBC's Red Network.

Despite WEAF's commercial success, the vast majority of its programs were sustaining (a radio and television term meaning unsponsored) and similar to WJZ's, judging from their respective logs. Both stations devoted more than two-thirds of their programming hours to music, consisting primarily of solo and small ensemble studio performances. The music ranged from classical to popular, with greater emphasis in the direction of the former. Most of the works were familiar—such as Beethoven, Chopin, and Tchaikovsky—but occasionally time was ceded to lesser known composers from different cultures in an effort to appeal to a broad cross section of New York's diverse population. Chinese songs were once performed over WJZ.

Not all music originated from the studio. Remote broadcasts of hotel bands or orchestras were daily staples, as were symphony concerts. Opera proved so popular that in 1925 WEAF established a resident company, sustained at the station's own expense. This set an important precedent for NBC, which would channel a portion of its advertising revenues into the production of costly classical music programming.

Choosing to play it safe, WEAF and WJZ were less receptive to jazz, which was creating a sensation in the recording industry by the midtwenties, but in many circles was still considered risqué. In general, the stations limited their presentation of such innovative music to lively hotel bands which incorporated jazz elements within a classically orchestrated framework—"decaffeinated jazz," in the words of historian Erik Barnouw.[4] More traditional musical forms of African-American influence, on the other hand, were frequently aired. WJZ's logs record performances by the Bordentown Male Quartet, which sang spirituals; the Tuskegee Male Quartet; and the Colored Entertainers, possibly a minstrel group. In 1924, WEAF featured weekly performances by "that group of talented negroes . . . [those] singers and jokesters," as the Eveready Battery Minstrels were described by their announcer. Minstrel shows remained popular with radio audiences through the 1930s.

Turning to nonmusical programming, there is enough material in the logs to sustain a horde of social historians. WJZ listeners received French lessons from Berlitz, lectures from Harper Brothers publishers on the latest game sensation pung chow (as mah-jongg was also called), daily vocabulary lessons, and at least one "radio boxing lesson." There were weekly talks on different dog breeds by Frank Dole of *Harper's Bazaar*; sporting lectures by Harold McCracken from *Field and Stream* (one entitled "Grizzly Bears I Have Met"); and occasional appearances by playwright Robert Sherwood, who served then as film critic for *Life*.

Weekday morning programming, primarily geared to women, invariably began with Mrs. Julian Heath's reading of "The Housewives' League Daily Menu." Typically, a lecture under the auspices of a women's magazine would follow—perhaps *Vogue*, offering tips on etiquette, or *Good Housekeeping*, instructing listeners on needlepoint. More substantive fare was provided as well, especially on those occasions when employment expert Helen Hoerle addressed the subject of "The Right Job for Your Daughter."

The content of nonmusical programming over WEAF was much the same, even if its "cast of characters," was somewhat more erratic. Still, the station hosted a few regular visitors, including Thornton Fisher, whose daily sports talks sponsored by the United Cigar Stores are recorded in the master books; weekly news commentator H.V. Kaltenborn, a controversial figure throughout his long career, as attested to by numerous letters of complaint in the archives;[5] and Adele Woodard, president of the National Motion Picture League.

Both stations devoted many hours a week to public service programming, as scores of university professors lectured on politics, literature, art, finance, and current events (one week over WEAF—"The Oil Mess in Mesopotamia"). Doctors and public health officials covered topics ranging from personal hygiene to the importance of keeping infants on strict feeding schedules. Religious programs, also standard fare on the rival stations, were not limited to worship services. WEAF reserved the 4:30 time slot on Tuesday afternoons for the Women's League of the United Synagogue of America, whose varied programs (sometimes recorded in the master books) encompassed Jewish music, lectures on ritual observance, and talks on contemporary issues, such as resettlement in Palestine and the plight of Jewish immigrants in Cuba.

Our best resource for assessing the quality, as opposed to content, of early radio broadcasting are the logbooks of WJZ and WJY, where we find comments or grades assigned to each program. "Ain't I a good boy, marking up the programs," wrote announcer Tommy Cowan, adding, "P.S. I'd get hell if I didn't." Mr. Cowan and his colleagues also recorded with utter candor the little accidents and incidents that continually beset "normal" station operations—never dreaming that their comments would be saved for posterity.

Clearly, these logs present a more reliable picture of early radio than WEAF's, which contain no critical commentary, nor for that matter, an indication of any problem other than last-minute programming changes and the occasional suspension of broadcasting due to an S.O.S.[6] Indeed, WEAF's nearly pristine logs create the impression that their broadcasts approached a level of perfection virtually impossible to achieve in those days, though with its superior equipment and much larger staff, the station presumably did conduct a more sophisticated operation than its rival.

WJZ's log for the afternoon of May 24, 1923, serves to illustrate a typical day at that station. Contralto "Miss Fabian," soprano Carmen Reuben, and pung chow lecturer Lewis Harr were judged to have turned out "good" performances, while Isabel Giles received only a "fair" for her talk, "A Little Law for Ladies." But "fair" was considerably better than the assessments given to the speaker from *Youth's Companion* ("rotten") and soprano Vivian Piero ("vile"), who at least had shown up. Though scheduled to perform at 4:00, pianist Elias Goldberg had not.

"No-shows" were a recurrent problem in radio's early days, when artists received no pay. In the event of such emergencies at WJZ and WJY, another performer usually filled the empty time slot or the announcer read from a book of short stories. Occasionally, the stations relied on the operatic skills of one of their announcers—Milton J.

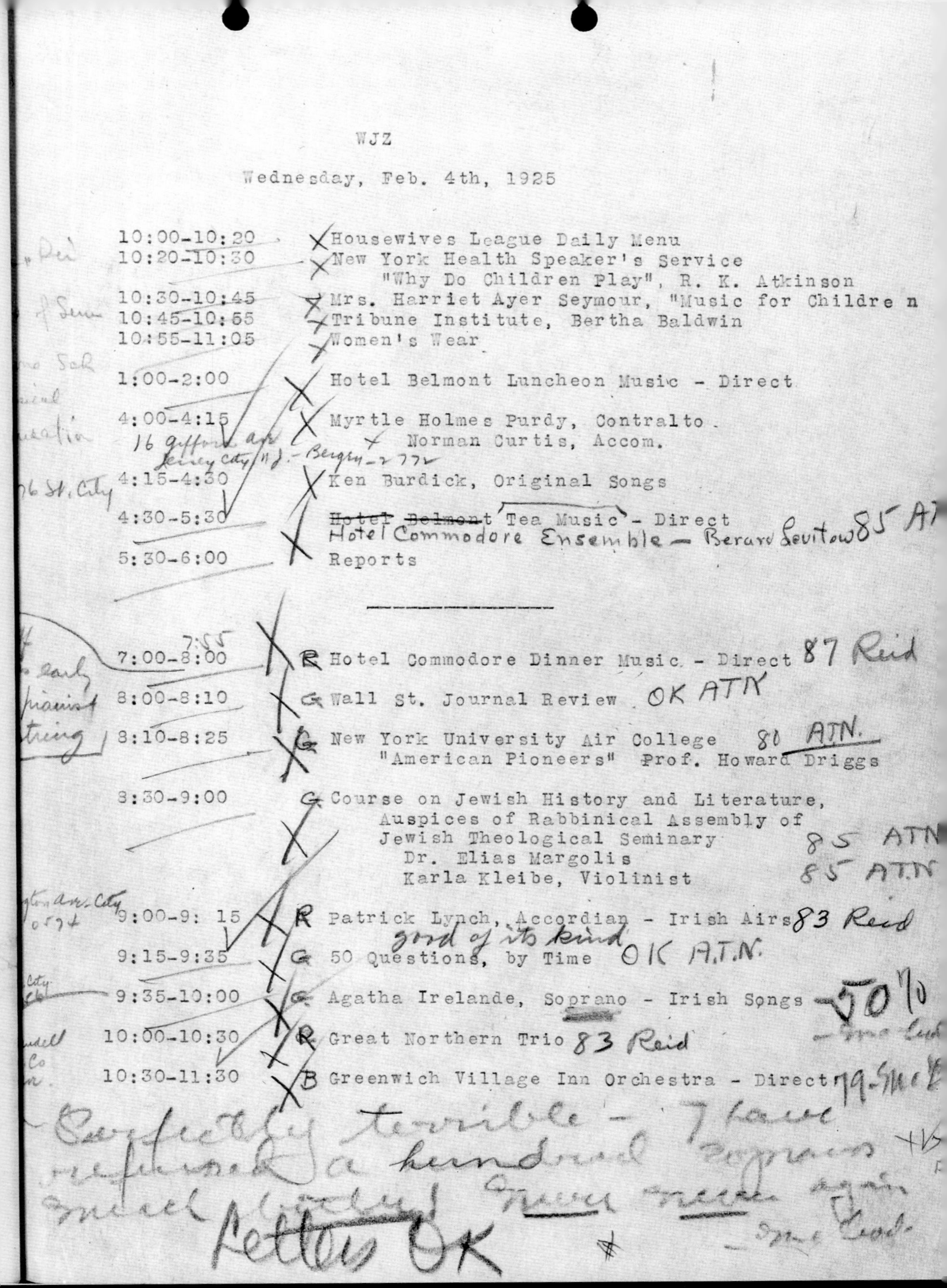

WJZ

Wednesday, Feb. 4th, 1925

10:00-10:20 ✗ Housewives League Daily Menu
10:20-10:30 ✗ New York Health Speaker's Service
         "Why Do Children Play", R. K. Atkinson
10:30-10:45 ✗ Mrs. Harriet Ayer Seymour, "Music for Children"
10:45-10:55 ✗ Tribune Institute, Bertha Baldwin
10:55-11:05 ✗ Women's Wear

1:00-2:00 ✗ Hotel Belmont Luncheon Music - Direct

4:00-4:15 ✗ Myrtle Holmes Purdy, Contralto.
         ✗ Norman Curtis, Accom.
  16 gifford ave Jersey City N.J. - Bergen-2772

4:15-4:30 ✗ Ken Burdick, Original Songs

4:30-5:30 ~~Hotel Belmont Tea Music - Direct~~
         ✗ Hotel Commodore Ensemble — *Berard Levitow* 85 A*T*

5:30-6:00 Reports

─────────────

7:00-8:00 7:55 ✗ R Hotel Commodore Dinner Music - Direct 87 *Reid*

8:00-8:10 ✗ G Wall St. Journal Review *OK ATN*

8:10-8:25 ✗ G New York University Air College 80 *ATN.*
         "American Pioneers" Prof. Howard Driggs

8:30-9:00 G Course on Jewish History and Literature,
         Auspices of Rabbinical Assembly of
         Jewish Theological Seminary 85 *ATN*
         ✗ Dr. Elias Margolis
         Karla Kleibe, Violinist 85 *A.T.N.*

9:00-9:15 ✗ R Patrick Lynch, Accordian - Irish Airs 83 *Reid*

9:15-9:35 ✗ G 50 Questions, by Time *good of its kind OK A.T.N.*

9:35-10:00 ✗ G Agatha Irelande, Soprano - Irish Songs *50%*

10:00-10:30 ✗ R Great Northern Trio 83 *Reid*

10:30-11:30 ✗ B Greenwich Village Inn Orchestra - Direct 79-*McL*

Perfectly terrible — I have refused a hundred sopranos mu... Never Never again — McLeod

Letters OK

PROGRAM — WEDNESDAY, FEBRUARY 4, 1925
STATION WEAF — AMERICAN TELEPHONE AND TELEGRAPH COMPANY
(492 Meters 610 Kilocycles) (Eastern Standard Time)
195 Broadway, New York City

11:00 A.M. Musical program to be announced.

11:10 A.M. "Tonsils and Adenoids" by Dr. Ralph Almour, speaking in connection with "Young Mother's Program" under the auspices of the New York Health Speakers Service.

11:30 A.M. Music.

11:35 A.M. Columbia University Lecture by Mary E. Rankin speaking under the auspices of Teacher's College direct from the College. Talk is the fifth in a series of "Character Building in Childhood" and is given in connection with "Young Mother's Program."

12:00 Noon Chapel Services direct from Columbia University. Address by Chaplain Raymond Knox and Music by Male Chorus and Walter Henry Hall, Organist.

12:20 P.M. Consolidated Market and Weather Reports by the United States Department of Agriculture and the New York State Department of Farms and Markets together with American Agriculturist.

- -

4:00 P.M. Jean Hannon, Lyric Soprano, accompanied by Winifred T. Barr.

4:10 P.M. Ruth Rosensweig, Pianist.

4:20 P.M. Jean Hannon, Lyric Soprano.

4:30 P.M. Ruth Rosensweig, Pianist.

4:40 P.M. Children's Stories under the auspices of the New York Public Library.

- -

6:00 P.M. Dinner Music from the Rose Room of the Hotel Waldorf-Astoria, New York City.

7:00 P.M. Synagogue Services under the auspices of the United Synagogue of America.

7:30 P.M. Rata Present, Pianist.

7:40 P.M. Grace Leslie, Contralto, accompanied by Catherine Widman. Program: In German - "Das Veilchen" (Mozart); "Madchen Lied" (Meyer-Hehmund); "Du bist wie eine Blume" (Schumann); "Mil Rosen bestrent" (Reger); "Erda's Warnung au Watan (Wagner).

7:50 P.M. "Increased Income" by Mr. H. K. Hutchens of the American Bond and Mortgage Company.

8:00 P.M. Rata Present, Pianist.

8:10 P.M. Grace Leslie, Contralto. Program: "Beloved" (Silberta); "The Changeling" "My Only Wish" (Titcomb); "My Lover is a Fisherman" (Strickland); "Recessional" (Foote).

8:20 P.M. Philharmonic Society of New York under the direction of Willem Mengelberg, in the sixth of a series of ten educational concerts for students direct from Carnegie Hall, New York City. Program: "Symphony C Major" (Schubert). Intermission. "Nutcracker Suite" (Tschaikowsky); "Overture 1812" (Tschaikowsky).

10:00 P.M. Artists Mixed Quartette.

10:40 P.M. Adam Carroll, Pianist.

11:00 to   Meyer Davis' "Lido-Venice Orchestra" direct from the Lido-Venice,
12:00 P.M. New York City.

wrote of Agatha Irelande's program of Irish songs. There was also a premature ending to the 7:00 Hotel Commodore program. From a sentence partly concealed by the binding, the words "off," "early," "pianist," and "string," presumably explain why. Surely in its early years WEAF must have endured its share of problems—from poor performances and broken strings, to scheduling mishaps and outbursts by temperamental performers. But on this date and all others, its impersonal logs disguise the truth.

Identifiable in this 1923 photo of WJZ's staff are announcers Milton Cross (last row, fourth from the left) and Thomas Cowan (front row, right), whose colorful personality is revealed not only in his log book commentary but in his dress. As that station's first announcer, Mr. Cowan established the precedent, adopted by at least some of his colleagues, for sporting formal attire when on duty.

It was customary at early radio stations for announcers to maintain their anonymity on air. Like telegraph operators, WJZ's announcers were identified in code. Tommy Cowan was known to listeners as ACN, which stood for "Announcer, Cowan, Newark (later, New York)," while Milton J. Cross employed the moniker, AJN—the letter C having already been appropriated when he joined the staff

in October 1922. This quaint practice was abandoned in 1925, presumably because WEAF's announcers, whose identities had never been hidden from audiences, had established a popular following.

The lone female in the photo, Bertha Brainard, assumed a variety of duties at WJZ. An occasional announcer (ABN), she also reviewed the stage in a bi-weekly segment called "Broadcasting Broadway" and recruited talent as the station's assistant program director. Miss Brainard was appointed NBC's first commercial program manager—the only woman to serve in an executive capacity at the network in its early years. She remained with NBC for twenty years, never obtaining top spot in her department despite her seniority.

Cross—a professional tenor who later became a legend at the Met without ever singing a note from its stage. (Mr. Cross announced and provided commentary for all but two Saturday afternoon Metropolitan Opera broadcasts, from their debut on NBC's Blue Network on Christmas Day 1931 until his death in January 1975.)

Unfortunately, the logs do not record the titles of the songs in Mr. Cross's radio repertory, but like a Rorschach test, they do provide some insight into his personality and his colleagues'. Assessing Allen Behr's performance of

"songs at piano" (jazz perhaps?) as "All right for that class of stuff," Mr. Cross was evidently elitist in his musical tastes and a stickler for detail. He once awarded a performer 69½ points out of a possible 100 and scrupulously noted every problem that occurred—even the most minor, as when a program ended a few minutes early or a singer complained that she had not received advanced publicity. Not only one of radio's greatest announcers, Milton Cross was, unwittingly, one of its most vivid chroniclers.

Using humor as his antidote to the stresses of the job, Tommy Cowan was Mr. Cross's antithesis. Reserving the highest marks for those occasions when he reported the news—10,000,000,000 percent on one occasion—Mr.

Cowan also filled the logs with such witty asides as, "Getting longer, Thank Gawd," in reference to a speaker from *Women's Wear*, and "No Come (Thank God)," when "The Threshold Players" failed to appear. Given their different temperaments, it was probably fortuitous that Tommy Cowan, rather than Milton Cross, was assigned to WJY on the evening of May 23, 1924, when a near disaster occurred during the "Hawaiian guitar" performance of Dettborn and Howard. Mr. Cowan scribbled in the log:

> We must compliment the Police Dept. Mr. Howard's wife whom he deserted two years ago, rushed in to the studio with two cops, "There he is." The cops told her "to close her face," "we won't ball up these people's program do your stuff and we'll take you when you are thru" etc. Some Radio Drama.

Further evidence that Murphy's Law seemed to govern life at the RCA stations was the time a diva refused to perform from a remote location, forcing a staff member to rush to the scene to "calm down the little witch," and repeated performance delays on the part of an orchestra leader, described by one announcer as having an "antagonistic attitude toward WJZ." There were also recurrent wire problems, including one puzzling incident in which AT&T—contrary to its usual policy—had apparently agreed to lease its phone lines to WJZ for a remote broadcast that was mysteriously delayed. Perhaps hinting at sabotage, Mr. Cross wrote in the logs, "It was Walker St.'s fault," boldly underlining the address—none other than WEAF's. It was radio warfare indeed, and we are left wondering how the two sides ever made peace.

Credit for setting the process in motion goes to the federal government which, in the midst of the radio wars, had threatened to charge both the Radio and Telephone Groups with creating monopolies as a result of the patent-licensing agreements. The warnings served to unite the adversaries on at least one issue: the pressing need to settle their differences. For nearly two years, while their case was being arbitrated in secret, both sides refused to give up the fight. Yet a letter from the history files, written shortly after the proceedings began, reveals that David Sarnoff—ever practical, if not downright prescient—urged his Washington station manager to adopt a friendlier attitude toward rival station WCAP.[7]

As the rulings came down, largely in favor of the Radio Group allies, AT&T gradually realized that, as a public utility company whose best interests were served by maintaining good relations with the government, it should withdraw from broadcasting. But how was it to do so without sacrificing its financial rewards? The Radio Group allies had devised an ingenious plan.

Using lines leased from the phone company, they would create a national network to be managed by RCA. AT&T would sell WEAF to the new network and relinquish control over its licensed stations. (WCAP, the phone company's Washington station, would be absorbed by rival station WRC.) The potential rewards of such a plan were enormous: AT&T could be assured generous, long-term line leasing profits from radio without having to assume the bur-

dens of broadcasting, while RCA, General Electric, and Westinghouse, would own the National Broadcasting Company, the first "permanent" radio network.

On September 13, 1926, RCA issued a newspaper advertisement which announced NBC's formation and purpose—"to provide the best program [sic] available for broadcasting in the United States"—as well as the new network's acquisition of WEAF for a million dollars.[8] RCA also assured the public it was "not in any sense seeking a monopoly of the air. . . . *If others engage in this business the Radio Corporation of America will welcome their activities, whether it be cooperative or competitive* [italics, theirs]." A year later, the Columbia Broadcasting System (CBS) entered the broadcasting arena, providing RCA with an even more formidable and enduring adversary than AT&T.

The announcement failed to mention that NBC would be supported by advertising—a foregone conclusion, given the success of AT&T's commercial venture, but better left unsaid. (Thanks to a lifting of the ban on direct advertising and to NBC's insistence that sponsors use discretion, early commercials over the network were both tasteful and brief.) Nor was there any reference in the announcement to the fact that NBC would be composed of two networks. According to "official" NBC histories in the archives, RCA originally had no intention of operating a second network. To explain its change of plans, the author of one such history cited David Sarnoff's testimony before the Federal Communications Commission (FCC) on November 14, 1938:

> As soon as our formation of a national broadcasting company was announced, independent station owners, local civic organizations and community leaders from every section of the United States wrote, telephoned or called in person to ascertain how soon network programs would be brought to their communities.
>
> To meet the popular demand represented by these requests, NBC rapidly expanded the experimental hook-ups of the Red Network into a regular service arrangement. . . . It quickly became apparent that a single network service was not enough to satisfy the demands of the radio audience for diversified programs of national interest and importance; that if broadcasting were to be popularized to all, there should be more than one type of program simultaneously available to listeners.[9]

If we are to believe Mr. Sarnoff's explanation, we must then conclude that RCA had planned to allow its premier station, WJZ, in which it had invested so much, simply to fade into oblivion like its sister station WJY. Perhaps that was the case, but it is also possible that, in an effort to appease a government increasingly suspicious of monopolies, RCA had deliberately suppressed mention of its intention to operate two networks. If so, it would not have been the last time its publicity department rewrote history.

Our story digresses for a moment to relate an amusing example. Among the NBC archives is RCA's unpublished "Biographical Sketch of Brigadier General David Sarnoff," which greatly exaggerates his importance in the immediate aftermath of the *Titanic* disaster.[10] Employed at the time as a radio telegraph operator at Wanamaker's department store

■ From the start, NBC's programming department carefully censored all scripts to ensure their suitability for broadcasting. As the number of straight musical programs declined in the 1930s and the number of more fully scripted programs, such as comedies and soap operas, rose, NBC established a department of "Continuity Acceptance"—a euphemism for censorship. It was headed by Janet MacRorie, whose background included work in theater, journalism, and public relations. She and her staff were responsible for seeing that program scripts and ad copy stayed within the bounds of good taste and that they conformed with NBC's ever-changing program policies. For instance, a script that presented divorce as an acceptable solution to a troubled marriage would have been rejected in the 1930s but accepted the following decade.

No doubt Miss MacRorie's most difficult task was determining where to draw the line with comedians, as too little censorship of their material might be seen as permitting tastelessness, while too much risked obliterating the intended comic effect. Clearly, she accepted the fact that humor, almost by definition, caused offense. In response to this ludicrous, but fairly typical letter of complaint from the history files, Miss MacRorie sent the following memo to her colleague Bertha Brainard:

Jack Benny is the only performer on NBC networks on Sunday evening who can be classed as a comedian. I feel certain that no joke told on the Jello program . . . was ever so objectionable as to shock a listener to the point of turning off the radio . . . I would ask her [Miss Geer] to point to any advertising medium, theatre or other form of entertainment, that is as free from the objectionable as is radio. In fact, it occurs to me sometimes that, insofar as the entertainment is concerned, it threatens to be cleaned up to the point where it will no longer be interesting. (June 12, 1936)

Miss MacRorie resigned from NBC in 1942, claiming that its program policies had become confused. Scattered pieces of evidence from the archives suggest that one network executive may have wanted her out, for reasons that remain unclear. The truth about her departure will probably never be known—lost, ironically, when the files themselves became subject to a censor's scrutiny.

in New York (where the wireless served primarily as a publicity gimmick), Sarnoff clearly was in radio contact with the rescue ship *Carpathia* and helped relay the names of victims and survivors to the outside world. That alone was quite an achievement for a twenty-one-year-old Russian immigrant who had arrived in America only twelve years before. But evidently it was not enough for RCA, which strongly implied in its account that David Sarnoff was the first American to receive word of the tragedy and was almost solely responsible for keeping an entire nation informed of the news from sea for three whole days until the *Carpathia* sailed into port. Citing such contradictory evidence as the fact that the first wireless reports of the accident were transmitted in the predawn hours of the morning, when Wanamaker's would have been closed—even to its dedicated young telegraph operator—recent scholarship has not only exposed the account as myth, but pointed a finger at Sarnoff himself as one of its perpetrators. [11]

Whatever the truth may have been concerning RCA's decision to operate a second network, WJZ did, of course, survive. And as the designated flagship station of NBC's Blue Network, it remained in competition with its old nemesis, WEAF, the key station of the Red. As for the origin of the networks' "colorful" names—AT&T engineers had used red and blue pencils to differentiate the wire paths of the two proposed networks on blank maps of the United States.

CHARLOTTE GEER

2 MELROSE PLACE, MONTCLAIR, NEW JERSEY

During the last few weeks I have caught a number of gags on your network that are certainly not fit for a mixed audience such as radio has. Only last week a socialite of Montclair told me that on a recent Sunday evening her debutant daughter had a bunch of youngsters at the house and turned on the radio. The comedian's lines were so bad that her father...a wall street man at that.. made a rule that the radio could not be turned on again for a group of youngsters to listen to..

Don't you realize down there that the listener is not the nightclub addict? He is a quiet conservative guy of suberbia or the farm and he will not tolerate dirty jokes in his home. If he happens to enjoy them with a group of cronies he is all the more determined that his children and his wife wont hear them. In other words you are losing out equally with the hick and the sophisticate.

If you knew how strongly the better class of Jerseymen object to such stuff as we hear lately you would appreciate the undoubted fact that radio receivers will be covered with cobwebs in this part of the world unless it is cleaned up. You just can't get away with it and you may wake up too late.

CHARLOTTE GEER

2 MELROSE PLACE, MONTCLAIR, NEW JERSEY

As you know I love my Broadway and I don't think I'd be accused of being a prude but through my fan mail and through the 60 or 70 speeches on radio which I make each winter I know a bit about honest public re-action and I know that unless radio is kept clean it is through.

I am also not a little upset at the way NBC has let down the bars to quacks and sex stuff, Is money tight or what? You always kept so clear of that sort of program and earned the respect of your audience thereby. Are you going to throw away what has taken ten long years to build up and to do it just when the better class of listener is finally becoming radio conciou

I just can't understand it and because I have watched radio grow up and because I love the NBC I can't let an opportunity pass to tell you how immediate and how bitter is the reaction of listeners you cant afford to lose.

Please don't get sore, I expect I've been pretty frank but I cant bear to see you throw away something so fine and so full of promise just because a few comedians want to get a belly laugh from their friends or an advertiser wants to reach a questionable audience through vulgar sensationalism. Do snap out of it---before radio like Vaudeville, is through.

As always...

June 10th

To introduce NBC to America, an inaugural broadcast fed to twenty-four stations from New York to Kansas City was scheduled for November 15, 1926, in the grand ballroom of the old Waldorf-Astoria. Promising in a press release "the most pretentious [sic] program ever presented in one evening on the air,"[12] NBC lived up to its word. Lighter programming fare was furnished by several popular dance bands, the comedy team of Weber and Fields, and a monologue by Will Rogers, broadcast remote from the backstage of a theater in Independence, Kansas. NBC also presented such exemplars of high culture as the New York Symphony Orchestra led by Walter Damrosch, the New York Oratorio Society under Albert Stoessel, and world-renowned opera stars Titto Ruffo and Mary Garden. To the estimated twelve million Americans who had tuned in, a clear message was conveyed: NBC would not only entertain America, but, more importantly, serve as its cultural mentor. That promise too was upheld.

And so AT&T's great experiment in broadcasting had come to an end. As a measure of its unqualified success, NBC not only adopted the phone company's stations and programs but its modus operandi. Like AT&T, NBC would reap huge profits from advertising, while maintaining its commitment to public service and projecting an unsullied image to the outside world. A publicity department modeled after WEAF's would aid in that effort.[13] Scripts would be scrupulously censored. No longer would the pages of WJZ's logbooks be marred by telltale comments and grades. Even the history files would be cleansed of potentially embarrassing contents. Still, they reveal the troubles that NBC faced in the coming years—many resulting from its bold gamble to operate two networks.

Before proceeding with the story of the Red and Blue Networks as it emerges from a study of the collection, we shall outline the major resources of that collection: the history files, logbooks, and master books; sound recordings, press releases, and a remarkable resource unmentioned so far—a comprehensive index card catalog of NBC radio programs and performers from 1930 to 1960.

The History Files

Approximately thirteen hundred files containing tens of thousands of documents comprise what NBC called its "history files." Consisting primarily of business papers, the files also include the reminiscences of early employees, printed memorabilia (such as anniversary programs), network histories, audience mail, statistics, charts, and maps. Most of the materials date from the mid-1920s through the late 1940s, when network radio was starting its decline as a result of television. Documents in the files relating to the newer medium, though less extensive, are still numerous. To facilitate access to this information, the Library created a 436-page

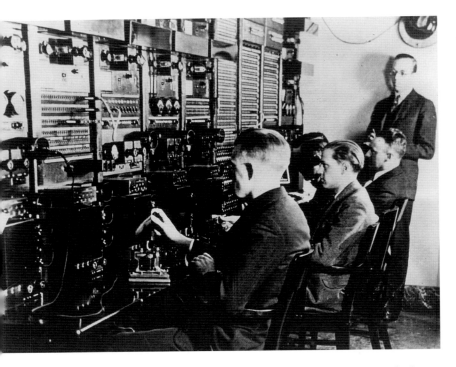

MATZENE
CHICAGO

■ **WEAF engineers on the night of November 15, 1926 relaying NBC's inaugural broadcast to twenty-four stations from New York to Kansas City, and some of the gala's featured performers: Metropolitan Opera baritone Titto Ruffo (dressed as Rigoletto, his most famous role); lyric soprano Mary Garden, who sang that evening from her studio/apartment in Chicago, with WJZ announcer Milton Cross in attendance to provide an introduction befitting her status as a star; and New York Symphony founder and conductor Walter Damrosch.**

From contemporary news accounts we learn that a photo of Miss Garden, taken shortly before she stepped up to the microphone in Chicago, was transmitted through the phone wires to the Waldorf, where it was shown thirteen minutes later to NBC's inaugural guests. Another performer, it was reported, barely made it to the hotel in time; arriving in New York that afternoon on the quarantined steamship *Franconia*, classical pianist Harold Bauer remained on board until NBC obtained special permission from Washington to allow him off the ship and into a chartered tug.

Although no portion of the broadcast was recorded, a reconstructed script of the program—including a list of its musical contents, Will Rogers's monologue, and a sketch by vaudeville comics Weber and Fields—is preserved in WEAF's master books.

computerized inventory which describes the most important contents of each file. Also listed in the inventory are hundreds of miscellaneous publications (many relating to advertising and to television) and the speech files of NBC executives, including those of Sylvester ("Pat") Weaver, creator of the *Today* and *Tonight* shows, handsomely bound.

Despite their great quantity, the materials in the files obviously represent only a tiny fraction of the documents produced or collected by NBC in those years, which raises an important question: Why did NBC save certain materials and discard others? Although we do not really know, we may assume that NBC disposed of most documents considered sensitive or potentially libelous, with the exception of a damning file on outspoken news commentator-gossip-monger Walter Winchell, a chronic headache for network executives. Possibly in deference to its sponsors—NBC's

chief source of revenue—the network also failed to save (or at least pass on to the Library of Congress) correspondence addressed to and from these advertisers and the agencies responsible for their programs.

To some extent, what was saved was probably a matter of chance. How else can one explain the fact that there are many documents that detail how NBC determined program policies (what was permissible or forbidden over the airwaves) but almost none about how specific programs were conceived and developed? Perhaps some departments or executives were simply more careful about saving their papers than others.

The files are particularly strong in certain areas. There are no secondary sources that chronicle in such detail NBC's early history or the problems resulting from NBC's operation of two networks. But what is perhaps most valuable about the history files is that, in spite of their omissions, they still present an excellent overview of how the network operated and, more specifically, how it juggled the difficult role of playing servant to many masters—sponsors, performers, and affiliates, as well as the government, special interest groups, and the listening public.

The Logbooks

The logbooks of WEAF (renamed WNBC in 1946) and WJZ list the daily programs and the call letters of all stations receiving those programs. As the number of affiliates rose, the combinations and permutations of networking became rather complicated. Thus, beginning with 1930 volume, the logs are no longer titled "Daily Programs," but rather, more descriptively, "Corrected Traffic Sheets." Only the

pre-NBC logs of WJZ and its sister station WJY contain critical commentary by the station announcers. However, some NBC logs provide supplementary information of a more objective nature, such as the musical contents of a program, the name of a guest artist, or the interruption of a scheduled program due to a news bulletin. Information of this type is usually found on the verso. The dates of the logbooks in the collection follow:

The WEAF/WNBC logs: 1922-1955

The WJZ logs: 1923 (the year RCA assumed control of the station)-1941 (when the Blue Network was divorced from NBC)

The WJY logs: 1923-1926 (the station's final year of operation).

The Master Books

In addition to the logbooks of WEAF (renamed WNBC in 1946) and WJZ, NBC donated microfilmed copies of the station master books. The master books contain the paper documentation of the programs produced at those stations. This documentation consists of program scripts, ad copy, news copy, and the so-called master music sheets, which list the musical contents of the programs. The documentation for programs aired over WEAF or WJZ, but produced elsewhere, are not included in their master books, but rather, presumably, in the master books of the stations where those programs originated. Many network programs were produced at NBC's regional studios in Chicago, San Francisco, and Hollywood.

A limited number of program scripts from the Chicago and Hollywood master books are included in the NBC Collection. These date from the war years. Under normal circumstances, those scripts would have been reviewed only by NBC censors in Chicago or Hollywood. But, perhaps for reasons having to do with the war, NBC was compelled to reexamine them at network headquarters in New York.

Also included in the collection are the microfilmed master books of NBC's International Network (sometimes called the White Network), composed of several shortwave stations whose broadcasts in six different languages were intended for overseas listeners. Altogether, 2,530 reels of microfilmed master books (including the Chicago and Hollywood scripts) were bequeathed by NBC to the Library. Comprising the largest radio script collection in America, they are inventoried below:

The WEAF/WNBC master books: 1922-1984

The WJZ master books: 1927 (when the station began broadcasting as the flagship station of the Blue Network)-1941 (when the Blue Network was divorced from NBC)

The Chicago scripts: May 1944-December 1945

The Hollywood scripts: August 1943-December 1945

The International Network master books: August 1936-September 1948.

The Recordings

The Library's NBC Collection includes less than two hundred sound recordings of network programs up to 1935.

LAYOUT OF
PROPOSED RED AND BLUE NETWORKS
WITH EXTENSIONS

KEY:

Proposed / Extended	Pernament Red Network
Proposed / Extended	Pernament Biue Network
Proposed / Extended	Temporary Red Network
Proposed / Extended	Temporary Biue Network

■ The growth of the Red and Blue Networks can be traced through numerous maps in the history files. This map from February 1927 is probably similar, if not identical, to the first network plan drawn up by AT&T engineers in the fall of 1926. Unlike later maps in the files, it does not indicate the station call letters. What it clearly does show is the Blue Network's disadvantaged position from the start with respect to station numbers—the Red boasting three times more.

As former licensees of AT&T and recipients of some of WEAF's popular programs, the majority of these charter Red Network stations enjoyed considerable prestige even before the formation of NBC. As a result, most of NBC's early sponsors wanted their programs placed on the Red Network. The Blue, by default, immediately established a less commercial character. It carried a greater share of sustaining programs and retained for a longer period of time vestiges of the so-called potted palm atmosphere of radio's early days, when studio performances of classical and light classical music predominated.

Most of these were produced by outside sources, such as RCA Victor, rather than NBC itself.[14] The invention of the lacquer disc in 1934 greatly facilitated the sound recording process, and as a result, NBC started recording many of its own programs, sporadically at first and with increasing frequency as the decade proceeded. From 1935 to 1939, the number of annually recorded programs retained in the NBC archive jumps from 661 to 3,007. The majority of

these recordings are of programs originating from New York. NBC's Chicago and Hollywood bureaus maintained their own recording archives, which were never incorporated within the network's primary, New York-based archive, now in the Library.

In general, the more important or prestigious the sustaining program, the greater the chance it would be preserved, as there are many recordings from the 1930s of opera, symphony, historic news broadcasts, and public affairs programs. The range of recorded commercial programs from this period is more puzzling and seemingly random. For some shows, such as Fred Allen's *Town Hall Tonight*, the inventory of recorded programs is nearly complete, while for others, no less popular, it is scant. One possible explanation for these discrepancies is that when NBC recorded a program at the behest of a sponsor or performer (the network established a commercial recording service in 1936), it sometimes produced a duplicate disc for its archive. Another factor to consider is that NBC did not save all recordings in its archive, but which ones were destroyed and why are not known. In the end, many questions about the recordings, like the history files, remain unanswered.

Following Pearl Harbor, the number of recorded programs in the archive soars, with Hollywood and Chicago programs now commensurate with their actual numbers. Peaking in 1944, the inventory for that year lists nearly nine thousand programs—including many news broadcasts. In addition to documenting the course of events, the wartime recordings provide vivid testimony of NBC's dedication to the war effort and of how Americans coped with the crisis. Naturally, humor was an important outlet, much of it at the expense of the enemy—the Japanese, far more commonly an object of ridicule than America's European foes.

Since receiving the NBC recordings in 1978, engineers in the Library's Recording Laboratory have been engaged in rerecording the fragile lacquer discs onto more durable polyester tape. So far, all discs through 1952 have been rerecorded. The remainder, which date to 1971, are still in the process of being preserved. In a parallel effort, Library catalogers, initially funded by a grant from the MacArthur Foundation, have created a comprehensive computerized inventory of the programs preserved on tape.

The Index Cards

Posterity owes an enormous debt to the scores of anonymous NBC employees who, between the years 1930 and 1960, compiled a comprehensive index card catalog of network programs, performers, and guests. It is the logical place to begin searching the collection for information in any one of these three areas. The catalog is composed of four major indexes: one for all commercial programs and another for all sustaining programs from 1930 to 1960; and two biographical indexes, comprising all "radio artists" (entertainment professionals) and "radio personalities" (basically everyone else, from authors and athletes to labor leaders and presidents) who appeared over the network during that thirty-year period.

The inspiration for the catalog came from AT&T, which kept summary records of WEAF's commercial programs on index cards. Some of these cards are still extant and incorporated within NBC's commercial program index. Typically, the NBC program cards contain a brief description of the show and also note its starting and ending dates, network affiliation (Red or Blue), hours of broadcast, advertising agency and agent (in the case of commercial programs), as well as the names of the stars, host, announcer, and orchestra.

Many program cards also include a complete rundown of every broadcast, where cast changes, guest performers, and sometimes even plot summaries are recorded. Notable facts, such as a cast member's final appearance, are often underlined in red. Carleton Morse's dramatic serial, *One Man's Family*, which ran over NBC for twenty-seven years, is described on forty-six, two-sided cards, some of which contain detailed genealogies of the fictional Barbour family.

The catalog is not only of interest to radio historians, but to specialists in almost any field of American history from 1930 to 1960, particularly World War II. In 1938, NBC created an index of all news and public affairs broadcasts relating to the "European War." Renamed the "World War II" index after Pearl Harbor, it comprises nearly two thousand

cards. Several hundred more cards are included in a separate "War Effort" index, which lists all programs broadcast from service bases, radio plays based on the war, programs which sold war bonds, and those in which war-related topics (victory gardens, for example) were incorporated into program scripts or ad copy.

NBC's careful documentation of the war years extends to the radio personality index where the speeches of important political figures, such as Churchill and Roosevelt, are summarized and frequently annotated with interesting details. For instance, Churchill's immortal, first speech as Prime Minister ("I have nothing to offer but blood, toil, tears, and sweat.") was originally heard only by members of Parliament on May 13, 1940, but redelivered for the purpose of broadcasting over the BBC two-and-a-half-years later.

A disconcerting feature of the index card catalog is that "Negro radio artists" (but not "personalities") were filed separately. The fact that NBC failed to "integrate" its artist index at some point after 1960, when revelations of the network's segregated filing system would have caused embarrassment, may reflect a desire to preserve the historic integrity of the index. But a more likely explanation is that by then most network executives were so focused on television they had little reason to consult the index card catalog. Indeed, few were probably aware of its existence.

The Press Releases

The press releases in the NBC Collection date from October 4, 1924, through 1989. (The 1940 and 1941 volumes were not included in the donation and are presumably lost.) The prenetwork press releases were produced by WEAF, while still under AT&T ownership. That WEAF regularly issued detailed press releases at such an early date is evidence of that station's greater wealth and sophistication in comparison to most, if not all other, early radio stations in America.

Far more legible than the microfilmed master books, the press releases are an invaluable resource for reconstructing early, unrecorded programs. They are also useful as a supplement to the card catalog. For example, a researcher wishing to obtain biographical information about an unfamiliar actor listed on one of the program cards could consult the press releases issued shortly before the date of his performance. In addition to releases on the programs and performers, there are many relating to the network's announcers, writers, musicians, corporate staff, affiliates, and to NBC's technical achievements, particularly its early experiments in television broadcasting.

Not to be overlooked is the fact that the press releases are simply a good read, providing tidbits on the stars and a vivid picture of day-to-day life at network headquarters. They describe: New York in the grips of a storm, as engineers rush to a top floor of Radio City to record howling gale-force winds for their sound effects library; studio audiences of the NBC Symphony being handed programs of soft, porous paper so that the musicians would not be distracted by the rustling of turning pages; and in those days when all performances were live, a weary Jack Benny deciding to move

```
    Murial Pollock(s)WEAF only
    Summary(s)WEAF only
    Martha & Hal(s)WEAF only     8:00  Malcolm Claire(s-Chi)WEAF BASIC CRCT
  -8:30  Good Morning Melodies(s-Chi)(WEAF on 8:20-8:25)BASIC CDN NW SE SC SW
  -8:20  Standard Oil of NJ(c)WEAF only
  -8:30  Consumers Market Guide(s-WNYC)WEAF CBS
    Cheerio Pgm.(s-NBC & Home for Incurables)WEAF BASIC CDN NW SE SC SW
    Harold Leveys Orch(s)WEAF BASIC
    Adela Rogers St John(s)WEAF BASIC
    Press Radio News(s)WEAF BASIC
    Amer. Home Products(c)WEAF KYW FBR RC TIC TAG NAC JAR CSH GY BEN CAE TAM SAI WJ MAQ
    (KSD off 10:30)OW DAF CRCT
    Pillsbury(c-Chi)WEAF KYW FBR RC TIC TAG NAC JAR CSH GY BEN TAM CAE CKY IRE WJ MAQ KSD
    HO OW DAF TAR RVA PTF WNC JAX FLA IOD TMJ KSTP EBC KY BAP KPRC OAI
    Babbitt Co(c)WEAF KYW FBR RC TIC TAG NAC JAR CSH GY BEN CAE TAM SAI WJ MAQ KSD HO OW DAF
    Sterling Products(c-Chi)WEAF KYW FBR RC TIC TAG NAC JAR CSH GY BEN CAE TAM SAI WJ MAQ
    KSD HO OW DAF TMJ KSTP
    Sterling Products(c)WEAF KYW FBR RC TIC TAG NAC JAR CSH GY BEN CAE TAM SAI WJ MAQ KSD OW
    DAF TMJ KSTP AVE MC API SB SMB KY FAA KPRC OAI
    Wasey Products(c)WEAF KYW FBR RC TIC TAG NAC JAR CSH GY BEN CAE TAM LW MAQ KSD HO OW DAF
    TMJ IBA KSTP EBC DAY KFYR KVOO KY FAA KTHS KTBS KPRC OAI KOA KDYL KPO KGW KOMO KHQ KFI
  9:40  Arlington Time Signal(s-WRC)WEAF BASIC CDN NW SE SC SW KOA
    Kellogg(c-Chi)WEAF KYW BEN CAE TAM LW WJ MAQ
    Kleenex(c-Chi)WEAF KYW FBR RC TIC NAC TAR GY BEN CAE TAM CKY IRE COL WJ MAQ KSD HO
    OW DAF KSTP AVE KOA KDYL KPO KGW KOMO KHQ KFI
  12:45  Gene Arnold & Ranch Boys(s-Chi)WEAF BASIC (Ex HO OW DAF)CDN
  -12:45  Sterling Products(c)KDYL KPO KGW KOMO KHQ KFI
  -1:00  Mystery Chef(c)KDYL KGW KOMO KFI
  -12:59  Soloist-Helen Jane Behlke(s-Chi)WEAF BASIC (Ex HO OW DAF)CDN
  -1:15  Soloist-Joe White(s)BASIC (Ex WEAF HO OW DAF) CDN KDYL
  -1:05  Standard Oil of NJ(c)WEAF only
  -1:15  Market & Weather Reports(s)WEAF only
  -2:00  Amer. Home Prod.(c)(KOA on 1:30)KDYL KPO KGW KOMO KHQ KFI
  -1:30  Hollywood High Hatters(s-Chi)WEAF BASIC(Ex HO OW DAF)CDN
  -2:00  Negro Education Radio Pgm(s-WSM & WRC)WEAF BASIC CDN

    NBC Music Appreciation Hour(s)WEAF BASIC CDN NW SE SC SW KOA KDYL REC
    Camay(c)WEAF KYW FBR RC TIC TAG NAC JAR CSH GY BEN TAM LW WJ MAQ KSD HO OW DAF TAR RVA
    PTF JAX FLA IOD TMJ KSTP EBC DAY KFYR SM MC API SB SMB KVOO KY BAP KPRC OAI KOA KDYL
    KFI KGW KOMO KHQ KPO
    Oxydol(c-Chi)WEAF KYW FBR RC TIC TAG NAC JAR CSH GY BEN TAM CAE LW WJ ENR KSD HO OW DAF
    TAR JAX FLA IOD TMJ KSTP EBC DAY KFYR SM MC API SB SMB KVOO KY BAP KPRC OAI KOA KDYL KFI
    KGW KOMO KHQ KPO KGHL
    Crisco(c-Chi)WEAF KYW FBR RC TIC TAG NAC JAR CSH GY BEN TAM CAE LW WJ MAQ KSD HO OW DAF
    TMJ KSTP NBC DAY KFYR KVOO KY BAP KPRC OAI KOA KDYL KFI KGW KOMO KHQ KPO
    Ivory(c)WEAF KYW FBR RC TIC TAG NAC JAR CSH GY BEN TAM CAE LW WJ MAQ KSD HO OW DAF TMJ
    KSTP EBC DAY KFYR KVOO KY BAP KPRC KOA KDYL KFI KGW KOMO KHQ KPO
    Longine Time Signal(c)WEAF only
    John Morrell Co(c-Chi)WEAF KYW RC TAG NAC GY BEN CAE TAM CKY IRE COL WJ MAQ HO DAF IBA
    KSTP EBC SM MC SB KOA KPO KGW KFI
    Claudine Macdonald Says(s)WEAF BASIC NW SE SC SW KOA KDYL REC

    Grandpa Burton(s)WEAF BASIC NW SC KOA KDYL REC
    Longines Time Signal(c)WEAF only

    Lee Gordons Orch(s-WTAM)WEAF BASIC KDYL REC
    Ralston Purina(c-Chi)WEAF KYW FBR RC TIC TAG NAC JAR CSH GY BEN CAE TAM SAI WJ OOD MAQ
    Genl Mills(c-Chi)WEAF KYW FBR RC TIC TAG NAC JAR CSH GY BEN CAE TAM WJ MAQ
    Wander(c-Chi)WEAF KYW FBR RC TIC TAG NAC JAR CSH GY BEN CAE TAM LW WJ TAR PTF JAX FLA
    Moorish Tales(s)WEAF BASIC NW SE SC SW KOA KDYL
  -6:30  Barry McKinley(s)SPLIT BASIC(WEAF off 6:28)
  -6:30  Ralston Purina(c-Chi)KSD KSTP
  -6:20  Standard Oil of NJ(c)WEAF only
  -6:30  Summary(s)WEAF only
    Press Radio News(s-Chi)WEAF BASIC SW MT BLC
  -6:45  Lucille Manners-Soloist(s)WEAF BASIC SW MT BLC
  -7:00  Sheffield Farms(c)WEAF only
  -7:00  Wander(c-Chi)KSD OW DAY KFYR AVE MC SB
  -7:00  Top Hatters(s-KYW)SPLIT BASIC(Ex.WEAF & TAM)
  -7:15  Pepsodent-Amos & Andy(c-Chi)WEAF KYW FBR RC TIC TAG NAC JAR CSH GY BEN CAE TAM LW
    WJ MAQ KSD HO
    Alka Seltzer(c-Chi)WEAF KYW FBR RC TIC TAG NAC JAR CSH GY BEN TAM CAE CKY IRE COL OOD
    MAQ HO OW DAF TMJ IBA KSTP EBC DAY KFYR KGEX KY BAP KTBS KPRC OAI
    Edwin C. Hill(s)WEAF BASIC CDN NW SE SW MT REC
    Norsemen Quartet(s)WEAF BASIC CDN NW SE SC SW MT
```

■ As WEAF and WJZ's logs from November 15, 1936 make clear, far more was required of NBC's control booth engineers than simply pushing a "red" or "blue" button and counting down the minutes till the ringing of the chimes. In addition to a basic core of stations carrying more or less the same programs as WEAF and WJZ, the Red and Blue Networks were composed of various appendages or so-called supplementary legs, each of which received a somewhat different package of network programs—in some cases, a mix of Red and Blue. Further complicating the process of networking was NBC's liberal policy of permitting an affiliate to turn down a network offering for a local program of greater interest to its listeners. Thus, few programs over WEAF or WJZ were received by an identical set of affiliates.

Sustaining programs, noted with an "s," are listed in the logs by title. Commercial programs, designated with a "c," are recorded by the name of their sponsor—a sure indication of who ran the show, both literally and figuratively.

0-8:30 Melody Hour(s)(WJZ off 8:28)BASIC
8-8:30 Summary(s)WJZ only
0 Tone Pictures(s)WJZ BASIC
0-10:00 Nat'l Spelling Bee(s)WJZ only
-10:00 Intl Salute to NBC on 10th Anniv(s-See Red sheet)BASIC(Ex WJZ)See Red sheet
0 Southernaires(s)WJZ BASIC CDN KLO BLC
0-11:30 Walberg Brown Ensemble(s-WGAR)BASIC(Ex WJZ)CDN KLO BLC
0-11:00 "Give us the Funnies(s)WJZ only
0 Press Radio News(s)WJZ BASIC KLO BLC
5 Soloist-Alice Remsen(s)WJZ BASIC KLO BLC
5 Alistair Cooke(s-London)WJZ BASIC CDN NW SE SC SW KLO BLC
0 Iodent Co.(c)WJZ FIL BAL MAL BZ-A LW XYZ MAQ KWK MT KSO KOIL REN IBA KSTP AVE SM MC API
SB JDX SMB
W Tastyeast(c)WJZ BAL MAL BZ-A SYR KDKA SAI XYZ ENR
0 Radio City Music Hall on the Air(s-Music Hall)WJZ BASIC CDN NW SE SC SW KOA KLO BLC
0 Our Neighbors(s)WJZ BASIC NW SE SC SW KOA KLO BLC
0 R C A (c-NBC NY)WJZ FIL BAL MAL ABY BZ-A SYR HAM GAR EBR
KDKA LW COL XYZ WOOD ENR KWK MT KSO KOIL REN CRCT CFCF FBC TAR RVA PTF SOC WNC IS
JAX FLA IOD CSC TMJ IBA KSTP KRC DAY KFYR AVE SM MC API SB JDX SMB KGBX KVOO KY
FAA THS KTBS KPRC OAI KOA KDYL KLO KGO KEX KJR KGA KECA KFSD KGIR KGHL KTAR KGU
Better Speech(c-Chi)WJZ FIL BAL MAL BZ-A SYR HAM GAR EBR KDKA SAI XYZ ENR MT KSO KOIL
REN TAR RVA PTF SOC WNC IS JAX FLA IOd KVOO KY FAA KTBS KPRC OAI KLO KGO KEX KJR KGA
KECA KFSd
5 Gen. Foods-Diamond Salt(c)WJZ FIL BAL MAL ABY BZ-A SYR HAM GAR EBR KDKA COL XYZ
0 Dorothy Dreslin-Soloist(s)WJZ BASIC CDN SE SC SW KLO BLC

0 Natl Vespers(s-Riverside Church & NBC NY)WJZ BASIC NW SE SC SW KOA KLO BLC
0 Sen. Fishface & Prof. Figsbottle(s)WJZ BASIC CDN NW SE SW KOA KLO BLC

0 Gen Foods-Calumet(c)WJZ FIL BAL MAL ABY BZ-A SYR HAM GAR EBR KDKA LW XYZ ENR KWK MT KSO
KOIL TAR RVA PTF SOC WNC IS JAX FLA IOD AVE SM MC API SB JDX SMB KGBX KVOO KY BAP KTHS
KTBS KPRC OAI KVOD KLO KGO KEX KJR KGA KECA KFSD KGIR KGHL
0 Gen Foods-Minute Tapioca(c)WJZ FIL BAL MAL ABY BZ-A SYR HAM GAR EBR KDKA CKY IRE COL XYZ
ENR KWK MT KSO KOIL KVOD KLO KGO KEX KJR KGA KECA KFSD
0 Benrus Time Signal(c)WJZ only
-7:00 Consolidated Edison Co(c)WJZ only
6:30 Echoes From The Orchestra Pit(s-San Fran)BASIC (Ex WJZ)CDN KLO BLC
-7:00 Golden Gate Park Band(s-San Fran)BASIC (Ex WJZ)CDN NW SE SC SW KLO BLC
Mobilization Human Needs(s-Topeka & NBC NY)WJZ BASIC KOA KLO BLC
Fleischmann(c)WJZ FIL BAL MAL ABY BZ-A SYR HAM GAR EBR KDKA CKY IRE COL XYZ LS KWK MT KSO
KOIL REN TAR RVA PTF SOC WNC IS JAX FLA IOd TMJ IBA KSTP EBC dAY KFYR AVE SM MC SB
JDX SMB KVOO KY FAA KTBS KPRC OAI KOA KdYL KFO KGW KOMO KHQ KFI KTAR

NBC 10th Anniv Symphony Orch(s)WJZ BASIC KLO BLC

Jergens(c)WJZ FIL BAL MAL BZ-A SYR HAM GAR EBR KDKA LW XYZ ENR KWK MT KSO KOIL REN
KLO KGO KJR KGA KECA KFSD KGIR KGHL KTAR
Woodbury(c)WJZ FIL BAL MAL BZ-A SYR HAM GAR EBR KDKA LW XYZ ENR KWK MT KSO
OIL REN KLO KGO KJR KGA KECA KFSD KGIR KGHL KTAR (KGU off at 9:30)
Real Silk(c-Chi)WJZ FIL BAL MAL BZ-A SYR HAM GAR KdKA LW XYZ ENR KWK MT KSO KOIL REN KLO
KGO KJR KGA KECA KFSd
Dreams of Long Ago(s)WJZ BASIC KLO BLC
Judy & The Bunch(s)WJZ BASIC NW SE SC KLO BLC
Press Radio News(s)WJZ BASIC NW SE SC KLO BLC
Shandor(s)WJZ BASIC CDN NW SE
11:30 Jergens(c)AVE SM MC API SB JDX SMB KY BAP KTHS KTBS KPRC OAI KOA KDYL
12:00 Hotel Stevens Orch(s-Chi)WJZ BASIC NW SE

12:15 Woodbury(c)AVE SM MC API SB JDX SMB KY BAP KTHS KTBS KPRC OAI KVOD

12:30 Chez Paree Orch(s-Chi)WJZ BASIC NW SE (KVOD KLO BLC on 12:15)
1:00 A.M. St Francis Hotel Orch(s-San Fran)WJZ BASIC SE NW SC SW KVOD KLO BLC

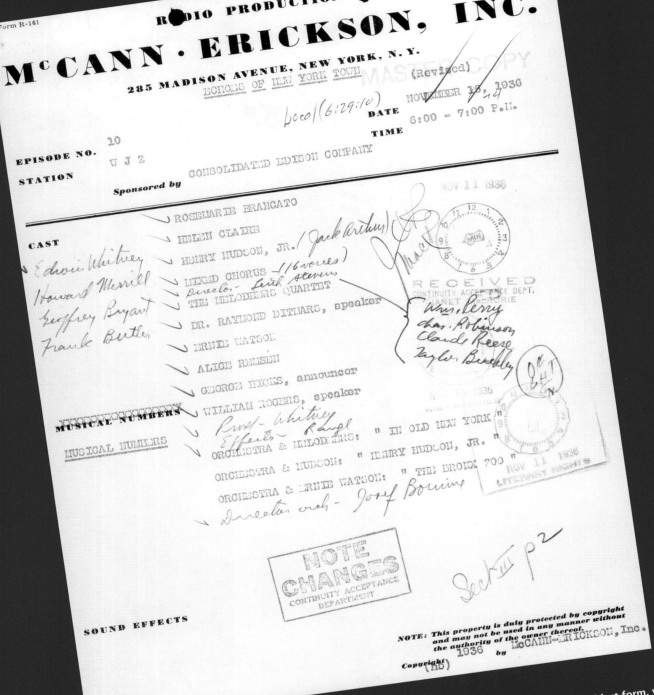

Form R-161

RADIO PRODUCTION OF
McCANN · ERICKSON, INC.
285 MADISON AVENUE, NEW YORK, N. Y.

ECHOES OF NEW YORK TOWN   (Revised)   MASTER COPY

Local (6:29:10)   DATE   NOVEMBER 15, 1936

6:00 – 7:00 P.M.   TIME

EPISODE NO.   10

STATION   W J Z   CONSOLIDATED EDISON COMPANY

Sponsored by

NOV 11 1936

RECEIVED
CONTINUITY ACCEPTANCE DEPT.
JANET MacRORIE

CAST

Edwin Whitney
Howard Merrill
Geoffrey Bryant
Frank Butler

ROSEMARIE BRANCATO
HELEN CLAIRE
HENRY HUDSON, JR. (Jack Arthur)
MIXED CHORUS (16 voices)
Director - Leith Stevens
THE MELODEERS QUARTET
DR. RAYMOND DITMARS, speaker
ERNIE WATSON
ALICE REMSEN
GEORGE HICKS, announcer
WILLIAM ROGERS, speaker

Wm. Perry
Chas. Robinson
Claude Reese
Taylor Buckley

MUSICAL NUMBERS

MUSICAL NUMBERS

Prof. Whitney
Effects   Ravel
ORCHESTRA & MELODEERS: " IN OLD NEW YORK "
ORCHESTRA & HUDSON: " HENRY HUDSON, JR. "
ORCHESTRA & ERNIE WATSON: " THE BRONX 700 "
Director orch - Josef Bonime

NOV 11 1936
LITERARY RIGHTS

Sect III p 2

NOTE CHANGES
CONTINUITY ACCEPTANCE DEPARTMENT

SOUND EFFECTS

NOTE: *This property is duly protected by copyright and may not be used in any manner without the authority of the owner thereof.*
Copyright 1936 by McCANN–ERICKSON, Inc.
(AB)

In addition to the microfilmed master books, NBC donated several so-called archival master books, which are actual (as opposed to microfilmed) samples from important dates, including D-Day and NBC anniversaries. Reproduced here is the cover page of a script from WJZ's archival master book for November 15, 1936—NBC's 10th anniversary.

Once an advertising agency submitted a commercial script to NBC, it was scrutinized by three departments: Continuity Acceptance (censorship), Literary Rights, and Music Rights, whose stamps are clearly visible on this page.

The censor reviewed the program script and ad copy to ensure their overall tastefulness and conformity with NBC's detailed, ever-changing program policies. As indicated on the bottom of this page, censor Janet MacRorie made a change in the script: She deleted the expletive, "damna-tion," since cursing, even in its mildest form, was deemed offensive.

While the primary responsibility of Literary and Music Rights Divisions was to guard against copyright infringements, an additional duty of the latter department was to scan the lyrics of songs for unsuitable language. As the following memo from programming director John Royal attests, NBC permitted greater leeway in this area than one might expect:

We should eliminate the word "nigger" whenever possible. Of course, these darkies put a lot of pressure on us and they are sometimes too exacting, and there are certain songs where the word "nigger" must be used. However it is wise to cut it out as much as possible. (May 1, 1935)

Not until 1939 did NBC issue a statement categorically forbidding the broadcasting of lyrics containing the words "nigger," "darky," and "coon."

60

PROGRAM TITLE Atwater Kent Radio Hour   DAY Sunday   TIME 9:15 –10:15 P.M.

CLIENT Atwater Kent Manufacturing Company,
ADDRESS 4700 Wissahicken Avenue, Philadelphia, Pa.
AGENCY Batten, Barton, Durstine & Osborn,
383 Madison Avenue, N.Y.

STARTING DATE Jan 22, 1925
NO. WEEKS
CLOSING DATE June 27, 1931 off
Aug 1931 returned
Oct 1931 off
One special pgm in Dec of 1931 & 1932
SALES CONTACT D. R. Buckham

PRODUCT Radio Receiving Sets
STATIONS WEAF and Network (34 Stations)

PROGRAM DESCRIPTION

Very high class musical program, with symphony-concert type orchestra and
outstanding soloists and artists. During the summer months the time is cust
to a half hour, and lighter music, and less prominent artists are substituted,
but a very high standard is maintained at all times. Full time series begins
October, and half time series begins in May of each year.

(see over)

SUN	MON	TUES	WED	THUR	FRI	SAT		COMM.	REG. SUST'G	NO PAY NO CHGE. SUST'G	ENT.	INFOR'IVE EDUC'L	OUTST'G EVENTS SERVICE	NEWS	/ REL.	OUTST'G ARTISTS OR SPEAKERS	INT'L
Atwater Kent Radio Hour																	

■ The vast majority of early radio programs were never recorded. Several collection resources, including the master books, press releases, and logs, permit us to partially recapture these "lost" programs. But no resource is as accessible as the index card catalog, where commercial programs are listed alphabetically by sponsor, and sustaining programs, chronologically by the year in which they ended.

Reproduced here are two program cards for the *Atwater Kent Radio Hour*, first aired over WEAF in the AT&T years. As a commercial program featuring classical music, it represents a type of program that flourished in the 1920s and all but disappeared the following decade.

Thanks to the broad range of documentation in the collection, a suspected error on a card can easily be checked. Here, "violinist" Andres Segovia is recorded as guest artist on March 2. One could consult his radio artist card to see if there is a notation of his ever having played the violin over NBC. (There is none.) For more definitive proof of an error, the press releases or master books are possible sources. In this case, the program script from WEAF's master book confirms that Segovia did not play the violin that evening, but rather, of course, his guitar.

MUSIC	ARTISTS	ACTORS	SPEAKERS	SPEC. ANNOUNCER

Joseph Pasternack,
Dir.

Special Artists
January 5 – Aida Doninelli, soprano, Metropolitan Opera Co.
    12 – Beniamino Gigli, tenor   "   "   "
1930   19 – Elizabeth Rethberg, soprano, "   "   ": Edward Austen Kane
    26 – Oscar Straus, Viennese composer (Chocolate Soldier, etc.) as Guest Conductor: American Radio Debut
February 2 Armand Tokatyan, tenor, Metropolitan Opera Company
    9 – Mme. Nina Koshetz, soprano: Geo. Cehanovsky, baritone, Metropolitan Opera Co.
    16 – Tito Schipa, tenor, Metropolitan Opera Co.: Kathleen Stewart, concert pianist
    23 – Mme. Maria Meuller, soprano "   "   ":
        Alexander Smallins, Musical Director and Conductor, Philadelphia Civic Opera C
March   2 – Andres Segovia, violinist
    9 – Martha Atwood, soprano: Renee Chemet, violinist
    16 – Edward Johnson, tenor, Metropolitan Opera Co.
    23 – Lawrence Tibbetts, baritone: "   "   "
    30 – Sigrid Onegin, contralto
April   6 – John Charles Thomas, baritone. (see above)
    13 – Mme. Maria Olszewska, contralto, Chicago Civic Opera Company
    20 – Lucrezia Bori, soprano, Metropolitan Opera Company
    27 – John Powell, concert pianist
        William Simmons, baritone

■ Press releases also served the purpose of damage control. As detailed in a later caption, a notorious skit featuring Mae West on the December 12, 1937, broadcast of *The Chase and Sanborn Program*, starring Edgar Bergen and Charlie McCarthy, had NBC's phones ringing incessantly within minutes of the broadcast. Issued only two days later, this release reminded outraged listeners that they were mighty lucky to have Charlie and should hold no grudge against him. Not only a lovable dummy, he was patented and inimitable.

National Broadcasting Company
RCA Building, Radio City, N.Y.
December 14, 1937

BIRTH RECORDS ON FILE
FOR CHARLIE McCARTHY

R2-2133

Charlie McCarthy, the saucy NBC dummy, is so important that his birth records repose in Government files in Washington.

The "birth records" of the hunk of pine to which Edgar Bergen has given such startling animation, are the documents that patent, register, copyright and trademark Charlie, the ventriloquist revealed recently.

Whenever Charlie opens his mouth to flirt with Dorothy Lamour, Carole Lombard or Mae West, the movement is protected against imitation by a patent which Bergen filed with the U. S. patent office six months ago. Even Charlie's name cannot be used in vain without incurring the wrath of Uncle Sam's sleuths. The name of McCarthy is a trademark. In case anyone wants to start a dispute over the style of Bergen's material, he'll have the copyright office to contend with. A typical script used on the NBC Chase & Sanborn Hour is duly registered with Uncle Sam.

Although every girl cries for him and the boys think him a regular guy, Charlie has basked in the spotlight of fame without a single threat from an imitator, Bergen said. "It may be that imitators find the job too difficult," the ventriloquist observed.

Bergan himself has hired one woodcarver after another to try to duplicate the dummy originally carved by Theodore Mack in Chicago some 14 years ago. So far, every attempt to capture Charlie's enigmatic personality has failed.

- - -

his program to Hollywood partly to avoid repeating his show late at night for the benefit of West Coast audiences. As explained in a press release on that subject, "It's all over by supper time out there."

The powers at young NBC must have breathed a collective sigh of relief when CBS announced its formation in September 1927. No longer the only radio network in America, NBC could now proceed with plans to extend two networks from New York to California with less reason to fear intervention from a monopoly-wary federal government. The existence of CBS served to fuel NBC's ambitions in ther ways as well. Indeed, the desire to outdo archrival "Columbia" became a goal in and of itself as we discover from numerous documents in the history files. The following memo from Chicago bureau chief Niles Trammell to NBC's second president, Lenox Lohr (1936-1940), is typical:

> Columbia has been promoting their network very successfully, and I feel we have to protect our leadership in the Red . . . otherwise, Columbia may be knocking at the door of our Number One network. We cannot afford to neglect our advantage because if we do, we will wake up some fine morning and find Columbia is on a par with us. Even now, they are claiming to have the best *single network* in the country. This is a fallacious claim, but we have to fortify our position.[15] (January 21, 1938)

In January 1927, there were nineteen stations on the Red Network and six on the Blue. By the end of 1930, NBC had acquired seventy-three affiliates, with transcontinental network service already in place on the Red. That year the government actually did file an antitrust suit against RCA, resulting in the dissolution of those patent-licensing agreements still in effect, and in an agreement by General Electric and Westinghouse to relinquish their respective ownership shares in both RCA and NBC. But NBC, now a wholly owned subsidiary of RCA, emerged from the proceedings unscathed, boasting 219 affiliates at the start of 1941 (the last year NBC operated two networks) as compared to CBS's 125.

Such impressive numbers, however, do not tell the whole story, for while the government may have permitted NBC's growth to go virtually unchecked for more than a decade, by the mid-1930s, NBC's own sponsors posed a serious threat to its dual network operation. Primarily due to a delay in the provision of coast to coast wire service for the Blue Network, it began to lose some of its most important sponsors to the Red. Even after the Blue Network became available nationwide in 1936, it never recovered.

Consequently, during the second half of the 1930s the Red Network's identity as the more commercial and popular of NBC's two networks became even more pronounced. The Blue assumed a somewhat "schizophrenic" character—on the one hand a showcase for NBC's most prestigious sustaining programs (opera and symphony), but on the other, the favored dumping ground for obligatory and usually dreary public service broadcasts (testimonial dinners, for example). With hours of unsold time on the Blue, it was also the primary residence for hundreds of sustaining programs "in search of sponsors"—some succeeding (in which case, their sponsors often requested a switch to the Red) but most succumbing to an early demise. Perusing NBC's sustaining program card index, one can understand why. Over the years the network's programming department churned out numerous shows as unpromising as *Don't Forget*, which aired over the Blue Network from April 1939 until February 1940 and is described below in NBC's words:

> An audience participation program, with Allen Prescott as Master of Ceremonies. It features the Mental Point of Contact as a means of helping listeners to remember names, numbers and places through thought association. Five members will be selected at random from the studio audience. Each contestant will receive five dollars, and for each question answered correctly additional sum of 68 cents, which represents the M.P.C. of the program as is broadcast on the sixth day of the week at eight o'clock. Listeners will be invited to send in M.P.C.'s which, if used, will win them three dollars. Prescott and Milton Cross, announcer, will quiz the contestants. (A sample question is "What three Americans were recently appointed Justices of the Supreme Court?" The answer is Frankfurter, Douglas, and Reed. The M.P.C. or thought to associate with the question is that their last initials make F.D.R. who appointed them.)

On a more positive note, as the less commercial of the two networks, the Blue offered listeners some relief from the intrusiveness of radio advertising—far less tasteful and restrained in the 1930s than in NBC's early years. Creative touches, such as the staccatolike chant of tobacco auctioneer L. A. ("Speed") Riggs for Lucky Strike, or the way in which announcer Don Wilson's pitch for Jell-O on the Jack Benny program was woven into the program script, were among the exceptions. More often than not, radio advertising was a bore—its entertainment value today chiefly lying in its anachronistic charms and the absurdity of sponsors' exaggerated claims. Indeed, gullible listeners in the 1930s and 1940s might have been inclined to replace all their prescribed medicines with an advertised "cure-all," such as Sal Hepatica (a laxative) or Fleischmann's yeast.

The Blue Network also fulfilled the mission attributed to it by David Sarnoff, who had testified before the FCC in 1938 that the creation of a second network was intended to meet the needs of a diversified national audience. The Blue not only carried a disproportionate share of public service programs catering to special interest groups and limited segments of the population, but also more programs than the Red with a distinctly regional flavor. Such programs included: *Magnolia Blossoms* (broadcast from Nashville and featuring the Fisk Jubilee Choir), *The Southernaires* (specializing in "negro folk melodies," according to their program card), *The National Farm and Home Hour* (sponsored by NBC in conjunction with the Department of Agriculture); and on the commercial side, country music programs, such as Anacin's *National Barn Dance*, one of the few truly popular shows to remain on the Blue Network after the mid-1930s, though it too eventually moved over to the Red.

Serving the needs of a diversified audience also meant catering to the intelligentsia. While the Red Network cer-

To press its allegiance with high culture, NBC not only produced outstanding musical programs of its own, but also actively recruited sponsors to aid in that effort. Many responded to the call, flooding the early airwaves with classical and light classical concert music. These programs (both sustaining and commercial) produced a cultural awakening of sorts, providing millions of listeners with their first exposure to serious music and creating a greater demand for live concert music. Indeed, from the late twenties to late thirties, there was a five-fold increase in the number of orchestras nationwide, attributable, at least in part, to the pervasive influence of radio concert music.

The Cities Service Concert, which joined the Red Network in 1927 after several trial runs over WEAF, was one such program. Somewhat lighter in programming fare than most of its counterparts (there was more Gershwin and Romberg than Beethoven and Schubert), it enjoyed greater longevity as a result. From 1930-1937, the program starred lyric soprano, Jessica Dragonette, pictured here with orchestra leader Rosario Bourdon (left), and announcer Ford Bond (center). As her broadcasting career ended before World War II and her film appearances were limited to cameo roles, she is mostly forgotten today. But in the 1930s Jessica Dragonette was more than just a household name, she was one of radio's most popular stars. Miss Dragonette left the program over creative differences with her sponsors, who insisted that she continue singing medlies from her versatile repertory, while she wanted them to produce fully dramatized operettas, her specialty. Their instincts were probably correct, for by then, the majority of radio listeners favored more modern and distinctly American forms of music.

tainly had programs that appealed to more educated audiences, the Blue had an edge in this category too, both with respect to public affairs programs and to those devoted to literature and the arts. Regardless of their merits, these programs were often short-lived. Take the case of the Blue Network's *Meet Mr. Weeks*. Though hosted by the erudite and amiable editor of the *Atlantic Monthly* and featuring such notable guests as Archibald MacLeish, then Librarian of Congress, this widely acclaimed program stood no chance against such formidable competition on the Red as *Fibber McGee and Molly*.

By the mid-1930s, the less commercial Blue Network unquestionably surpassed the Red in the area of classical music programming, whose sponsored support had steadily declined since the previous decade. Still obliged to provide such programs to ensure its prestige, NBC now sustained most of these programs at its own expense. But apparently the majority of listeners stayed "tuned out," as evidenced by the response to a brilliant program added to the Blue Network's sustaining lineup in 1940. *The Chamber Music Society of Lower Basin Street* satirized classical music programming by applying its language ("celebrated young diva Dinah Shore") and format (intermission commentaries, like Milton Cross's at the Met) to describe and structure a

program devoted to jazz. Using its recently developed "program analyzer" to test audience response to the show, NBC discovered the predominant reaction was one of bewilderment.[16]

Not even the NBC Symphony, led by renowned conductor Arturo Toscanini and created in 1937 partly as a way of giving the Blue Network a much needed shot in the arm (and partly to keep up with CBS, which at the time was featuring the New York Philharmonic), achieved the ratings NBC had anticipated. Indeed, they never approached those of its Red Network competitor, *The Lucky Strike Hit Parade*, prompting one network executive to recommend in 1938 that "all classical or semiclassical music . . . be eliminated or buried [between popular programs] where possible."[17]

So while the Red Network—with an all-star line-up featuring Jack Benny, Bob Hope, Edgar Bergen, Rudy Vallee, Fibber McGee and Molly, and Fred Allen—amassed huge profits from the mid-1930s on, the Blue remained a constant liability in the books and in most cities a perennial third or fourth in the ratings. Numerous documents in the history files also indicate that the Blue Network was the object of an intensive effort on the part of NBC executives to reverse its ailing fortunes.

Capitalizing on one of its strengths—the regional flavor of much of its programming—NBC opened supplementary legs of the Blue Network throughout the South and other less populous regions, offering discounts to its regular advertisers who purchased time on these outlets. Subsequently, to encourage more aggressive salesmanship on the Blue and the development of better programs, NBC separated its sales and programming departments into Red and Blue divisions. With its own director by 1939, the Blue Network was operating more or less as a distinct entity within the organization.

As a result of these measures, the network showed signs

■ To at least some extent, the changing fortunes of the Blue Network were the result of a single program—*Amos 'n' Andy*. Written by and starring Freeman Gosden (Amos and The Kingfish—left) and Charles Correll (Andy), the program joined the Blue Network in August 1929. A "comedy sketch of the events in the lives of two negro characters, owners of a taxicab, and proprietors of 'The Fresh Air Taxicab Company,'" as described on its NBC program card, *Amos 'n' Andy* was the most popular radio program of all time.

As success breeds success, the program attracted numerous sponsors and affiliates to the Blue Network in the early 1930s. Conversely, when Pepsodent decided to transfer *Amos 'n' Andy* to the Red Network in 1935, the Blue started on its irreversible decline.

Originating in Chicago, *Amos 'n' Andy* moved to Hollywood in 1936. Like most non-New York programs, it is not well documented in the NBC Collection. There are few recordings from the 1930s—the decade in which it enjoyed its greatest popularity—and no scripts save for the years 1943-1945. (The Library's Manuscript Division, however, holds a complete set of scripts on microfilm.) Among the few references to *Amos 'n' Andy* in the history files is the following excerpt from the minutes of a Chicago division meeting, which suggests this photo of Gosden and Correll may be unusual:

> Mr. Williamson read a letter from New York asking for 100 pictures in white face of Amos 'n' Andy. It was decided that only black face pictures are to be released for that purpose, so as to maintain in the mind of the public the impression of Amos 'n' Andy as two living darkies. (December 27, 1929)

NBC's insensitivity to race was obviously not unique to that organization, but it was certainly endemic. To publicize the upcoming appearance of the black face comedy team, Pic and Pat, on *The Quaker Party* (a musical program sponsored by Quaker Oats), a January 4, 1939 press release reads: "Aunt Jemima, who speaks their own language, will be on hand, of course, to welcome them to the party." Other groups were stereotyped (for example, greedy characters with thick Yiddish accents were occasionally portrayed in comedy sketches) but none as persistently as African Americans—often presented as lazy, conniving, obtuse, or semiliterate.

Negative stereotyping even occurred where we might least expect it. Broadcasting his December 15, 1940 program from New York, rather than its usual venue, Hollywood, Jack Benny is looking for his servant Rochester in one sketch. "To find out once and for all if he's California's Ambassador to Harlem or working for me," Benny makes three phone calls—the first to the "Harlem Social and Benevolent Spareribs Every Thursday Club," where he learns Rochester has been shooting craps; the second to a woman friend, who leaves no doubt as to how Rochester has passed the time at her place; and the third to the "Lenox Avenue Gin Till You Spin Club." We may assume there was little or no protest to the script at the time, for it was recycled by Benny's writers the following decade, at which point objections were raised, prompting an apology from the star. Similar protests in the mid-1950s resulted in the cancellation of the *Amos 'n' Andy* television program.

With respect to race, NBC, and radio in general, had been blind, rather than intentionally malevolent. They did not create the stereotypes, but were certainly guilty of impressing them even more indelibly into the American consciousness.

of reviving in the late 1930s. Joining its ranks were a number of popular programs, such as the *Aldrich Family*—a comedy revolving around the life of its vulnerable adolescent hero, Henry; and *Information Please*, a quiz show distinguished for the wit and urbanity of its expert panel. But

In 1930 at age thirty-nine, David Sarnoff became president of RCA and chairman of the board of NBC. Seen here in a much later photo examining an electronic light amplifier, designed by RCA for applications in television and medical science, he appears to be gazing into a crystal ball. Whether intended or not, the metaphor is apt, for David Sarnoff was indeed visionary.

In 1916, when most radio experts still saw its future as a means of message transmission via wireless telegraphy and telephony, Sarnoff envisioned the medium as a source of entertainment and education in the average American home. He developed a plan for an affordable "radio music box"—"a 'household utility' in the same sense as the piano or phonograph," as he described it. But his superiors at American Marconi (a leader in the field of wireless telegraphy) promptly shelved the idea as impractical.

With NBC radio barely off the ground in the mid-1920s, Sarnoff was already looking ahead toward television and certainly the driving force behind NBC's experimental broadcasts in that medium in the early 1930s. But the archives fail to disclose the full extent of his involvement with NBC.

Although he is referred to in numerous documents, the files contain little correspondence addressed to or from him. Whether this was because he was too preoccupied with other matters to pay much attention to NBC (only one facet of RCA's vast communications empire), or because most records documenting his involvement with NBC were destroyed, we do not know. Both perhaps were true.

Where Sarnoff emerges in the archives as a real person, rather than a shadowy presence, is in connection with RCA's early Washington station WRC (see text), and later, in connection with the Blue Network. In a handwritten memo, he expressed his views on that subject to NBC president Lenox Lohr:

Mr. Lohr: This much seems clear from what you told me yesterday. Unless we can increase sales on the Blue (Red being almost filled) our rising costs will diminish our profits; while at the same time Columbia will add to its sales and profits. Thus to widen the gap between NBC and Columbia net results, [sic]would be to bring the severest criticism on all of us. (December 7, 1937)

He was both a blessing and a curse to NBC. Throughout the late thirties and early forties, Walter Winchell's Sunday night broadcasts sponsored by Jergens Lotion were the most popular program on the Blue Network—a page from his script of November 15, 1936, leaving little doubt as to why. The problem for NBC was not that Winchell dished up the dirt on the rich and famous, but rather that he applied that same no-holds-barred style of journalism to more serious news as well.

Clearly, Walter Winchell could be insufferable, and it was probably no accident that when the history files were purged of potentially libelous contents, his file remained intact. But it is also true that many of his "outrageous" comments were justified. In 1939, he is reproved for referring to Hitler as a "madman;" and later, for calling (Nazi diplomat) Von Ribbentrope—"Von Ribbentripe." As "one of the chosen people, he [Winchell] is causing undue hardship and anti-Semitism throughout the Middle West," wrote NBC news director A. A. Schechter in 1939. The Winchell file in the archives says as much about America as it does about its subject.

as NBC continued to bow to the wishes of its sponsors, these programs, and many others, ultimately established residency on the Red—ironically, a greater beneficiary of the Blue Network's intermittent successes than the Blue Network itself.

Given the persistent problems plaguing the Blue Network, one can only wonder why NBC did not simply offer it up for sale. Clearly, that was a consideration, possibly as early as 1934,[18] and certainly by 1936, when RCA president and NBC board chairman David Sarnoff directed the network's treasurer to study the possibility.[19] But the history files also suggest that some executives were stubbornly determined to maintain NBC's dual network operation for two reasons. Without a second network, NBC would have to give up some of the sustaining programs which conferred prestige upon the organization as well as the gratitude of loyal listeners. But even more importantly, two networks afforded NBC nearly twice as many saleable hours as CBS. Thus, NBC was able to offer substantial discounts to its best advertisers, which served to keep them away from Columbia. If indeed there is one lesson to be learned from the history files, it would be never to underestimate NBC's fierce sense of competition with CBS and the extent to which it affected network policies.

Credit NBC with expressing that rivalry openly and with humor on at least one occasion—the March 31, 1939, broadcast of *The March of Time*, which usually dramatized recent events in a straightforward fashion. That week, however, NBC took a more lighthearted approach to its subject—the loss of one of its most popular programs, *Amos 'n' Andy*, to CBS. (The program would return to NBC in 1943.) The point of the sketch was, who on earth listens to CBS? Evidently no one in NBC's fantasy, as it portrays bereft Americans and foreigners alike "slowly twisting their tuning dials" in a futile effort to find the "lost" program. The skit ends when radio signals of *Amos 'n' Andy* are picked up from Mars—a place so strange its inhabitants tune in to CBS. (This climax, incidentally, alluded to a recent CBS

broadcast—the *Mercury Theater of the Air's* infamous adaptation of H. G. Wells's *War of the Worlds*, which had uncounted listeners convinced of a Martian invasion.)

Eventually, the problem of the Blue Network was solved, not as a result of any corrective measures on NBC's part, but rather due to the determination of a staunch antimonopolist—James Fly, Chairman of the FCC. In 1938, his department began a lengthy investigation of CBS and NBC, culminating in the FCC's *Chain Broadcasting Report* of May 1941.

Among the numerous orders contained in that report was one of particular consequence to NBC: "No license shall be issued to a standard broadcasting station affiliated with a network organization which maintains more than one network."[20] NBC challenged the legality of that order in the courts, and also put up a strong defense of its modus operandi in testimony delivered before the Senate Interstate Commerce Committee in June 1941 by president Niles Trammell (1940-1949).[21] Retained in the archives, his remarks provide a cogent explanation of NBC's policies, as well as an excellent overview of the network's growth and accomplishments during its first fifteen years.

But Mr. Trammell's testimony was also laced with bitterness and sarcasm, suggesting he could barely contain his rage toward the FCC chairman. Years later, James Fly would recall that he had been "attacked, lampooned, and vilified" for forcing NBC to divest itself of one of its networks.[22] He may not have been exaggerating. Despite the fact that NBC must have produced hundreds of memos and position papers relating to the FCC order, only Mr. Trammell's statement is contained in the archives. Possibly,

GOOD EVENING, MR. AND MRS. NORTH AMERICA, AND ALL THE SHIPS AT SEA -- let's go
to press!

FLASH! LOS ANGELES! -- The Reid Russell mystery, which involved Gouverneur Morris,
the novelist, has been solved, according to the police...They announced all
clues indicated suicide.

FLASH! NEW YORK! -- Broadway just learned that Peggy Hopkins Joyce of the stage,
screen, and altar, has been named co-respondant in the divorce suit of Mrs. Stella
Jackson of London -- daughter of Lord Newborough...Miss Joyce only recently
announced that she would marry Mrs. Jackson's husband.

FLASH! NEW YORK! -- Clyde Pangborn, who flew around the world with Hugh Herndon --
announced today he would start on a non-stop flight to England in about two weeks.
He expects to break the current speed record between New York and London.

FLASH! RICHMOND, VIRGINIA! -- Further sensational developments are expected within
a few days from the G-Men's recent arrest of Congressman Heppel and his son. The
Congressman and his junior were recently convicted of selling appointments to West
Point. But no football players, eh? (1st show only.

NEW YORK! -- Bernard F. Sandler is the new trial counsel for Peggy Garcia whose
lawsuit against Rubinoff, the violinist, will come up in the local courts shortly...
She alleges Rubinoff broke her poor little heart.

■ If NBC reacted to the FCC's order of divorcement kicking and screaming like a spoiled child, the government itself was partly to blame. Overly permissive for nearly fifteen years, it had allowed the network to realize its grandiose dreams of expansion. For the most part, government interference in NBC affairs had been limited to little more than a severe reprimand over the impropriety of a skit on *The Chase and Sanborn Program,* starring Edgar Bergen and Charlie McCarthy, of December 12, 1937.

Preserved in a recording, the sketch featured Mae West as the Biblical Eve, and Don Ameche as an unaroused but contented Adam. Bored by a life untainted with original sin, though oblivious to the cause of her ennui, she passes the time playing solitaire with a deck of fig leaves and devising a way to get her "long, lazy, and lukewarm" husband to break his Garden of Eden lease. Knowing that it stipulates banishment in the event that they eat forbidden fruit, Eve beseeches a "long, dark, and slinky palpitating python" to retrieve not just any piece of fruit, but "a big one [because] I feel like doing a big apple." Turning the apple into apple-sauce, she feeds it to her unsuspecting husband, as dramatic music signals their sudden exile from Paradise.

Immediately, NBC was flooded with a torrent of angry phone calls, telegrams, and letters—not one of them saved when the history files were cleansed. Joining the chorus of protesters were the Legion of Decency, members of Congress, and James Fly's predecessor at the FCC, Frank McNinch, who described the sketch as "offensive to the great mass of right-thinking, clean- minded American citizens."

Racy content alone did not create the furor. As Mae West biographer Emily W. Leider notes, few objections were raised to an earlier skit on the program (also recorded) in which Mae tells her bedroom visitor, Charlie McCarthy, "I like a man who takes his time. . . . Come here, I'll let you play in my wood pile." (At least Charlie had saved his good reputation by walking out on her.) Rather, it was that sex and Biblical parody were a lethal mix in 1930s America. To make matters worse, the sketch was aired on a Sunday, only two weeks before Christmas.

Arch Oboler, the personification of innocence itself in this photo, and one of radio's most talented playwrights, had written the Garden of Eden skit specifically with Mae West in mind. She did not embellish his words. What is more, network censors in Hollywood, where the program originated, had approved the material in advance. But none of that seemed to matter to NBC. To save its skin, it allowed Mae West to take the fall, just like the character she had portrayed.

Oboler not only went unpunished, but was rewarded in 1939 with his own Red Network program, *Arch Oboler's Plays.* Don Ameche continued as a regular performer on *The Chase and Sanborn Program,* and America continued its love affair with Charlie McCarthy, whose program's ratings remained consistently high in the late 1930s and 1940s. Mae, on the other hand, received the same harsh punishment as Eve—banishment. Her radio artist card indicates she did not reappear over NBC until October 28, 1948, eleven years after the incident. That appearance was restricted to audiences of a local New York program, *Hi! Jinx.* Presumably, listeners in that city would be more likely to recall the old sketch with laughter than righteous indignation.

the other documents were deemed unfit for the public record.

At the time of the Senate hearings, NBC knew the writing was on the wall. So even before it was legally forced to divest itself of one of its networks, it prepared for the Blue Network's inevitable sale. As a first step, NBC wrested from the Blue some of its most popular programs, possibly at the behest of their sponsors. Then, in January 1942, the Blue Network was divorced from NBC and made an independent subsidiary of RCA, where it would remain pending the outcome of the appeal. The playing field had been leveled. From now on, NBC would face CBS as that network had always faced NBC—as a single network operation.

Even those executives, like Niles Trammell, who had hoped to hold onto the Blue probably experienced the divorce with a sense of relief. After all, the "marriage" of the Red and the Blue Networks had been troubled for years, perhaps even doomed from the start—each partner, the offspring of bitter corporate rivals. If there was any regret over the loss of WJZ and its affiliates, there is certainly no evidence to that effect from the history files. But there was also no time to look back, for by then America was at war, and NBC's energies were fully engaged in that effort.

On May 10, 1943, the Supreme Court upheld the constitutionality of the FCC order, and the pressure was on RCA to find a buyer for the Blue Network. That July David Sarnoff accepted an offer of eight million dollars from former Undersecretary of Commerce Edwin Noble, who had made his fortune in Lifesavers. In 1946, the Blue Network was renamed the American Broadcasting Company—ABC.

■ To publicize an upcoming appearance by Jack Benny (left) on Fred Allen's *Town Hall Tonight*, NBC issued this photo of the two comedians in early 1936. At the time they appeared over the Blue and Red Networks respectively, though in the wake of *Amos 'n' Andy's* defection to the Red the previous summer, Benny's sponsor, General Foods, would soon transfer his show to that network. Later that year, Benny and Allen became sworn enemies over the ether, engaged in a mock feud that became one of radio's most enduring gags.

From their NBC program and artist cards, the origin of the feud can be traced back to the December 30, 1936 broadcast of *Town Hall Tonight*, preserved in a recording. That evening, ten-year-old violinist Stuart Kanin played Schubert's "Bee" with astonishing virtuosity, prompting Allen to remark, ". . . a little fella only in fifth grade and already [he] plays better than Jack Benny." Some of radio's funniest moments occurred when Benny or Allen appeared over the other's program—their radio artist cards listing twelve such appearances (ten recorded) from 1936-1949. (Presumably, there were more, as Allen was with CBS from 1940-1944.) Occasionally, Allen found a willing accomplice—Eddie Anderson as Rochester, chief victim of Benny's stinginess. Anderson's radio artist cards, filed in the segregated "Negro artist" index, list three appearances over Allen's program, all recorded.

Due to a decline in his program's ratings, Fred Allen temporarily retired from radio in 1949. Two years later, he returned to NBC as writer and performer on *The Big Show* starring Tallulah Bankhead—an all-out but short-lived effort to keep the radio variety show alive in the new age of television. Benny, meanwhile, had left NBC in 1948 for the greener pastures of CBS. Cleverly devising a way for performers to incorporate themselves and thus reduce their tax burden, that network also captured, among other top NBC stars, Freeman Gosden and Charles Correll (Amos and Andy), and Edgar Bergen. The CBS raid was a devastating blow, but as the history files suggest, given the same opportunity, NBC would have acted no differently.

Notes

1. The patent agreements had awarded AT&T exclusive rights to commercial wired and wireless telephony–that is, the right to charge businesses for long distance telephone service. Since radio broadcasting was viewed as a form of radio telephony, AT&T reasoned that it also had the exclusive right to permit businesses to use the airwaves for commercial purposes. Although the phone company would demand a licensing fee from stations which profited from radio advertising, few stations complied.

2. All documents relating to the WRC-WCAP rivalry can be found in File 1000. Affiliates–Radio.

3. Erik Barnouw, *A Tower in Babel: A History of Broadcasting in the United States*, vol. 1 (New York: Oxford University Press, 1966), p. 160.

4. Ibid., p. 131.

5. File 429. Programs–Criticism, 1942-1948.

6. Following the *Titanic* tragedy, federal law required the immediate cessation of all nonessential radio activity within a 500-mile radius of a ship in distress.

7. File 1000. See the December 6, 1923, letter from F. P. Guthrie to David Sarnoff, which was returned to Mr. Guthrie with Sarnoff's comments detailed in the margins.

8. File 93. Historical Facts and Figures (3 of 3). See "Highlights of NBC's Contributions to Radio Broadcasting," app. 1.

9. File 92. Historical Facts and Figures (2 of 3). See Horton Heath's "A History of the National Broadcasting Company."

10. Pamphlet 63. Radio Corporation of America, Department of Information, "Biographical Sketch of Brigadier General David Sarnoff," 1945.

11. Tom Lewis, *Empire of the Air: The Men Who Made Radio* (New York: HarperCollins, 1991), pp. 105-107.

12. Although this release is missing from the set of network press releases in the NBC Collection, a copy can be found in File 7. Tenth Anniversary (3 of 3).

13. File 505. RCA-NBC Cooperation. See the September 14, 1926, eleven-page proposal for a publicity department for NBC from the Broadcast Company of America. (NBC's placement of the document in this file is misleading; the Broadcast Company of America was an arm of AT&T, not RCA).

14. The author is indebted to Prof. Michael Biel of Morehead State University (Kentucky) for information on NBC's broadcast sound recordings.

15. File 306. Networks–Red Network 1936-1942.

16. File 420. Programming–General. See November 6, 1941, memo from H. M. Beville, Jr. to Sidney Strotz.

17. File 31. Broadcast Advertising. See "Committee on Sales Improvement," p. 19.

18. File 998. NBC Network Affiliates. See June 28, 1934, letter from Harry Wilder to Richard Patterson, Jr.

19. File 300. Networks–Blue Separation or Sale 1937 (1 of 4). See November 5, 1937, memo from David Rosenblum to Lenox Lohr.

20. Pamphlet 187. "Statement by Niles Trammell President National Broadcasting Company Before Senate Interstate Commerce Committee," June 17-18, 1941, p. 77.

21. Ibid., entire document.

22. As quoted in James Fly's obituary in the *New York Times*, January 7, 1966, p. 29.

Listed below is an inventory of all the materials in the NBC Collection which are not covered by this article:

*Approximately 1300 reels and 340 cassettes of selected radio news broadcasts from 1961 through 1985. These include presidential news conferences and speeches, as well as coverage of important events, such as the first moon landing.

*Transcriptions of *Meet the Press*, 1954-1984, on microfiche

*NBC Television Logbooks, May 1949-November 1988

*NBC Television Master Books, 1936-1991, on microfilm

*NBC Television Kinescopes, approximately 18,000 programs, from 1948-1977.

KATHLEEN MILLER, currently a cataloging technician in the Arts and Sciences Cataloging Division of the Library of Congress, has also worked in the field of art museum education as a researcher, lecturer, and writer. She has contributed to several publications, including *Views and Visions: American Landscape Painting before 1830*, and is sole author of *American Neoclassical Sculpture in the Corcoran Gallery of Art*.

Heartfelt thanks to playback technicians Larry Miller, George Kipper, David Sager, Neil Gladd, and James Wolf for bringing radio's golden age back to life; Recorded Sound Section Head, Samuel Brylawski, and reference librarians, Edwin Matthias, Janet McKee, and Bryan Cornell, whose collective patience and kindness count among the Library's most valuable treasures; and Michael Biel, Professor of Radio and Television at Morehead State University (Kentucky) for sharing with this author his extensive knowledge about NBC.

The photographs are from the Recorded Sound Reference Center's collections.

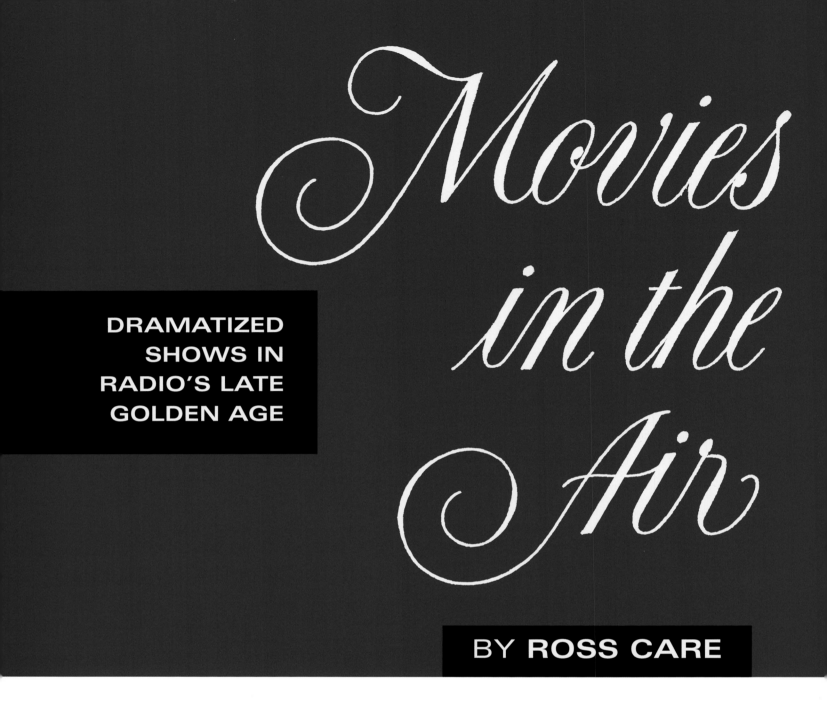

Movies in the Air

DRAMATIZED SHOWS IN RADIO'S LATE GOLDEN AGE

BY ROSS CARE

Commencing in the 1930s and persisting well into the 1950s, two entertainment mediums dominated the American imagination: movies and radio. As it later did with television in the early 1950s, Hollywood at first shunned the burgeoning phenomenon of radio, even to initially forbidding film stars to participate in the new medium. Unlike its reaction to television, however, Hollywood soon learned to exploit the airways, and film and radio entered into a lengthy, mutually supportive, and profitable alliance. While only a few radio stars made the leap into movies (such as the several radio-inspired *Big Broadcast* films of the 1930s), established film stars were soon (and sometimes despite severe attacks of mike fright) regularly appearing on the air, and the phrase "star of stage, screen, and radio" entered the national jargon.

American network radio in its heyday of a few brief decades offered its devoted mass audience as varied a bill of fare as did motion pictures. There were programs showcasing music, news, variety, and (most colorfully of all) a wide spectrum of dramatized radio encompassing Broadway and Hollywood adaptations, soap operas whose involved tales of woe literally went on for decades, genre offerings such as *radio noir* crime and suspense, fantasy and adventure shows, and children's fare which incorporated the increasingly popular science fiction that flowered both aurally and visually in the early 1950s.

Radio Days

For a youngster growing up in the late forties and early fifties, a typical media weekend might run something like this. Waking up on Saturday morning, the precious strains of "The Teddy Bears' Picnic" heralded a program which set the tone for the entire weekend: *No School Today* [1] with Big Jon (Arthur) and Sparkie, the "beloved radio pixie." Big Jon was one of those adults who (like *Howdy Doody's* Buffalo Bob) had an appealing if somewhat curious (and nonfamilial) relationship with a diminutive fantasy pal, in this case

Radio actress Clara Horton seems rather unimpressed by the latest in "decorative radio," an early (circa 1925) model embellished with photos of film stars Corinne Griffith (left) and Colleen Moore. *Prints and Photographs Division.*

pixie Sparkie, who, like Disney's Pinocchio, "wanted more than anything in the world to become a real boy." Big Jon's hour-and-a-half network show featured a mix of instructive patter and recorded music and stories, mostly kiddie story albums from record labels such as Capitol and RCA (which produced kiddie albums that were like radio shows on record, without commercials, of course), but also short musical numbers with kid appeal (such as "March of the Siamese Children" from *The King and I*, probably my first exposure to an original Broadway cast recording, a genre I instinctively loved). As the show grew in popularity, a greater amount of original dramatized material relating Sparkie's adventures with the various characters who evolved around him was developed.

Originally a syndicated show from Cincinnati in the late 1940s, at its peak *No School Today* (NST) and Big Jon and Sparkie achieved national fame. A "TV Radio Mirror" survey voted it 1956's "Favorite Radio Children's Program" (up there with *Howdy Doody* on television) and, while never

resulting in a television edition, NST did engender spin-offs, such as comic books and records, illustrating the commercial clout radio still wielded in the mid-1950s. The comic books gave pleasing images to Sparkie and the other characters kids had previously only conjured up in their mind's eye over countless school-free Saturday mornings. But with one of Sparkie's first records, "Little Red Caboose," a song popularized on the show, also came one of childhood's first major reality checks. Experimenting with my nifty new leatherette portable three-speed phonograph, I played the 45 rpm record of "Caboose" at 33 $\frac{1}{3}$ rpm, and was shocked and somewhat devastated to discover that Sparkie was actually only the adult voice of Big Jon speeded up to sound like a less manic version of the mice in Disney's *Cinderella*. Thus, with technology also came disillusion.

Circa 1955 to 1956 *No School Today* was on ABC at the civilized hour of 9 a.m., and for a time (around 1954 to 1955) it was followed (at 10:30) on the same network by *Space Patrol*, one of the latest fifties manifestations of a

■ Two photos of radio shows being performed before live audiences illustrate the variety of the fare offered in the medium's Golden Age. The broadcast of an unidentified CBS show, probably originating from New York in the early 1940s, is shown from a backstage perspective in the first photograph. *Prints and Photographs Division.*

The second shows the audience's viewpoint of a more upscale broadcast of Kay Thompson and her Rhythm Singers being accompanied by conductor Andre Kostelanetz in a show from one of CBS's lavish Broadway radio theaters in 1936. *Motion Picture, Broadcasting, and Recorded Sound Division.*

Radio was often a proving ground for talent that moved into other mediums: Thompson gained fame as a nightclub performer and vocal coach-arranger for Hollywood's MGM studios, and Kostelanetz maintained a successful recording career with Columbia Records through the 1950s.

genre that stretched back to the long-lived *Buck Rogers in the 25th Century* series of the thirties and forties, but which was now called science fiction. At the helm of *Space Patrol* (which was on five times a week, Monday through Friday, during its original 1950 to 1951 season) was Commander-in-Chief Buzz Corry (who may or may not have influenced the name of the Buzz Lightyear character in the recent *Toy Story*) with Cadet Happy as Buzz's wisecracking young sidekick. *Patrol* also spun-off cheap but charismatic radio merchandising, pop artifacts such as a "Jet-Glow" code belt with decoder buckle, or a "Cosmic Smoke" gun which could shoot 100 "absolutely harmless" blasts per loading, and either of which could be had for twenty-five cents, a Ralston Cereal boxtop, and a cosmically endless wait for the U.S. mail to deliver either or both of the breathlessly awaited treasures.

Space Patrol's competition for extraterrestrial territory and audience ratings was ABC's later (1952 to 1954) *Tom Corbett, Space Cadet*, a show which (like *Patrol*) quickly made the transition to television, but with a bigger budget and greater commercial success. *Tom Corbett* dealt with the adventures of three Space Academy cadets, hero Tom, the obligatory wise cracker, Roger Manning, and Astro who, though a man, was still from Venus. Both series inspired comic books, but unlike *Space Patrol* (issued by second-string Approved Comics, Inc.) the *Corbett* comics were high-end Dells that included an impressive cover painting, a scene from the television show on the inside front cover, and no advertising. Other merchandising in the form of books and toys (such as a way cool Space Academy play set), a dynamic Sunday color comic strip, and tie-ins with Kellogg's "Pep" Cereal certified *Tom Corbett's* status in the pop culture of the first half of the fifties. And with the emergence of the drug culture of the late sixties, the term *Space Cadet* launched a successful reentry into the American mind-set.

Though both *Space Patrol* and *Tom Corbett* are probably best remembered as classically clunky early fifties television shows, their radio originals, with their over-the-top Hammond organ scores, blast-off sound effects, and cliff-hanging situations, remain classic fifties dramatized radio in their own right. Indeed, bearing in mind the primitive production values of early television (and the power of a collective juvenile imagination as yet unsullied by overexposure to the insidious new medium), the radio versions of both shows probably evoked derring-do in outer space with more power and credibility than their television counterparts ever could or did.[2]

In the late forties and for a time in the early fifties, the less bombastic, indeed rather genteel *Let's Pretend* was heard at 11 a.m. (and later at 2 p.m.), this venerable children's program also had a history extending back to the thirties. The show's creator was Nila Mack, an actress who had appeared in both vaudeville and Nazimova's famous production of Ibsen's *A Doll's House*. Mack had made her radio debut on CBS's *Night Club Romances* in 1936, a role that led to her writing and directing the dramatized classic fairy tales of *Let's Pretend* for the ensuing two decades. For a good deal of its history, *Let's Pretend* had the unique status of being one of the few shows without an ongoing sponsor,

but sometime in the early fifties it came under the aegis of "Cream of Wheat," implanting in a generation of young minds the opening jingle: "Cream of Wheat is so good to eat you should have some every day."

Which brought things up to Saturday lunch, after which media time was pretty much taken over by movies, almost always a matinee jaunt downtown or to one's local neighborhood movie house, with varying possibilities for Saturday evening and Sunday matinee screenings as well. Sunday evening was, however, usually a radio night, with school the next day and memories of a backlog of movies from the rest of the weekend to digest and savor. Quiet Sunday afternoons (with blue laws still strictly in effect) could also be taken up with cultured fare such as *Symphonette* or *The Woolworth Hour* (with Percy Faith), followed by an hour-and-a-half broadcast by the New York Philharmonic or some other prestigious orchestra (just as, if one had the stamina, Saturday afternoons could be spent with Milton Cross and his hours-long live opera broadcasts from the Met in New York). One of my last truly nostalgic memories of real radio is of springtime Sunday drives with my parents through the orchard country of central Pennsylvania, of meandering through acres of white apple trees under silvery overcast skies while the classical music broadcasts of the celebrated Concertgebouw Orchestra wafted out of the car's tinny sounding AM radio from far-off Amsterdam.

Other varied offerings of a Sunday afternoon might include *The Catholic Hour, Old Fashioned Revival Hour,* or Dr. Oral Roberts. Much more interesting to me in that line, however, was *The Greatest Story Ever Told*, a half-hour dramatized series at 5:30 which draped Bible stories in a many-colored coat of stirring voices, ethereally uplifting music, and portentous echo chambers. *Greatest Story* was based on the Fulton Oursler book which also became a George Stevens epic in 1965.

Sunday evening was definitely the primest of the prime, CBS's fall 1954 lineup of half-hour shows including: *Gene Autry* at 6, followed (at 7) by *Jack Benny, Amos 'n' Andy, Our Miss Brooks,* and *My Little Margie,* and peaking with the hour-long *Edgar Bergen Show* (synonymous, of course, with Charlie McCarthy and pals) at 9. After that it was news for the adults, and bedtime for the children with school again looming on Monday morning. Thus, there was something almost desperately enthralling about these Sunday evening shows (which were often as not enjoyed along with a much-anticipated, informal Sunday evening supper of hamburgers with all the trimmings), delaying as they did the drudgery of another five-day school week.

Daytime Drama

Weekday daytime radio remained something of a mystery, only experienced on those memorable days when a kid was blessed with a fever and thus officially too sick to go to school. Those days gave tantalizingly brief insights, often filtered through a dreamy fever haze, into the turbulent daily lives of characters and locales such as *Old Ma Perkins, Young Doctor Malone, The Second Mrs. Burton,* and *Hilltop House.* Again CBS was the home of these popular shows,

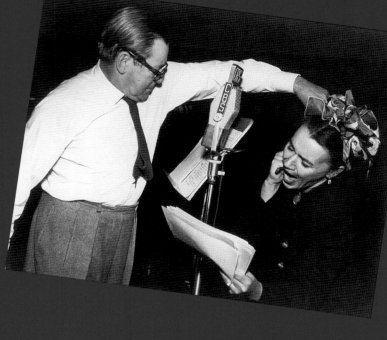

■ *Suspense* was a popular, long-running half-hour radio thriller that featured both leading and supporting Hollywood performers in its major roles. Around 1949, World Wide Photos captured several *Suspense* stars emoting in a series of seven action photographs that illustrated how the violence that thrilled radio listeners was simulated. In the three examples shown here John Garfield realistically takes a bullet for the show "Death Sentence," Herbert Marshall murders Jeanette Noland in "Back for the Holidays," and Kay Brinker attempts to murder Gregory Peck by running him down with her car (but instead misses and plunges "screaming to *her* death") in "Hitch-Hike Poker."

Obviously, the subject of most *Suspense* shows was murder in all degrees. The collections in the Library of Congress Recorded Sound Reference Center include a tour de force *Suspense* episode, "Death and Miss Turner," vividly performed by Agnes Moorehead on May 19, 1957. Was Miss Turner guilty? Tune in and see. *Prints and Photographs Division.*

while later in the afternoon *Young Widder Brown, Backstage Wife, Stella Dallas,* and *Pepper Young's Family* all valiantly fought for their *Right to Happiness* through the dinner hour on NBC.

However elusive the above-mentioned afternoon shows were, I still vividly recall the noon-hour weekday lineup on CBS. Before the impending middle-class migration to the suburbs of the later fifties, I still lived in a city in the early half of the decade, and thus walked home from school for lunch each noon and was able to catch parts of four durable fifteen-minute programs. I usually missed the news section of *Wendy Warren and the News,* a show that resourcefully managed to fuse news casting and soap opera. But the news was no great loss to me even in the early fifties, and the ongoing ups and downs of female newscaster Wendy's tempestuous personal saga were ever so much more compelling anyway: "Stunned by grief, but not shattered, Wendy knows she must and will make something of the new life that now opens before her."[3] I seem to have vaguer memories of the 12:15 slot, only recalling someone named Aunt Jenny (probably because I also had an Aunt Jenny who lived in distant, exotic Atlantic City).

However, 12:30 is still memorable for *The Romance of Helen Trent,* the program that (to the gentle strains of a guitar and an androgynous male voice humming "Juniata") asked the question, "Can romance still come to a woman of thirty-five and over?" Helen had been thirty-five for years and was probably way over that age by the 1950s, a fact which did little to dampen her ongoing romantic pursuits:"The shock of her broken romance with Brett Chapman has forced Helen Trent to admit what she was trying to forget —that she has never stopped loving Gil Whitney!"[4] At 12:45 each day *Our Gal Sunday* also relentlessly questioned whether "a girl from a little mining town in the west" could find happiness "as the wife of a wealthy and titled Englishman." I never found out if Sunday could or did, because about five minutes into her show I was hied back to school, the many denouements of Sunday's perpetual quest for happiness with Lord Henry Brinthrope in Black Swan Hall thus remaining an eternal mystery.

The utter sameness of the soaps, emphasized by the catchphrase "Tune in tomorrow, same time, same station," might have been amended by the addition of "same plot," but there was also a comfortable pattern to the daily routine of daytime drama. With a freedom and single-mindedness often missing or denied in real life, radio's Helen Trent sought romance, and Our Gal Sunday happiness, everyday "same time, same station," and life went on, the reassuring regularity of the mostly female quests for happiness and order brightening and ordering the daily monotony of a generation of pre-Liberation housewives and other housebound listeners. One of the many great things about radio was all the things you could do while listening to it: eat lunch, read a comic book or magazine, or do homework or chores. Unlike the more demanding medium of television, you could get on with your life, indeed have a life, while still enjoying radio.

In the early fifties, daily soap opera time continued through the afternoon and into dinner hour which brought with it the quartet of *Just Plain Bill, Lorenzo Jones, Hotel for Pets,* and *It Pays To Be Married* (these on NBC), and only varied slightly from the late forties when *Portia Faces Life, When a Girl Marries, Just Plain Bill,* and *Front Page Farrell* occupied the same slot. A bit earlier (circa 1947) the irresistible quartet of *Terry and the Pirates, Sky King, Jack Armstrong,* and *Tennessee Jed* captured the younger audience every weekday at 5 on ABC.[5]

Evening dramatized radio was too varied to recall in

■ Rosalind Russell (right) and Lurene Tuttle in a life-and-death struggle on a *Suspense* episode entitled "The Sisters." Note the soundman ready to create the effect of a shattering railing as Russell struggles to push Tuttle to her death. (In the script it is Russell who falls to her demise in the botched attempt.) Lurene Tuttle was a busy, versatile radio actress and in an August, 1947, *Radio Mirror* article commented on the many role changes required by the medium: "I wonder if the first 'split personality' a psychologist ever discovered wasn't an actress? And if you're a radio actress as well— my personality isn't just split, it's in little pieces." Tuttle made her radio debut on Louella Parsons's *Hollywood Hotel* and in 1938 she played Hedda Hopper's daughter in a show called *Brenthouse,* but her role on an hour-length show based on the lives of famous people, *White Fires,* really launched her career in radio. Later she was Sam Spade's secretary, Effie, on CBS's *Adventures of Sam Spade* in the late forties, and Mother Day in the late fifties television series developed from the long-running Broadway play, *Life with Father.* One of her last screen appearances was in Hitchcock's *Psycho* in 1960. *Prints and Photographs Division.*

detail here. By 1955 it encompassed (to name but a few classics): *Fibber McGee and Molly,* whose running closet gag was an introduction to the power of radio sound effects and the imagination; *Suspense* with its shrieking, hysterical climaxes and unforgettably creepy Bernard Herrmann musical theme;[6] that other aural descendent of the Edgar Allan Poe short story, *Inner Sanctum; Mr. Keene, Tracer of Lost Persons,* its musical theme (I was amused to discover much later in life) being Noel Coward's "Someday I'll Find

Lux presents Hollywood

to America's largest audience

In its 17th season

the Lux Radio Theatre again presents
famous Hollywood stars in
Hollywood's finest screen plays

**Mondays 6 P.M.
Los Angeles Time**

**K
N
X**

*Every Monday night more people
listen to the Lux radio program than listen
to any other program on the air!*

and Coast to Coast Columbia Network

■ A *Lux Radio Theatre* advertisement from the industry publication *The Hollywood Reporter*, January 1949.

You"; and *The FBI in Peace and War*, the stirringly quirky music theme of which (I also much later realized) was—very ironically for the "better dead than Red" fifties—Russian composer Serge Prokofiev's "March" from *The Love for Three Oranges*. In 1956, as television slowly dismantled radio, the most popular evening dramatized radio shows were Mutual's *Gang Busters* (8 on Wednesdays) and CBS's *Gunsmoke* (6:30 on Sundays).

I also have pleasant after-dinner memories of a comedy show called *Beulah*, which was one of the few spin-off series in radio history. Beulah was a character who had originally appeared on *Fibber McGee*, and a bizarre piece of triva about the series is that Beulah and her gentleman friend were, for a short period after the show's debut in 1945, *both* played by a white male, Marlon Hurt. When Hurt died in 1947, Louise Beavers and Hattie McDaniel both took over the title role for varying stints. So when I finally saw a revival of *Gone with the Wind* sometime in the mid-1950s, I was intrigued and a bit disoriented to discover that Scarlett's Mammy was actually the well-loved Beulah of many a humorous weekday radio evening.

Lux Presents Hollywood!

These shows have been randomly but indelibly implanted in my memory and on many an impressionable young consciousness. But for a time, as if to cure the post-weekend blahs and to make the beginning of another interminable school week just somewhat more bearable, what was perhaps the most charismatic dramatic radio show of all time was heard at 9:00 p.m. (EST), Monday evening: *The Lux Radio Theatre*. Aside from being one of the most entertaining shows in radio history, in the pre-video age when movies came and then went, mostly forever, *Lux Radio Theatre* also provided the pleasure of reexperiencing a favorite film, or of discovering an unknown one (not to mention its bringing the cream of Hollywood stardom into one's own living room or bedroom). Aside from its lavish production values, one of the show's most unique qualities was its ability both to evoke a film one had already seen and to arouse interest in an unknown one.

Premiering in the mid-1930s from New York with a season mostly adapted from Broadway dramas, Lux shifted networks and coasts to open the following season with the classic pronouncement "Lux Presents Hollywood!" and now from Hollywood itself. Commercial radio was born in the early 1920s, and with it, almost from the start, radio drama. (The two major networks, NBC and CBS, appeared in 1926 and 1927, respectively). But, as noted earlier, prestigious film stars were at first forbidden by their studios to appear on the upstart medium.

Lux Radio Theatre soon changed that. The original show, premiering on NBC on October 14, 1934, did not prove immediately popular and was close to being canceled when Danny Danker, an advertising man from the famous J. Walter Thompson agency (which handled the Lever Brothers/Lux account), hit upon the Hollywood emphasis. Actually Lux toilet soap had always been hyped via the glamour angle, with celebrity (often motion picture actress-endorsed) magazine advertisements that were first seen in

■ When *Lux Radio Theatre* moved from New York to Hollywood in 1936 it found a home in a real theater, the Music Box at 6126 Hollywood Boulevard (today known as the Henry Fonda Theater). Audiences, who had not been a part of the New York broadcasts, became an essential element of the Hollywood show which was performed live at 6:00 p.m. Pacific Time. As this June 1, 1936, photo shows, the show became immensely popular with audiences, and those who could not obtain a free ticket— the theater seated about a thousand people—were sometimes inclined to riot. In 1940 *Lux* moved to the Vine Street Theater where it remained until its last broadcasts in 1953. *Recorded Sound Reference Center.*

the 1920s and continued into the 1950s.[7] In addition, Louella Parsons's radio show, *Hollywood Hotel*, had already proven a popular West Coast broadcast, and with other shows soon dispersing Tinsel Town glamour across the country like pixie dust on the airwaves, *Lux Radio Theatre* moved to Hollywood in 1936, its first show emanating from Hollywood Boulevard's Music Box Theater on June 1.

The shift to the West Coast cued a number of changes in the show's format. It was now performed in front of a live audience that became an integral part of the show's total ambiance. The production team was also new, retaining only one writer from the New York company. Sanford Barnett (who would be with the show until its demise in the 1950s) was brought from New York to write the framework (or nondramatic) portions of the show—commercials, framing episodes, and the general "ad-lib" chitchat with celebrity guests. In the late forties and fifties, as S. E. Barnett, he would also adapt the screenplays themselves. Louis Silvers, a studio musician who also worked at Warner Bros. and Columbia, now supervised the expanded use of music in the Hollywood productions, and the new program director was Frank Woodruff, a young director fresh to Hollywood but gifted in handling its distinctive temperament on the air.

Perhaps the most notable addition to the Hollywood *Radio Theater* was the legendary showman, Cecil B. DeMille. As host/moderator, DeMille brought to *Lux* more charisma than actual creative involvement. Though he was hyped as the show's "producer," in reality he was not, nor was he ever *Lux Radio Theatre*'s director. What he was, however, was a personable host who imbued *Lux* with an audible air of quality and prestige, and for a time DeMille and *Lux Radio Theatre* became synonymous.

DeMille stayed with *Lux* until the notorious incident in 1945 when the American Federation of Radio Artists (AFRA) assessed each of its members a dollar in a campaign to strengthen union control in radio. DeMille (who had been making 2,000 dollars per broadcast and was adamantly antiunion) refused to pay the dollar and in addition instigated a lengthy court battle which the producer lost when it was pursued to the U.S. Supreme Court. Thus, commencing with the January 29, 1945, broadcast (hosted by Lionel Barrymore), DeMille was no longer associated with *Lux Radio Theatre*, though the mogul continued to play the gracious host in his own epic motion pictures, providing the voice-over narration for films such as *The Greatest Show on Earth* in 1952, and even appearing in the prologue to his 1956 epic, *The Ten Commandments*. A number of "guest" producers filled DeMille's shoes for most of the remaining 1945 season. On November 5, William Keighley, a veteran Hollywood director, took over the job, remaining with the show for six years. The last *Lux* host was another director, Irving Cummings, who joined the show in 1952, staying until its last broadcast on June 7, 1955.

For its final season on the air *Lux* switched from CBS back to NBC (on Tuesday evenings at 9:00 p.m.), the network where the program had originally premiered in 1934. The shift to NBC is well-documented in the Library of Congress by a series of program cards on microfiche in the NBC Collection in the Recorded Sound Reference Center of the Motion Picture, Broadcasting, and Recorded Sound Division. The *Lux Radio Theatre* data, found in the "sponsor" section under "Lever Bros.," includes two introductory cards with a brief overview of the show and its credits, plus an ensuing chronology of shows in the 1954-1955 season by title, plot, and cast.

The card also notes: "In honor of the past twenty years of broadcasts, the current series presents hour-long adaptations-for-radio of 20 great films of the past 20 years—those films, from the 'greats' of all the Hollywood Studios, in many cases were based on novels and classics of Literature." Just how "great" many of the films on the final NBC season ultimately were is open to opinion, but as usual, they ran the gamut from musicals and comedies to dramas and some genuine classics. Though this final season pushed the "greats" angle, each season of *Lux Radio* presented an equally varied bill of screen fare, past and recent, with later seasons placing an emphasis on current releases. The 1952-1953 season, a goodly cross-section of which may be found as part of the voluminous Armed Forces Radio Collection in the Recorded Sound Reference Center, was a typically varied season. Commencing with the nostalgic MGM musical, *Two Weeks with Love* (with three of the 1950 film's original stars, Jane Powell, Debbie Reynolds, and Ricardo

Montalban), on September 8, 1952, the second program was the equally lightweight *Here Comes the Groom*, from the 1951 Paramount comedy, with original star Jane Wyman and Fred MacMurray in the Bing Crosby role.

The Library's Armed Forces Radio series of *Lux* broadcasts begins with the season's third on September 22, 1952, 20th Century-Fox's 1951 *I'll Never Forget You*. The film was based on John Balderston's 1929 play, *Berkeley Square*, which in turn had first been adapted for *Lux* sometime during its first season when material was mainly drawn from Broadway dramas. The property was rebroadcast (with Ronald Colman and Maureen O'Sullivan) in 1944. In the 1952 radio adaptation, Tyrone Power reprised his original role (in the 1951 film remake), and the "lovely new star" Debra Paget essayed the role created by Ann Blyth.

Though apparently considered inferior to the 1944 broadcast, the 1952 *I'll Never Forget You* remains a touching and atmospheric romantic fantasy about a cross-century romance between a contemporary American and a nineteenth-century English belle. Though leaving the English accents to one of Lux's consistently competent supporting casts (including Eleanor Audley as Lady Ann Pettigrew), Paget, hyped as "the pride and joy of 20th Century-Fox" in the show's regular closing star interview, gives a sincere performance as young Helen Pettigrew, the play's female love interest, and the final farewell scene when Power returns to his own era remains quite touching. (Paget's receding and naturally plaintive voice is here enhanced by the spacey sound of that classic radio special effect, the echo chamber.) Music, which is seldom overemphasized in these later adaptations, is again used sparingly, here for the usual transitional cues but also to emphasize emotional peaks. An unusual touch is the use of an electronic instrument, probably some kind of organ or possibly a Novachord, to evoke the story's fantasy, time-tripping elements.

The next broadcast in the Library's collection is the ensuing week's September 29 *Adam and Evelyne*, based on the 1949 J. Arthur Rank film (released in the United States by Universal International). For *Lux* the real-life husband and wife (and genuinely British) team of Stewart Granger and Jean Simmons recreated their original roles in this light English comedy. October 6th's show returned to American

■ "When a dramatic script calls for a scene in a vast temple, or an adventure series depicts action in a cave far underground, then the ingenuity of the engineer is displayed in the construction and use of echo chambers, or more correctly, reverberation chambers. The echo or cave effect is created by feeding a portion of the studio microphone output into a loud speaker which is mounted in a room, called an echo chamber. The hard, inside surfaces of this room reflect the sound issuing from the loud speaker in a heterogeneous pattern. This sound is then picked up by a microphone also mounted in the echo chamber. The outputs of the microphones in the echo chamber and the studio are electrically mixed in the desired intensity relation. On the air the result of this mixing is a surprisingly realistic illusion of sound in a highly reverberant room or cave."

It was also a popular recording effect in the 1950s. Today we call it "reverb" and it comes in a little black box. "NBC's Air Castles," 1947 NBC publicity pamphlet, *Recorded Sound Reference Center.*

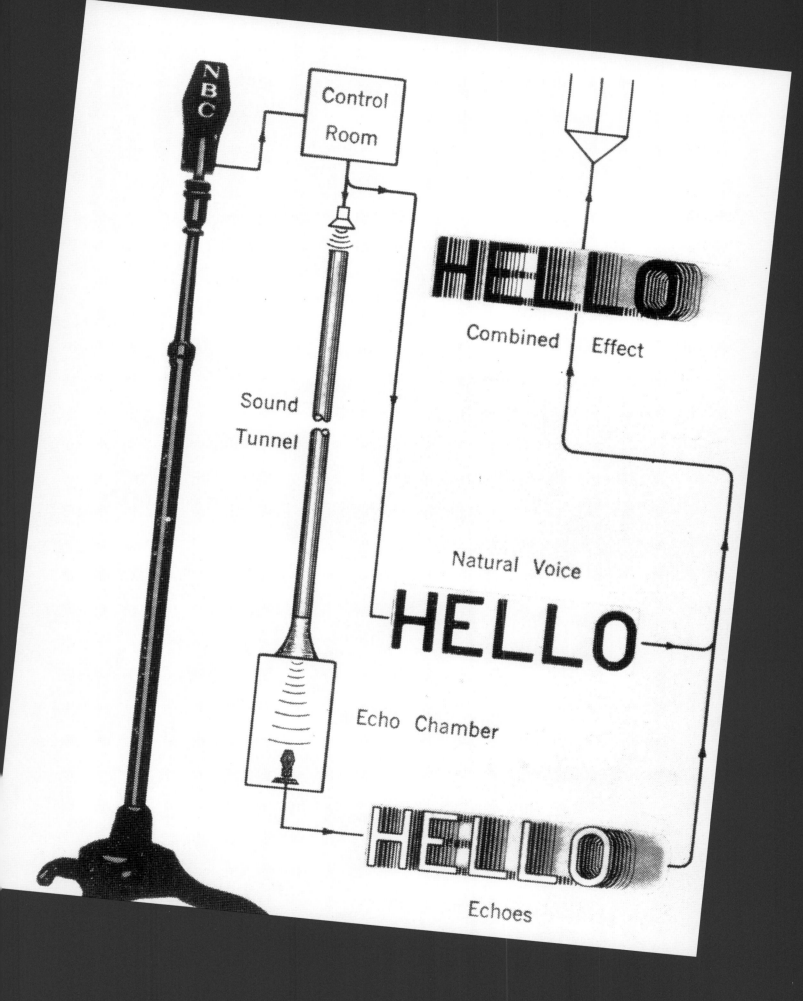

Control Room

Sound Tunnel

Echo Chamber

HELLO

Combined Effect

Natural Voice

HELLO

HELLO

Echoes

comedy with one of the season's most entertaining, well-scripted shows, *The Model and the Marriage Broker*. A kind of contemporary version of Thornton Wilder's *The Matchmaker*, Thelma Ritter and Jeanne Crain both reprised their original 20th Century-Fox film roles.

Ritter, whose distinctive New York accent and "just-folks" earthiness made her a popular supporting character actress and a perfect comic foil for haute 1950s glamour in nearly a decade of Hollywood films, was an absolute natural for radio comedy as well. This *Lux* script, adapted from the original Charles Brackett–Walter Reisch–Richard Breen screenplay, provided a rich showcase for the actress whose appeal and no nonsense, self-deprecating charm comes across as vividly aurally as on-screen. Brief touches of seriousness interspersed into the humorous script about a contemporary New York matchmaker who surreptitiously arranges the love life of a model involved in an affair with a married man (e.g., "you never get used to being lonely," or "who knows who's right for who?") give Ritter an opportunity to aurally convey a serious side to the romantic intrigue. In the less rewarding role of the model, Jeanne Crain's attractive voice nonetheless evokes the fresh-scrubbed, all-American beauty and charm that the Fox actress conveyed on-screen. The various bits of ethnic shtick woven into the script are well-handled by Verna Felton and Hans Conried, whose voices were also well-utilized by the Disney studio in *Cinderella*, wherein Felton was the Fairy Godmother, and *Peter Pan*, where Conried essayed the major vocal role of Captain Hook. (In the early days of the studio, Disney frequently drew his vivid cartoon voices from radio actors.)

The next three shows of the season (and in the Library's collection) are all adaptations of 1952 films: Fox's *Five Fingers* on October 13, Columbia's *My Six Convicts* on October 20, and Paramount's *My Son John* on October 27. On November 3, an adaptation of John Steinbeck's original screenplay for 20th Century-Fox's *Viva Zapata* was aired with Charlton Heston in the title role (originally played by Marlon Brando) and Jean Peters, who appeared in the film. The show was the first of the season to take on an epic quality (though *King Solomon's Mine* would be coming up in about a month) and while remaining rather engrossing, *Zapata* suffers from a talky script and the abbreviated, often abrupt climaxes which the nonvisual medium necessitated. *Zapata* also employs a noncharacter narrator, in this case a voice-over by Paul Frees, whose neutrally stentorian tones evoked a kind of cosmic "Voice of the Future" association due to his narration of several George Pal sci-fi epics of the early fifties, as well as an oddball RCA Victor narration-choral sci-fi album, "Exploring The Unknown," a kind of radio show on LP.

In *Zapata*'s introduction, Heston and Peters are introduced as "newcomers, outstanding artists of tomorrow," and while the visually charismatic Peters proves a less-than-riveting vocal performer, hearing Heston without his impressive physical presence makes one aware of how vocally distinctive and dynamic some film stars could be. While (perhaps wisely) eschewing any attempt at a Spanish accent—on *Lux* (and elsewhere) most Hollywood stars tended to avoid the attempt at anything like an authentic foreign or ethnic accent—one hears in his *Zapata* emphatic pre-echoes of Ben Hur and Moses, and a rich and distinctive style of vocal delivery which, however appropriately it served each, varied little from gruff circus boss (in *The Greatest Show on Earth*) to Old Testament patriarch. At one point in the script (to denote a character's honesty) Heston rather sensuously murmurs "I like the look in his eyes."

In the concluding star chat, Heston notes that he "came up from radio," and current *Lux* host Irving Cummings recalls his work on a silent serial, *Diamond from the Sky*. Peters, a Fox contract player, also lauds Heston's performance in a new Paramount release, *The Savage*, and mention is also made of the same studio's *Bloodhounds of Broadway*. Aside from the ongoing star plugs for Lux toilet soap, it was a standing practice of each show to hype the latest product of the studio which originally released the current adaptation or, in some instances (as here), the studio of the broadcast's major star. Thus, we have the otherwise unthinkable instance of a Fox star plugging a Paramount film. Sometimes, though, managing to work these references into the script put an audible strain on the supposedly spontaneous and ad-libbed dialogue. In a further example of *Lux Radio Theatre*'s role as studio publicity tool, each show of this era included an interview with a starlet from the studio whose film was being adapted, 20th's Helene Stanley with *Zapata*, and Dawn Addams with the following MGM script.

Another change of pace was MGM's *Grounds for Marriage*, more a comedy with music than an actual musical comedy. Kathryn Grayson and Van Johnson reprised their film roles, and a challenge for nonvisual transcription was how to maintain interest (and air time for Grayson) in a script about an opera singer who loses her voice in a psychosomatic snit over an attempted reconciliation with her estranged husband. In spite her voice failing halfway through the show, *Grounds* nonetheless offered Grayson the opportunity to perform arias from *La Traviata* and *Carmen*, as well as Coward's "I'll Follow My Secret Heart," the script reuniting husband and wife after a series of (somewhat tedious) comic misadventures.

Ensuing film adaptations found among the Library's *Lux* broadcasts from the 1952-1953 season include *The African Queen*, *The Will Rogers Story*, *With a Song in My Heart*, and *Lady in the Dark*, and many other *Lux Radio Theatre*

■ Two stills from films in which the original stars recreated their screen roles for adaptations on *Lux Radio Theatre*: MGM's *Grounds for Marriage* (1950) and 20th Century-Fox's *The Model and the Marriage Broker* (1952). The *Lux* script for *Grounds* managed to work in several operatic scenes from the film. Here Van Johnson and Kathryn Grayson (right) are seen in a dream sequence in which Grayson (as Johnson's estranged opera-singer wife) performs the "Habanera" from Bizet's *Carmen*. Scott Brady, Jeanne Crain, and Thelma Ritter are seen in a still from *The Model and the Marriage Broker*. Both Crain and Ritter appeared in the *Lux* version (in which Ritter proved a highly effective radio performer), but the Scott Brady role was played by Stephen Dunne, a *Lux* semiregular who also played the second male lead in *Grounds for Marriage*. *Model* was aired on October 6, 1952, and *Marriage* on November 10.

Both programs may be found in the Armed Forces Radio Collection in the Library's Recorded Sound Reference Center. *Motion Picture, Broadcasting, and Recorded Sound Division.*

recordings from the 1950s can also be found in the huge Armed Forces Radio Collection. However, due to government policy, AFR recordings delete the shows' commercials thus eliminating some of the show's regular features, such as the starlet interviews and Hollywood gossip because (as noted in the ensuing discussion of two 1940s broadcasts) these sections always slyly segue into Lux commercials.

As on all Armed Forces Radio broadcasts, the *Lux Radio Theatre* commercials are replaced by public-service announcements geared for service men and women, these providing as insightful a glimpse into the ideology and assumptions of the times as do the commercials. In the still postwar climate of the early 1950s, the pervasive message of many of these military segments was one of reunification. Human interest stories took precedence, with an emphasis on America's and (in particular, of course) the Armed Forces' role in helping rehabilitate countries such as Germany and Korea. Recurring motifs are "make a friend and you make an ally," and "in helping others you help your country," echoing lessons learned in World War II (which was less than a decade into history at the time of the original airing of these shows), and tacitly evoking Cold War Communist paranoia which was also escalating in the United States during this same period. Thus, these Armed Forces Radio recordings are replete with stories of German citizens brought to Los Angeles to learn first-hand about American democracy, American towns collectively rallying to help Korean orphans, and personal vignettes of specifically cited individuals, such as a GI who organized a young peoples' orchestra in the German town where he was stationed. The shows did, however, retain the studio plugs worked into the conclusion of each broadcast, and thus Armed Forces members of all sexes around the world were not deprived of messages such as (re Fox's *The Snows of Kilimanjaro*) "For glamour, don't miss it!"

Fine and entertaining as these fifties shows consistently are, two 1940s *Lux Radio Theatre* broadcasts in the Recorded Sound collection suggest that the 1940s were nonetheless the Golden Age of the show. The Library has only a fragment of the December 20, 1943, broadcast of *Dixie*, a musical biography of the composer of the song of the same name, starring Bing Crosby and Dorothy Lamour; but fortunately there is a complete recording for May 10, 1948's *Intrigue*. Both include the original commercials, Hollywood features, and public service announcements, the last being particularly interesting because of the mid-World War II *Dixie* broadcast.

Dixie picks up with the Act I intermission feature, an interview with a nurse who "served with the Navy at Pearl Harbor." The feature urges housewives to save household fats for recycling into "modern miracle medicines" and "opiates to ease pain," and the urgent plea concludes with the added incentive that housewives will receive "two meat ration points for every pound of fat" recycled, and a detailed "how to" spot. Act III of *Dixie* is then introduced by the distinctive voice of Cecil B. DeMille, who sets the scene for the next act. Immediately discernible in *Dixie* is the sound of a larger orchestra and more lavish production values in general. The show concludes with an elaborate sequence in which the song "Dixie" is premiered to calm a panic as the

theater in which the minstrel show is being performed rather abruptly catches fire. Sound effects are well-utilized throughout the script, such as crowd and background noises in the theater where a singer is also performing with voice and piano, crowd confusion and fire effects, and earlier in the act atmospheric cricket sounds effectively evoke a Southern ambiance for a scene between Crosby and one of the female leads.

Intrigue, a contemporary drama dealing with the black marketeering and greed that erupt in inflation-wracked postwar China, illustrates the production values that *Lux* lavished even on a George Raft B-picture from United Artists (here cited by producer William Keighley as "Star Films"). Costarring with Raft is June Havoc, and the distinctive voice of Jeff Chandler is heard in a minor supporting role. (Chandler, a *Lux* regular at this point, went on to become a popular leading man in many 1950s films.)

William Keighley, who took over hosting chores from DeMille in late 1945, opens the show with the familiar "Greetings from Hollywood" and his personal reminiscences of a prewar visit to Shanghai, then quickly shifts into a Lux commercial, describing how Chinese citizens of the preinflation era had taken Lux products to their collective bosom. A grandly exotic orchestral introduction, really a quasi Main Title, introduces an extended musical transition that continues under the opening dialogue scene, immediately accentuating the more profuse use of music in the broadcasts of this decade. The overall big orchestra sound with the free use of that characteristic soundtrack effect of the era, the string tremolo, added a highly cinematic ambiance to both the Main Title and the ensuing underscoring as a whole. The more expansive use of music is also exemplified in a series of bar/nightclub scenes, all underscored by a sequence of continuous cues which shift from source cocktail piano to dramatic underscoring and scene changes to more source dance music for the nightclub cues. Louis Silvers, who had worked at both Warner Bros. and Columbia before joining *Lux* when it moved to Hollywood, was still the show's musician-in-residence through the forties, but in 1950 Rudy Schrager, an Austrian-born musician who had been Silvers's assistant, took over.

The Act I intermission features Lux columnist Libby, doing a plug for the Fox film *Iron Curtain* that, according to Libby, managed to work "18,000 pieces of previously unrevealed evidence"—though evidence of what is not explained—into its script. The Hollywood news again abruptly shifts into a commercial for Lux Diamonds, "dif-

■ **Hollywood quickly established itself as a center for radio and television as well as motion picture production, and the quaintly named environs of Los Angeles soon became nationally known via such radio shows as *Jack Benny* with its running "Anaheim, Azuza, and Cucamonga" gag. This photo shows a state-of-the-art Los Angeles broadcast center in the late forties: the Mutual Don Lee Broadcasting System building which was equipped for simultaneous radio, television, and FM productions. Built in Hollywood at a cost of three million dollars, the facilities opened in May of 1948. As the photo notes, it was also the home of Los Angeles station WKHJ. *Prints and Photographs Division.***

New Hollywood Home of "KHJ" — Hollywood, California

ferent from any other soap." Following the Act I station identification—"We pause now for station identification"—the weekly starlet interview (here with Martha Hyer of RKO) is heard. Hyer's ostensible "interview" consists mainly of a plug for RKO's *Miracle of the Bells*, smoothly eliding into another commercial when Hyer describes how, due to long scenes under the lights in heavy armor (as Joan of Arc), actress Valli was constantly supplied with fresh changes of lingerie, each of course laundered in gentle Lux flakes.

It is easy to take a tongue-in-cheek attitude toward radio-era commercials with their naive jingles and sly writing which bends over backwards to link seamlessly commercials and Hollywood plugs, but in spite of the countless inventive ways Lux writers manage to make abrupt, almost disorientingly fluid transitions from studio hype to Lux soap plugs, the overall impression of the *Lux Radio Theatre* is one of

drama, not commerce. The title of the show implants the name of the product in the mind of the listener at the beginning and end of each program, but the overriding impression remains one of lavish, indeed dense, wall-to-wall drama, which today would heavily tax the attention spans of audiences conditioned by television's endless commercial breaks. Indeed, compared to the commercialization of most 1990s broadcasting, be it movies butchered for television or prime time shows, the commercial ambiance of most Golden Age radio is a model of taste and restraint.

Lux Spin-Offs

Besides evoking the commercial-free flow of a real movie, Hollywood-inspired radio drama also echoed studio era cinema in the sheer volume and range of its output during the peak network production period. Being the pioneer in the use of Hollywood stars on the air, *Lux* soon coexisted with a number of other film-derived dramatic programs of equal or even higher quality. Drama on radio has been traced back to 1922 and a program called *The WGY Players* which broadcast radio versions of stage plays from Schenectady, New York. But these and other regional dramatic shows seldom featured well-known performers, and even after the emergence of network radio, drama was still the province of amateurs and lesser-known players and was still mostly aired as part of a variety show format.

As *Lux Radio Theatre* gained in popularity, a number of similar shows inevitably appeared, among them *The Silver Theater, The Gulf Screen Guild Show*, the short-lived (1944-1946) *Theater of Romance*, and *The Campbell Playhouse* which, on dropping its sponsor, became one of the most celebrated series of the era: Orson Welles's *The Mercury Theater of the Air* (which of course made history during its brief twenty-two- week run with its H. G. Wells's *The War of the Worlds* broadcast). For a brief period, even prestigious MGM produced two radio shows: *MGM Theater of the Air* (1949-1952), and the *MGM Musical Comedy Theater* (1952). Of particular interest for their screen connections are several shows which are well-documented in the NBC Microfiche Collection in the Library's Recorded Sound Reference Center.

The *Screen Guild* Series

The *Gulf Screen Guild Show* underwent several title changes after opening on CBS in January of 1939, becoming the *Gulf Screen Guild Theater* when it switched from its original variety format to doing half-hour movie adaptations in November of 1939, and *The Lady Esther Screen Guild Players* in 1942. NBC records indicate that it was aired as *Screen Guild Players*, a "new program," when it premiered on NBC on October 7, 1948, in a 10:00 to 10:30 Thursday evening slot. NBC also notes the series "consists of dramatizations of recent motion pictures, with the stars of the motion picture doing their original roles" and, adhering to the show's original policy, stars "give their services free, fees that they would ordinarily demand are instead turned over to the Motion Picture Relief Funds, Inc., a philanthropic project which is financed principally by the *Screen Guild Payers*" (one assumes this glitch to be an amusing if appropriate typo). The introduction also notes that each week *Screen Guild Players* sponsor Camel cigarettes sends free cigarettes to servicemen's hospitals "throughout the nation," and that the names and addresses of the hospitals are announced on the show weekly.

The initial 1948 NBC *Screen Guild Players* broadcast featured James Stewart in *Call Northside 777*. The NBC card also notes: "(for history of program on other networks, see 'Screen Guild Players' sponsored title files)." Ensuing shows included *The Babe Ruth Story* with William Bendix, *Kiss of Death* with Victor Mature, and *Rebecca* with Loretta Young. Two holiday broadcasts on December 23 and December 30 were adaptations of Disney's *Snow White* with Edgar Bergen and Charlie McCarthy (with Mortimer

■ The long-running *Theater Guild on the Air* series offered some of the most prestigious productions and talent on radio. Director Homer Fickett (second from right) is seen with Linda Darnell (left), Ezio Pinza, and Madeleine Carroll as they rehearse a 1950 radio dramatization of the play *Goodbye Again*. John Gielgud with Pamela Brown (left) and Dorothy McGuire are seen performing *Hamlet* for a 1951 broadcast. The Shakespeare broadcast was named the outstanding dramatic show of the year by the Academy of Radio and Television Arts and Sciences. The shows all originated from the stage of the Belasco Theater in New York.

The final *Theater Guild* show, Shakespeare's *Julius Caesar* with Maurice Evans and Basil Rathbone, was heard on June 7, 1953. It included a feature on behalf of a proposed American Shakespeare Festival Foundation, and Armina Marshall, the show's executive producer, thanked listeners and sponsors for making the show, which aired over "300 representative plays" in the past eight years, possible. *Prints and Photographs Division.*

Snerd featured as Bashful), and *Pinocchio*, moderated by Fannie Brice and Hanley Stafford in their familiar radio roles of Baby Snooks and her Daddy. NBC notes that the March 31, 1949, program was canceled "in order to have a special broadcast talk by Winston Churchill," and after a summer break *Screen Guild Players* returned on October 6 as *The Camel Screen Guild Theater*, maintaining the policies (and the free cigarettes) of earlier editions. The fall season included *Suspicion* with Cary Grant and Joan Fontaine, *Little Women* with June Allyson and Peter Lawford, and *It's a Wonderful Life* with James Stewart and Donna Reed. The last NBC *Camel* was *You're My Everything* on June 29, 1950, the "last program in the current series."

The Theater Guild on the Air

A prestigious NBC series, heard from summer 1949 through June 1953, was *The Theater Guild on the Air* (*TGA*), the summer replacement for which were broadcasts by NBC's celebrated symphony orchestra. Noted in the NBC records as "*The United States Steel Hour* presents NBC Summer Symphony," the series presented the orchestra "under direction of world-renowned conductors with different famous singers and instrumentalists as guest soloists" playing works "selected for summer listening." The June 12, 1949, show featured Fritz Reiner and Dorothy Maynor, and a special feature "revisiting the scenes of D-Day, on this, the fifth anniversary of D-Day" was included. A segment for children was called "The Children's Corner," and when the 1950 summer series recommenced on June 11, Fritz Reiner programmed a short piece by Béla Bartók, "The Bear's Dance," in the children's slot, illustrating the conductor's continuing support of a major composer who was much neglected during his unhappy last days in America (where he died in 1945). Ensuing guests included Dimitri Mitropoulos, Antal Dorati (listed as "Anatol" Dorati), and Harold Levey, conductor for the winter *TGA* program, who premiered his original concert piece, "Concerto in One Movement," adapted from one of his *TGA* scores. Recordings from these concerts are listed under the heading of "Theater Guild on the Air" in the card catalogs for non-

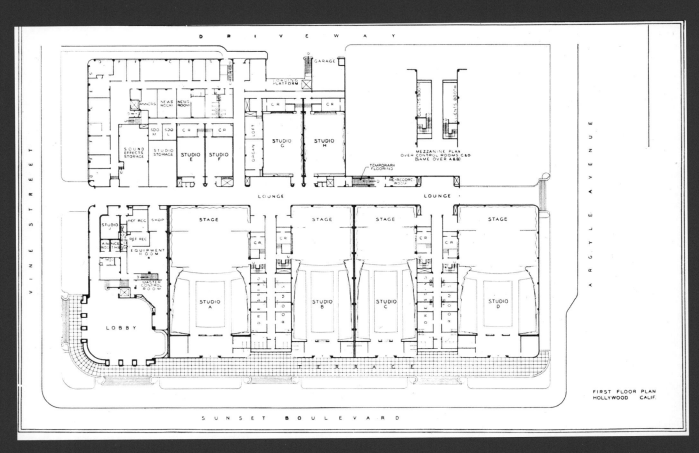

FIRST FLOOR PLAN
HOLLYWOOD   CALIF.

■ A 1947 publicity booklet, "NBC's Air Castles," aptly summed up the magic of the young medium of radio (with a fleeting reference—"images"—to the then even younger medium of television): "All that has been related in this booklet has sprung from a beginning only twenty-seven years ago when Dr. Frank Conrad, operating his experimental radio station, KDKA, in the garage of his home in Wilkinsburg, Pennsylvania, broadcast the first prescheduled radio program in history, the Harding-Cox presidential election returns on the evening of November 2, 1920, to an audience of an estimated 500 wireless fans.

"Who will question that the wonders worked in this brief quarter of a century by the radio wizards of today are not more wonderful than anything retold in the Arabian Nights Tales? In the long history of mankind, twenty-seven years is a mere twinkling of an eye, and in that 'blink of time' our modern magicians have waved their electronic wands and Lo!—voices, music and images—a whole new world of entertainment, news, culture, and instruction—appear from the void at the casual touch of our fingertips."

Two illustrations from "NBC's Air Castles" show a photo of NBC's Radio City at Sunset and Vine in Hollywood and a floor plan of its first floor studios. The booklet also presents detailed descriptions of six other NBC facilities across America. *Recorded Sound Reference Center.*

commercial recordings in the Recorded Sound Reference Center.

When the *TGA* resumed its winter 1949 drama series, NBC's program description noted it was "one of radio's foremost dramatic shows," featuring a weekly hour-long "radio adaptation of a different Broadway production starring the top actors and actresses of the American theater—whenever possible, the stars who did the original Broadway roles," bringing "the high standards of the Theater Guild's Broadway productions to radio listeners." Underlined is *"The Theater Guild on the Air has been sponsored by United States Steel since its first performance on Sept., 9, 1945."*

As with many series, NBC records then list detailed entries for each show with title, date, and credits from September 11, 1949, through June 7, 1953, this section taking up nearly one hundred two-sided cards in the microfiche collection. Card 16 for April 23, 1950, notes that *TGA* "today departs from the usual policy of dramatizing stage plays in order to offer an adaptation of the novel, and later the screen play, *National Velvet*" (with Peggy Ann Garner and Mickey Rooney). In spite of the occasional movie show, *TGA* mostly adhered to its policy of both classic and unusual legitimate drama, ensuing adaptations including Joshua Logan's Americanized version of Chekhov's *Cherry Orchard*, *The Wisteria Trees* with Helen Hayes and Joseph Cotten on September 14, 1952, Kaufman and Hart's *George Washington Slept Here* on the ensuing September 21, Shirley Booth (as Amanda) in Tennessee Williams's *The Glass Menagerie* (April 12, 1953), and Robert Anderson's *The Petrified Forest* with Tyrone Power (April 19). Film adaptations tended to be on the classy side, for example, *All About Eve* which starred Tallulah Bankhead as Margo on November 16, 1952, but occasional lighter film fare (*The Major and the Minor* on October 14, 1951) was also aired. The NBC microfiche collection provides a plethora of detailed information about this and many other NBC shows, both famous and lesser-known.

Screen Directors' Playhouse

An interesting footnote to the *Lux* school of dramatic radio is *Screen Directors' Playhouse*, which featured as its weekly guest the original director of the film being adapted. Though the quality of the films varied, the show gives brief but immediate glimpses into the relatively unknown personalities of many directors from Hollywood's late Golden Age. Running from 1949 to 1951 (and for a time known as the *NBC Theater*), guest directors included John Ford, William Wyler, Michael Curtiz, George Marshall, and Lewis Milestone. Musical director for the early shows was William Lava, who later composed film music for Universal International. In 1950 the show's music was handled by Robert Armbruster, who had composed for the first (New York) season of the *Lux Radio Theatre*. Adaptations included *Fort Apache*, *Portrait of Jennie*, *Champion*, *Flamingo Road*, and *A Star Is Born*. The final June 30, 1955, broadcast was Disney's *Cinderella* for which NBC notes: "No guest director today. Ilene Woods gives credit to 'three directors': Wilfred Jaxon, Clyde Geronomi, and Ham Luske, of Walt Disney Studios."

The Library of Congress collections include many *Screen Directors'* shows, including *Fort Apache* from August 5, 1949, the computer readout for which notes "On this program John Wayne and John Ford appear together in a beer commercial." Another curiosity is a *Screen Directors' Playhouse* dated October 15, 1949, on which Ford, Wyler, George Marshall, Cary Grant, and Rosalind Russell join forces to perform a fairly hard-sell promotional for the "men of RCA Victor." (Pabst and Anacin were the the show's previous sponsors.) Promising "only the most successful screenplays" and "star testimonials" with guaranteed "sales appeal" for a "nation of moviegoers," the show opens with a brief plug for the Screen Directors' Guild, an organization which offers aid to industry professionals "when misfortune strikes." The promo concludes with a sample show, *Mr. Blandings Builds His Dream House*, with director H. C. Potter and star Cary Grant.

Signing Off

Sometime between its August 1947 and September 1948 issues, the national magazine *Radio Mirror* became *Radio and Television Mirror*. *Mirror* was the *Photoplay*, *Modern Screen*, and *Movie Stars Parade* of radio, and presented features, spots, gossip, and full-page color photographs on radio stars and shows. Though the September 1948 cover had "television" in small print, the change nonetheless marked the beginning of the end for the kind of radio that had been a national institution for several decades. By 1962 the magazine had become *TV Radio Mirror* (with *TV* in big print) but it did maintain the "radio" part of its title into the 1960s (when covers asked: "Is the honeymoon over for Jackie?") and into the even more lurid seventies (when a February 1971 article promised to reveal Pat Boone's "Sex Problems with His Wife").

By the early fifties many radio shows had already made the transition to television, while others simply faded away. In 1956, *Mirror* still featured its "Inside Radio" pages, a monthly day-by-day timetable of shows on the four major networks, and there were still features on the few shows (such as *Fibber McGee and Molly* and *The Woolworth Hour*) still available only on radio. But the impact of television was also unmistakable. Some shows, such as *Our Miss Brooks*, *Dragnet*, and *The Guiding Light*, had dual radio and television listings, but new television exclusives, variety programs like *The Ed Sullivan Show*, new sit-coms (some with stars who dated back to the 1930s!) like *The Adventures of Ozzie and Harriet*, television-only soaps such as *Search for Tomorrow*, and musical hours such as *The Lawrence Welk Show* (which was already a Saturday night institution in 1956) were obviously the wave of the future. By September of 1960, there were no longer any monthly radio listings in *TV Radio Mirror*, and within less than a decade a unique, imagination-nurturing era of American popular entertainment came to a close forever.

■ It must have been Cub Scout Day in Doodyville when this 1948 photograph was taken. One of the earliest of the five-times-a-week television kiddie shows, Buffalo Bob Smith's *Howdy Doody Show* dated back to 1947 when it premiered as *Puppet Playhouse Presents* (though the puppets were really marionettes). By 1956 the most popular children's show on television was even televised "in color and black and white." As this photo shows, it was performed in front of a live audience of children, the "Peanut Gallery," and those shown here probably grew up to be among the first victims of the nation's ensuing obsession with the dominating visual medium. *Howdy Doody* was a television original, i.e., a show *not* derived from a radio version, and was also one of the first television series to contribute to America's popular mythology, with characters such as Dilly Dally, Phineas T. Bluster, and the Flubadub. *Prints and Photographs Division.*

Notes

1. The 1950s *No School Today* show is not to be confused with a show of the same title which was broadcast on Saturdays for a brief period in the late 1930s. In several books on Golden Age radio the Big Jon show is cited as *Big Jon and Sparkie*, but a mid-1950s *TV Radio Mirror* lists it as *No School Today* at 9:00 a.m. (EST) Saturdays. *TV Radio Mirror*, September 1956.

2. An insert in the first issue of *Space Patrol* comics (Summer 1952) listed all the stations across the nation which broadcast the show on both radio and television. The list was in the form of a dialogue between two proto-type children of the fifties: Gus, whose family already had a television set, and Tommy, whose family did not. After Tommy rather impossibly recites (from memory) the two-page litany of stations and cities to the understandably impressed Gus, he is invited over to watch *Space Patrol* on television. "Nope," Tommy replies, "I'm going home and listen to *Space Patrol* on the radio! It's just as wonderful!"

More wonderful, some might reckon today. The comic book features three stories illustrated in classic (and rather racy) "whap, zzzzoom!" fifties graphic style and illustrated ads for various mail order *Space Patrol* merchandise. *Space Patrol Comics*, vol 1, no.1, Summer 1952. Approved Comics, Inc., Chicago, New York.

3. *TV Radio Mirror*, March 1955.

4. Ibid.

5. At least one soap opera title has survived from 1940s radio to present-day television: *The Guiding Light*.

6. A Donald Duck short, *Duck Pimples* (1945), amusingly shows the potent effect of radio suspense shows on the imagination of the period: the cartoon opens with the Duck is alone in the dark by his radio as the loud aural violence depicted on the show (combined with his own volatile imagination) suddenly plunges him into a surreal dream world of bullying cops, loud, flying bullets, and a seductive gun moll who strongly suggests the later Jessica Rabbit in *Who Killed Roger Rabbit*. Thus, *radio noir* inspired some of the most fantastic and surreal imagery and sequences in the usually fairly staid Disney shorts oeuvre.

7. Lux magazine ads peaked in the late 1940s ("A Lux Girl? Indeed I am!" said Maureen O'Hara promoting Fox's *Sitting Pretty* in 1948), but by the early 1950s products like Lustre-Creme Shampoo and Jergens Lotion had usurped the Lux glamour angle. Jergens especially fused ads for its lotion with publicity for specific films and their stars. Thus, Deborah Kerr lauded the moisturizing effects of Jergens after the taxing chore of filming the burning of Rome in *Quo Vadis*: "Nero fiddled while I burned." Around 1952 Lustre-Creme launched a series of full-page ads with portraits of the top stars of the era in color and with beautiful but usually totally unreal-looking hair.

ROSS CARE is a free-lance composer, MIDI musician, and author based in Ventura, California. Especially interested in theater and film, his music for regional theater productions includes, among many others, incidental scores for *The Cherry Orchard, The Death of a Salesman, The Glass Menagerie*, and the original score for the award-winning play for young people, *This Is Not a Pipe Dream*. Concerning his first work in sound design in Ventura, California, the *Los Angeles Times* commented: "every theatrical sound person in town should show up just to hear how sound designer Ross Care handles the cues and effects." His musicals include a version of Gibran's *The Prophet* performed at Philadelphia's Annenberg Center, and an adaptation of Lewis Carroll's *Alice Through the Looking Glass* which has been seen nationally. His concert works include song cycles to poems of James Joyce, A. E. Housman, and Frank O'Hara, and a choral cycle, *The Sacred Harp*.

In 1999 Care orchestrated Philippe Blumenthal's epic score for an independent European film, *General Sutter*, with the composer, and also cosupervised its recording with the City of Prague Philharmonic. Care has also composed scores for a number of short documentary and animated films that have been seen on CBS, PBS, HBO, and the BBC, among them *Crepe Flower, Otto Messmer and Felix the Cat*, and *The Wizard's Son*. His music for *Bottom's Dream* can be heard in the feature film *The 19th International Tournee of Animation*, and his score for *Byron B. Blackbear and the Scientific Method* was cited for "Best Music" at the ASIFA East Animation Awards in New York.

Among his recent writing credits are essays for the multivolume *St. James Encyclopedia of Popular Culture* and the revised edition of *The International Directory of Film and Filmmakers*. He does a regular column for the genre magazine *Scarlet Street*, and reviews for the new Los Angeles pop culture journal *Worldly Remains*. He has also contributed to various American and European journals such as *Film Quarterly, Sight and Sound, Millimeter, The Writer, Soundtrack/CinemaScore*, and *Elmer Bernstein's FilmMusic Notebook*. His article "Threads of Melody," a detailed study of the collective evolution of the musical score for the Disney animated feature *Bambi*, based on scores in the Music Division of the Library of Congress, has been published in the book *Wonderful Inventions* (Library of Congress, 1985), and it won an award in the International Film Literature Contest in the criticism category. For the premiere volume of the Library of Congress's *Performing Arts Annual* in 1986, he wrote "Memoirs of a Movie Childhood in Harrisburg's Movie Palaces," tracing the architectural and entertainment styles of bygone movie houses from their Golden Age to their demise as parking lots and porno movie houses. For ensuing volumes he penned "Hot Spells," a two-part essay on Alex North's scores for *A Streetcar Named Desire, The Sound and the Fury*, and other cinematic adaptations of Southern literary classics; "Out of This World," a detailed study of the lesser-known songs, musicals, and films of Cole Porter, which was based on Porter's personal manuscripts and papers in the Rare Materials Collections of the Music Division of the Library of Congress; and "The Great (Almost) American Novel Becomes The Great American Film Score," an in-depth analysis of Johnny Green's score for the film version of Ross Lockridge, Jr.'s novel, *Raintree County*.

Care is currently at work on a book on Hollywood music, *Main Title, End Title*, inspired by his article, "Twilight's Last Gleaming: The Americanization of Hollywood Film Music, 1950-1965," published in the Library's 1998 *Performing Arts—Motion Pictures* volume.

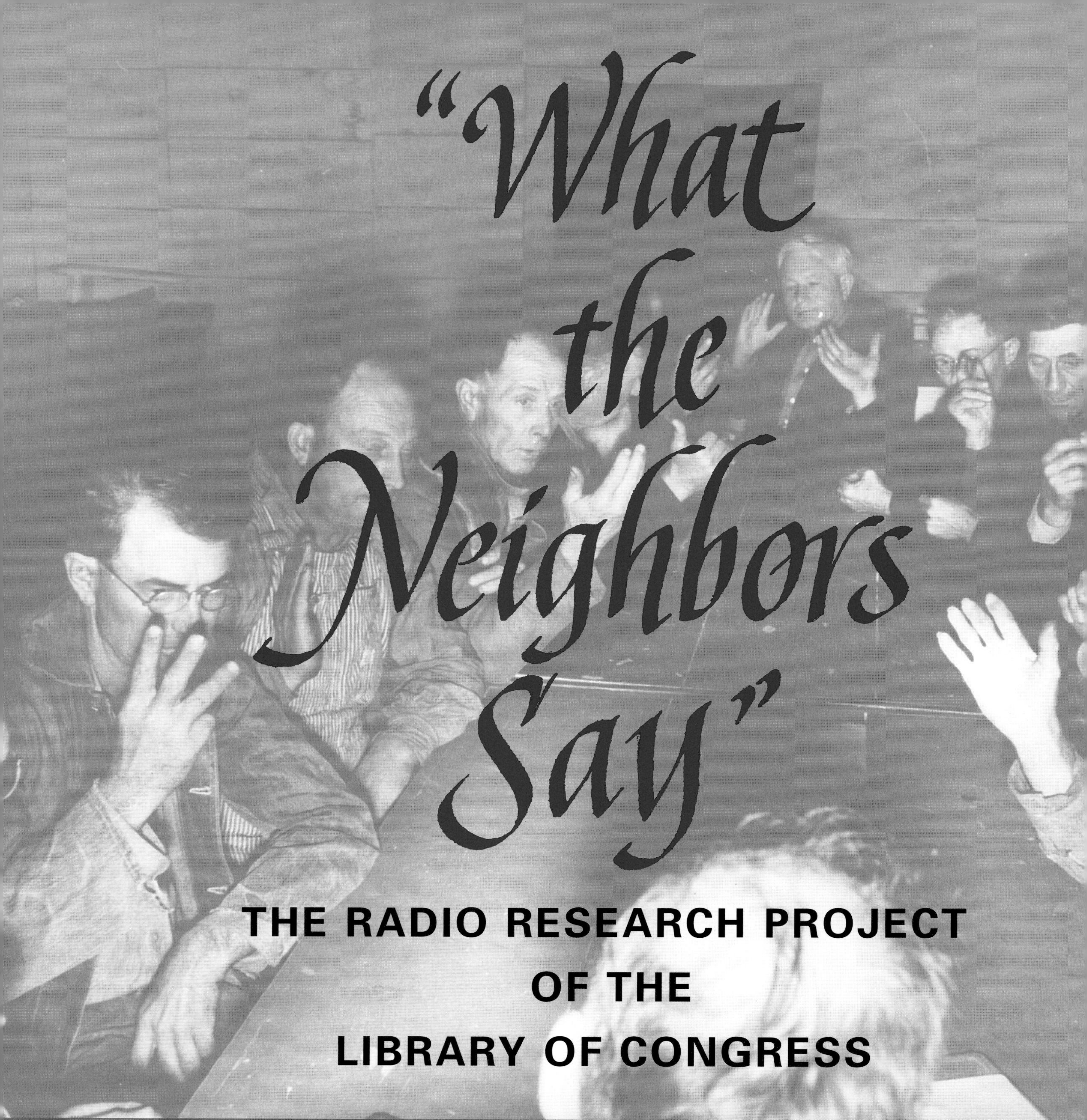

"What the Neighbors Say"

THE RADIO RESEARCH PROJECT OF THE LIBRARY OF CONGRESS

BY

ALAN GEVINSON

The Library of Congress is the place for the American Record.

> The most important thing in life
>   Is what the neighbors say.
> The quickest thing to stir up strife
>   Is what the neighbors say.
> No matter what the cause may be
> Just look around and you will see
> The thing that troubles you and me
>   Is what the neighbors say.

Novelty song by Will H. Ruebush from *Delaware and the Eastern Shore of Maryland* broadcast

During 1941, as war gripped Europe and democracies fell, an experimental project operating out of the Library of Congress and funded by the Rockefeller Foundation produced "popular education" radio programming with the expressed aim to prevent Fascism from taking root in America. Called the "Radio Research Project of the Library of Congress,"[1] the project began by producing programs that relied upon historical documents, most of which came from collections housed at the Library relating to local, regional, and national history, traditions, and lore. The intention was to exhibit to listeners the values inherent in the American tradition and way of life. Since the shows were based on documents, they sometimes were called "documentaries" even though they used actors and were scripted in advance.[2] The experiment took a turn in mid-1941, as the project's team of writers, researchers, and recording engineers ventured out of their government enclave to communities in rural and urban America to interview and record the speech, music, and songs of common folk of diverse ethnicity. After returning with a wealth of raw, unscripted material, the team produced edited recordings for broadcast about these communities—many of which were undergoing considerable transformations as the country prepared for war. These programs used the actual voices of the people recorded, not actors.

The later shows were made possible by an experimental editing technique that the project's chief recording engineer devised. They marked the first extensive use in America of the kind of documentary that is prevalent today in radio, television, and films: documentary that is not built on dramatized reconstructions. Previously, documentary radio in America relied on actors reading scripted speech. They were called "documentaries" because they were based on historical documents, and thus were reputedly factual, not fictional, accounts. Most American documentary films of the time did not use synchronized sound recorded at the same time as the picture, but instead, essentially were silent films with narration. Today, sync-sound documentary television, radio, and film are taken for granted. We can easily forget that these genres had a beginning, that they emerged from earlier forms at a precise historical moment, and that the concerns that led experimenters to try new techniques were concerns deeply inscribed in the culture of the times.

The producers of the Library of Congress's Radio Research Project's documentary series knew they were creating something new. Alan Lomax, the principal creator, enthusiastically described the significance of the develop-

■ Jerome Wiesner, Chief Engineer of the Library's Music Division, on the sideboard of the Recording Laboratory's sound truck equipped for location recording, circa 1940. As technical director for a number of the Radio Research Project's documentary programs, Wiesner traveled with the writers and interviewers, providing technical support. In the lab, he pioneered the development of a technique to edit sound recordings made in the field that allowed the project to produce what may have been the first synchronized-sound documentary radio programs in this country. In later life, Wiesner served President Kennedy as a science advisor and was the president of M.I.T. *Manuscript Division.*

ment in a report he submitted about the project: "Out of the extension of this [editing] technique, whether or not we are able to carry out the ideas ourselves, will emerge a new function for radio; that of letting the people explain themselves and their lives to the entire nation."[3] Commentators on the programs also noted their significance. Charles Siepmann, formerly the director of the British Broadcasting Corporation's departments of Talks and Regional Relations, evaluated the project for the Library and made the following comments about the documentary programs: "These must be judged as pioneer, experimental efforts in new radio techniques. The experiment is promising but incomplete. It is important. . . . It was discovered, naturally, by trial and error and only lately." In 1945, Erik Barnouw (who some thirty years later would become the chief of the Library's Motion Picture, Broadcasting, and Recorded Sound Division) wrote about one of the documentary shows: "Alan Lomax uses as his material not merely the voices but the minds and emotions and impulses of the people themselves. It was Lomax's job *not* to put words into their mouths, but to draw the people out, to get 'on the record' their currents of thought, the feelings they had about their environment. . . . There is unfailing fascination in hearing, in a dramatic broadcast, one's own kind of talk.

■ **Alan Lomax (b. 1915) began recording Southern folk songs as a teenager in the 1930s with his father, John Lomax. Alan became Assistant in Charge of the Library's Archive of Folk Song in 1937 and was the major impetus behind the Radio Research Project's Documentary Series. In the previous two years, he had written and produced two successful shows for CBS: a weekly morning folk music series for** *American School of the* **Air; and a three-night-a-week series called** *Back Where I Come From,* **that was directed in New York by Nicholas Ray. Early in 1940, Lomax hoped to work with Ray, political film documentarist Joris Ivens, and Joseph Losey (later to become, as would Ray, one of America's most respected film directors) on a series of documentary films for the Library about folkways and folk music of America. By August 1940, when funding for that project did not materialize, Lomax authored a memorandum in which he requested funds to make five "Out Our Way" radio programs using the Library's soon to arrive sound truck, but MacLeish was unable to raise the necessary money. The Radio Research Project provided Lomax an opportunity to experiment with documentary production.** *Prints and Photographs Division.*

[It]could not have been duplicated by any actors in the world."[4]

The project's creators wanted its listeners, the American public, to think of themselves as "neighbors." They wanted to record and present to diverse communities the lives, struggles, and speech of Americans in neighboring communities, many of which previously had been underrepresented in the media. "The most important thing in life is what the neighbors say," as the novelty song of "homespun philosophy," used as an epigram for this essay, tells us. As the year 1941 progressed, "What the Neighbors Say," became the most important thing for the project's creators to record and transmit, more important than the treasured history, lore, songs, and traditions of the past, collected by the Library. They feared a future in which Americans had little connection with each other, as much as they feared a future run by dictators, so they used the medium of radio to try to solidify that connection based on something stronger than

shared heritage: the shared present and future, and the sharing of opinions, talk, jokes, songs, and laughter, even of fears and troubles.

At the risk of pushing an already strained reference point even further, the last line of the song—"The thing that troubles you and me is what the neighbors say"—stresses an aspect of this project that becomes apparent once the collected recordings that were not included in the broadcasts are heard. Some of "What the Neighbors Say" would have been troubling to many listeners had the material not been edited to block remarks that broached on touchy subjects, such as isolationism, labor unrest, and unpopular political beliefs, such as Communism. In addition, the interviewers own points of view, evidenced in questions, asides, and discussions not included in the broadcasts, showed concerns about the fragility and limits of democracy. These also may have troubled some listeners had they been aired. Because the ultimate goal of this project remained one of educating the public to stave off the appeal of Fascism, speech that threatened to seriously challenge American traditions of democracy was kept away from the "neighbors."

Origins

Pulitzer Prize-winning poet Archibald MacLeish accepted President Roosevelt's request that he become Librarian of Congress, despite some resistance from the professional librarian establishment, and assumed that office in October 1939. On October 19, MacLeish delivered an address entitled "Libraries and the Contemporary Crisis," at the Carnegie Institute in Pittsburgh, in which he detailed his views of the choices facing the nation in the coming period. He contended that the country was in an "either/or" situation: "The 'either,' as I see it, is the education of the people of this country. The 'or' is fascism. We will either educate the people of this Republic to know, and, therefore, to value and, therefore, to preserve their own democratic culture, or we will watch the people of this Republic trade their democratic culture for the nonculture, the obscurantism, the superstition, the brutality, the tyranny which is overrunning eastern and central and southern Europe."[5]

Earlier in the decade, MacLeish had forged a reputation as a pacifist. In 1935, he wrote, "I should do everything in my power to prevent the United States going to war under *any* circumstances." As the decade wore on, however, his stance changed dramatically. During the Spanish Civil War, MacLeish helped establish a production company for the anti-Franco documentary film, *The Spanish Earth*, for which he coauthored the screenplay, and met with Roosevelt to ask why U.S. forces had not been sent to aid the democratically elected Spanish government. In 1937, MacLeish's first radio play, *The Fall of the City*, eerily presented a Fascist takeover in an unidentified city. Its theme, according to MacLeish, was "the proneness of men to accept their own conqueror, accept the loss of their rights because it will in some way solve their problems or simplify their lives."[6]

A week after his address to the Carnegie Institute, MacLeish applied for funding to the Carnegie Corporation for a recording laboratory at the Library, and to the

SHINER: That oath still remains in my heart and when I taken

that oath I taken it in the presence of God, without

prejudice or enmity to any man and I intend to sustain

that oath with the assistance of the Almighty God

until I die. For when a man takes an oath for a just

cause it's more than taking a drink of water or settin'

down to his breakfast...

MUSIC: UP TO TAG.

NARRATOR: Such is the diary of Michael Shiner, the unknown slave

who wrote history - - Michael Shiner - - America Maker!

MUSIC: UP AND DOWN BRIEFLY THEN TO BACKGROUND

■ The *Diary of Michael Shiner*, an account written by an exslave covering his life in Washington, D. C., from 1813 to 1865, survives in the Library's Manuscript Division; a corresponding page from the script of the *Hidden History* program, "The Slave Who Wrote History" is shown. In the show, an actor read Shiner's actual words, dramatized with background sound effects and music. The decision to dramatize this diary, which climaxes with Shiner taking an oath of allegiance to this country, no doubt was made in part to encourage unity among Americans of diverse backgrounds as the country prepared to enter the war in Europe. *Recorded Sound Reference Center.*

■ Archibald MacLeish (1892-1982), Librarian of Congress, 1939-1945. In addition to obtaining funds for the Recording Laboratory and guiding the Radio Research Project, MacLeish, in 1942, inaugurated a new Library policy regarding film acquisition, selection, and retention, taking the first steps that led eventually to the accumulation at the Library of one of the world's great film collections. Regarding radio, which he deemed "one of the most potent forces in our present-day culture," MacLeish, himself a creator of acclaimed radio programs, vowed to attempt the "special effort necessary to preserve them." *Prints and Photographs Divison.*

Rockefeller Foundation for an information staff, so that portions of the Library's vast collection of audio materials could be copied and circulated through libraries and broadcast over the radio. The Carnegie Corporation had turned down a smaller request in 1938 but, due primarily to MacLeish's efforts, they gave the Library a grant of $41,520 in April 1940. MacLeish's stated aims for the lab were broader than those of the previous librarian who made the earlier request. The new sound lab was to be used not only for phonoduplication, but also for originating broadcasts and for making transcriptions. In addition, the Library purchased a sound truck and six portable recording machines to make field recordings. MacLeish's press release about the grant ended with the following statement: "It is foreseen that the Library of Congress will originate educational programs and make radio transcriptions that will draw from all its resources. . . . These radio broadcasts and transcriptions will create channels through which the Library's buried treasures of art and knowledge can be brought directly to the people to whom they belong."[7]

In the application to the Rockefeller Foundation, MacLeish wrote: "It is assumed that there will be agreement upon the proposition that one of the greatest, if not the greatest, need at the present moment in this country, is an effective program of popular education, which will familiarize the people of this country with their own cultural tradition and heritage as citizens of a democracy. Unless such a program can be developed, there is an evident possibility that the democratic culture of the people of this country may be supplanted by another very different culture and tradition. The point need not be labored. The facts-not only abroad but in this country-speak for themselves." The application to the Rockefeller Foundation contains a copy of MacLeish's speech to the Carnegie Institute as printed in the *Congressional Record*, on which he had marked the following section: "Those who, like myself, assert that the threat to democratic civilization in this country is the threat of fascism mean that the culture of the Republic is threatened by the existence in the United States of the kind of situation which has produced fascism elsewhere, and that that situation in the United States has already given indications, human and other, of developing in the known direction." Calling Fascism "the image of a condition, not the invention of a man," MacLeish offered an analysis of the social and economic situation that produced Fascism in Germany and Italy and warned that "the condition which has created fascism in Europe may very easily create fascism here, unless we act, and act now, to prevent it." Briefly, he blamed the creation of fascism on the creation of a new economic class frozen into a social order—"the so-called lower middle class"—members of which do not fit in with the workers below or the intellectuals above. It is this new class, without the moral, intellectual, and emotional inheritance of traditions of those below or above it, whose leaders ("its Mussolinis and its Hitlers") create their own new traditions and symbols, MacLeish believed. He advocated that "democracy can be saved by educating the people to value the kind of life democracy makes possible."[8]

MacLeish contended that it was the job of American libraries to provide that education. In this belief, he defined the "burden" of libraries, as he called it, and as Librarian of Congress, embarked on an activist course to take the lead in promoting what he termed "popular education" through radio.

The Rockefeller Foundation had been funding projects to conduct research into the uses of radio and film for public education and national security purposes since 1937. John Marshall, Assistant Director of the Foundation's Humanities Division, who formerly had been a medievalist at Harvard, broached the subject of funding experimental radio and film studies in 1936 because of their potential "great importance alike for formal education and for the general diffusion of culture." In late 1939, Marshall and the foundation's Humanities Division director, David Stevens, administered a portion of the foundation's financial resources for communications studies on propaganda. Like MacLeish, Marshall and Stevens worried about the public's attraction to Fascism. Marshall blamed advertising and politicians for inducing the public to substitute, in terms he used in a memo, "incomplete" knowledge of a subject for "genuine knowledge." Although he condemned commercial and political influence on the public as "propaganda," Marshall expressed the need for a "genuinely democratic propaganda" to protect democratic practices."[9]

Various writers on radio have analyzed the medium's potential for propaganda. Charles Siepmann wrote in 1950, "The disembodied voice of radio exerts a peculiar fascination and a degree of identification . . . that is quite unusual. It is said that Hitler, in his hour-long radio harangues, achieved a mastery of his audience unmatched even by his hold over the mass meetings he addressed." Siepmann distinguished, however, between "good" and "bad" propaganda, contrasting a quote from Hitler ("Mental confusion, contradiction of feeling, indecision, panic—these are our weapons") with his own dictum: "Good propaganda . . . is rooted in reverence and concern for the individual." Writer Max Wylie insisted that an author of documentary-based broadcasts must "entertain as he informs." He argued: "For unless he does, he loses that vast section of his audience that are looking for escape rather than enlightenment in their

■ **Philip H. Cohen, Director of the Radio Research Project, with his son, Philip Lee. Before working on the project, Cohen gained solid experience in the production of educational and experimental programs as radio production director of the New York unit of the U.S. Office of Education and director of the Radio Workshop at New York University—the first of many radio workshops set up primarily at colleges and universities to encourage the use of radio for educational purposes. In 1938, Cohen went to the British Broadcasting Corporation as a Rockefeller fellow to study broadcasting techniques. Photo from *The Journal of the Association for Education by Radio*, 1942.**

radio listening. And usually it is of vital importance that such people be reached with the message that the documentary broadcast carries. For, it must be frankly admitted, the documentary broadcast is a form of propaganda." Radio playwright and director William N. Robson, author of the acclaimed 1943 radio play *Open Letter on Race Hatred*, argued stridently that radio's aptness for propaganda had been ignored for too long: "Radio sells soap and automobiles—by propaganda—known as commercial announcements. Radio is now beginning to sell democracy and justice and honesty and tolerance. The step is inevitable—a consummation devoutly to be wished—and long overdue."[10]

In his original grant request, MacLeish sought to create positions at the Library for directors of information, radio programs, and phonoduplication, but he soon learned that

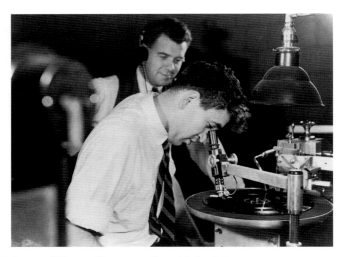

■ Jerome Wiesner (foreground) and John R. Langenegger (rear), engineers in the Recording Laboratory, examine the grooves of a record while it is being cut on a Scully recording machine. Both men worked as technical directors on Radio Research Project programs. *Manuscript Division.*

Congress probably would not agree to this. Stevens then suggested a more modest proposal: conduct an experimental radio project for a year or two to determine how best to utilize the Library's resources for broadcasts. MacLeish agreed, and after some haggling, preliminary work on the project began in September 1940 as two Rockefeller fellows, Philip H. Cohen and Charles T. Harrell, arrived at the Library to plan the series with Alan Lomax, of the Library's Archive of Folk Song, and chief recording engineer Jerome Wiesner. The project was under the direct supervision of MacLeish.

For the project to reach masses of people as MacLeish desired, the programs would have to be broadcast over one of the major networks, NBC or CBS. Besides broadcasting their own commercial programs, the networks at the time had numerous open slots in their schedules for sustaining, or noncommercial, programming financed independently. The networks were especially amenable to broadcasts of educational programs, as they had won a major battle in 1934 over the control of radio broadcasting fought against groups representing educational interests and had since attempted to ease conflicts with the educational broadcasting community by providing time for specialized broadcasts. In the late 1930s, networks had begun to program a number of public affairs programs dealing with social issues. They welcomed the Library's plan, and by August 1940, William Paley, head of CBS, and representatives of NBC had offered their cooperation.

On December 5, 1940, the Rockefeller Foundation announced that they were appropriating $23,320 to the Library "toward its work in RADIO BROADCASTING during the year beginning January 1, 1941." The proposal detailed that the Library "should undertake to make its holdings and the services of its staff available through broadcasting." The major series mentioned in the grant was one designed "to portray various American regions and communities in terms of their cultural and historical diversity and of their individual formulations of the traditions they have in common." It was noted that the Library could use more

than 20,000 recordings in its Archive of American Folk Song, its vast collections of written materials, including over 37,000 pages of unpublished materials, its voluminous Manuscript Division source materials, and the surveys of the Federal Writers Project covering local, state, and regional folklore and histories of twenty-five states."[11]

Cohen, who formerly had been the radio production director of the New York unit of the U.S. Office of Education and the first director of the Radio Workshop at New York University, was made director of the project. Joseph Liss, a writer for CBS's acclaimed *Columbia Workshop*, joined the group and by mid-December had completed the first half-hour script of the project, a Regional Series program entitled "Williamsburg." MacLeish, at the time, was "going over" it, and throughout the project's existence, he would review all programs before they were aired.

Cohen, with his radio workshop experience, especially appreciated the ability to experiment with shows. In a letter to Marshall, he noted, "To me the fact that we can experiment, record, revise, re-record and revise again is the thing that makes our opportunity here unique. We are not under the pressure of the commercial broadcasters."[12]

On January 1, 1941, Cohen, Harrell, and Liss officially became Library employees with offices in the Recording Laboratory. The first two series to be produced, *Books in the News* and *The Ballad Hunter*, were recorded in the lab. *Books in the News*, a series of six five-minute programs on current news topics and related books, was distributed free to over 150 radio stations, libraries, schools, and broadcasting organizations. *The Ballad Hunter* series of ten fifteen-minute recordings was made in six weeks by John A. Lomax (Alan Lomax's father and honorary curator of the Archive of American Folk Song), who selected and recorded commentaries on folk recordings he had made over a period of thirty years. A flyer for the series states that the programs "offer an unequaled opportunity to hear the everyday music of the people-the simple, human stuff-the roots of democracy." MacLeish is quoted on the flyer, stating that the programs "search one of the deepest currents in the development of American culture—the current of American folk song." It was the next series the project prepared, however, that best fit MacLeish's ideas on using the Library's resources for popular education.

The Regional Series

The intention of this series was to present half-hour dramatized programs based on documentary evidence dealing with contemporary problems faced by different types of American communities. Under the supervision of project editor Joseph Liss, six scripts were prepared by late April 1941 from materials at the Library, most of which came from the Local History Division. At the time of the Librarian's Annual Report for 1941, nine additional scripts were being prepared. MacLeish wrote in the report, "If this is accomplished, the result should represent a documented story of the roots of America which must sustain American progress."

The conception of the series stemmed in part from Philip Cohen's experience as a Rockefeller fellow with doc-

THE BALLAD HUNTER—the man who discovered "Home on the Range", "Good-Bye Ol' Paint", "Git Along, Little Dogies", and "The Boll Weevil". The man who has spent a lifetime searching for the stirring and melodious songs that belong to the American people. Now, at last you can hear some of the thousands of folk songs recorded in the field by John A. Lomax, author of "Cowboy Songs", "American Ballads and Folk Songs."

■ Advertising brochure for *The Ballad Hunter* series of ten recordings for radio broadcasts, schools, and libraries, selected and narrated by John Lomax from folk music he had recorded during the previous decade. *Prints and Photographs Division.*

■ Prison Compound No. 1, Angola, Louisiana, July 1934, where Lomax recorded songs of prisoners that were included in *The Ballad Hunter* series. Huddie Ledbetter, better known as Leadbelly, can be seen standing in the foreground of this photograph. In his commentary to *The Ballad Hunter*, Lomax relates: "In the Louisiana Penitentiary I heard Leadbelly, now a famous singer, sing this song about the Boll Weevil. The negro balladist seems to sympathize with the Boll Weevil when the entomologist attempts to destroy him." *Prints and Photographs Division.*

The Regional Series focused on once vibrant communities in trouble, including ones like this Hudson River fishing village that thrived before steamer trade up the river destroyed its herring fisheries. Photos by John Collier, U.S. Department of Agriculture, Farm Security Administration, October 1941. *Prints and Photographs Division.*

umentary radio shows of the British Broadcasting Corporation. Since the early 1930s, the BBC had been sending recording vans to the countryside to document and preserve for posterity the speech and sounds of English regional communities. Documentation on the Regional Series emphasizes the focus on communities: "We show how specific industries, land, the way of life and the culture of the people contribute to democracy and at the same time—if such be the truth—show why certain communities or parts of communities lack either a traditional or historical or economic background for democracy and how such shortcomings may lead to the establishment of undemocratic procedures and influence. In short, we show . . . the real significance of the big-concept words such as democracy, liberty, and America by breaking them down into their everyday manifestations in communities or regions throughout the country."

More than any other programs that the project produced, the Regional Series bore MacLeish's stamp. Instructions to script writers of the series contained the following warning by MacLeish: "Let us avoid at all costs an anthology of quaint customs, curious history and antiquarian charm." MacLeish also instructed the writers with a succinct statement of the theme he hoped the series would get across: "The significance of America is the fact that it is a country—a society—which millions of *anonymous* men and women of many generations *tried to make for themselves* and were unwilling to accept readymade from the hands of any ruler or dictator or whatever." This description echoes the antithesis of the situation in MacLeish's acclaimed radio play, *The Fall of the City*, noted earlier, "the proneness of men to accept their own conqueror, accept the loss of their rights because it will in some way solve their problems or simplify their lives."[13]

In defining his concept of democracy, MacLeish, in 1939, had written, "We mean by democracy a society in which the dignity of man is of first importance, a society in which everything else must be subject to, and must support, the dignity of man." At the close of the Regional Series script "Williamsburg," an African-American guide to the city reads a gravestone that is most meaningful to him: "As the most exalted station may be debased by vice, so there is no situation in life on which Virtue will not confer Dignity." In a 1941 *Reader's Digest* article, MacLeish expressed his belief that the survival of democracy necessitated action: "Democracy is never a thing done. Democracy is always something a nation must be doing." This conception is echoed in a scene in the "Williamsburg" script when the African-American guide introduces a scene of patriot George Mason reading the first Bill of Rights to the people of Virginia at Raleigh's Tavern. The guide instructs his audience, "Listen to de words—words meant not just fo' repeatin'—but for doin'."[14]

While the initial impetus for the series stemmed from Cohen's previous experience with BBC documentary radio, and the sense of the series derived from MacLeish's beliefs about the threat of Fascism and the necessity to live democracy, not just mouth democracy's words, the idea of documenting regional locales, rather than urban centers, had circulated among a number of intellectuals and writers since

the 1920s. Just as MacLeish traced the threat posed by Fascism to his understanding of the creation of a new economic and social class of individuals lacking a tradition, a group of "regionalists," including Lewis Mumford, Waldo Frank, and Van Wyck Brooks, created their own understanding of the rootlessness in present-day American life. Frank, in 1929, wrote that urbanization had led to the "death-spasm of all the Sections [of the country], of all our pasts." His depiction of this pastless present was all but apocalyptic: "America emerged . . . without sectionalisms, without organic past at all. It was swept to a flat atomic formlessness." Mumford blamed the modernity of urban America of the 1920s for giving Americans "a blankness, a sterility, a boredom, a despair." He condemned modern life in America for failing "either to absorb an old culture or create a new one." Mumford and Frank prescribed as a cure for society's ills, "programs of regional development" to create a culture that integrates, what a historian of the regionalist

■ Before his work with the Radio Research Project, Arthur Miller (b. 1915) had built a reputation as a radio dramatist, writing for CBS's *Columbia Workshop* and for *Cavalcade of America*, the Du Pont series on American history. Miller contributed a script to each of the project's Regional Series and to *Hidden History*, in addition to conducting interviews and providing narration for the Documentary Series program "Wilmington, North Carolina." A former coworker recalled that during his work on the project, Miller, later to become one of this century's top playwrights, received only a small honorarium and was "starving at the time." About the "Wilmington" program, Lomax, in a report on the project, wrote, "Mr. Miller was more direct than we had been in other field efforts and simply walked up to people that he met in trailer camps, factories, and on the streets and interviewed them about what was going on in the city." The finished product, Lomax judged, "is the most stirring program which we have completed." *Prints and Photographs Division.*

From WOSU - Ohio State Univ.   *June 5, 1942*

LIBRARY OF CONGRESS   AMERICANS TALK
BACK

Radio Research Project

Here is the series of documentary programs which you ordered. As soon as your station has finished putting this series on the air, please return the records to the Radio Research Project, Library of Congress, USING THE FRANKED LABEL ENCLOSED WITH WHICH NO POSTAGE IS REQUIRED.

On the next sheet you will find brief announcements which should, if at all possible, be used to introduce the programs. We would appreciate it very much if, after the series has been completed, you would fill out the questionnaire below and return it with the records. There may be two more shows of this type to follow.

1. What do you think of the documentary type of program? *Excellent* . 2. Do you think there is justification for further experiments in this direction? *Yes* . 3. Which of the programs did you like the best? *Ledford & his friends* . 4. Why? *It tied together as a more complete show, thus it sounded like it had "more meat" in it.* 5. Do you think that these programs could be played a number of times? *The Ledford show perhaps & any* 6. Which ones? *future programs like it. The others are a little spotty.* 7. Do they have entertainment value? *I think so* 8. Each program consists of 50 or more sections from various field recordings dubbed together. Do you think that this is a technique that can be used in local originations? *Yes, altho I think the number is a little high* 9. Did this technique trouble you at any point in the program? *In some places where it was "rough"* 10. What was your estimated audience? *At least 200,000* . 11. Did you receive any mail response? *No* . 12. Did you receive cooperation with your local library? *The whole state library organization* 13. Comments? *There wasn't much to demand mail response on these programs.*

* *There are 2 million or more in our primary area. We estimate conservatively that we are now reaching at least 10% of that audience at any one time, thus the figure of 200,000.*

The basis of these programs is good. If their mass production could be speeded up before the material gets "cold" - I think you would develop a tremendous audience. Too bad you can't have the help of the networks in some instances. However, Mutual doesn't object to some recordings; perhaps there are some topics which could be discussed on a split basis, i.e., some recording, some live talent.

Someday, we'll have those facilities here, then we can do that (over) kind of job for Ohio. The idea can be adapted to telling community success stories also, working in some drama, perhaps, & other techniques of the documentary which you know better than I.

When we get the facilities in Ohio, for example, I hope to work out something with the Ohio Commission for democracy, which is chairmaned by Harrison Sayre, of the American Educ. Press.

This has developed into a letter ... I hope you don't mind. But it's now important technique, & the more you do, the more it helps us in the hinterlands. Some day, I believe we'll be in a position to help each other.

Sincerely yours

Wilbert Pettegrew
Program Supervisor - WOSU

movement, Robert L. Dorman, has designated, the "new and *indigenous.*" A similar remedy is proposed in the Regional Series programs.[15]

The scripts carried out MacLeish's beliefs about citizenship. In "New Orleans," scripted by a youthful Arthur Miller, a scene from 1766 is dramatized in which a Spanish fleet of ships arrives at the harbor of the city, and the governor explains to the city's French settlers that France had lost New Orleans to Spain in accordance with a treaty. Unlike the acquiescent populace in MacLeish's *The Fall of the City,* who welcome their new conqueror ("They wish to be free of their freedom: released from their liberty: —The long labor of liberty ended! They lie there!"), a man of New Orleans cries out to his fellow citizens: "I'm sure we have a certain right to say who shall govern us! . . . If our government won't rule us, we'll rule ourselves. I say we have that right!" In "Williamsburg," the elderly African-American guide shows a young girl (and the listening audience) around the town and points out the question that most tourists neglected to ask when they viewed the town's historical sights: "How kin a man have self respeck for hisself if he ain't a free man?" Coming from a black man, the question undoubtedly relates to the practice of slavery that was in existence in the colony and state of Virginia while patriots spoke of freedom; however, the question asked in 1941 also speaks to MacLeish's fear that Fascism might overtake the land in the present day and wipe out all existing freedoms.[16]

A number of themes appear again and again in these scripts. Communities in flux or in decline, and with pasts of changing fortune were selected as subject matter for the series. In "Nantucket, Ahoy!" one-third of the present-day population is said to be on relief. In "Williamsburg," the tourists to the newly restored town seem to have little real interest in the American tradition, and the inhabitants who recreate colonial life for them only playact at a version of patriotism. In "Hudson Valley," pollution threatens the once-vital river communities. In "New Orleans," the city of "play" for the rich has decayed and is now strewn with filth. Self-reliance of communities, rather than of disjointed individuals, is prescribed for the rejuvenation of these depressed regions. Community gatherings, in the form of town meetings, conservation societies, or just discussions at the general store, are depicted as the way to begin to find solutions to problems. Interactions and codependency between ethnic groups, races, and classes is shown to be a part of many communities' heritages, and mixed ancestry is depicted positively. The key to resolving the dilemma of whether to hold on to traditions that are no longer viable economically or try new ideas that might destroy old communities is shown to involve using innovative measures to bring moderate and appropriate industries into the communities, such as a quahaug chowder factory in Nantucket.

The programs show little interest in personal exploits. The people portrayed are subordinate to the place; history of communities takes precedence over biographies of individuals. While the community becomes the "star" of the programs, the "supporting role" usually goes to a character functioning as a "guide" to one or more visitors, who stand in for the radio listener. The guide directs us, the disconnected radio public, in understanding the potential of community life and values.

The tendency towards fragmentation common in these narratives that willy-nilly cross barriers of time as they chart a community's rise and fall, is controlled by the guide's narration and explanation. As MacLeish points out in an interview about *The Fall of the City,* radio facilitates this type of controlling role: "The Announcer is the most useful dramatic personage since the Greek Chorus. For years modern poets writing for the stage have felt the necessity of contriving some sort of chorus, some sort of commentator. . . . This chorus, this commentator, has always presented an extremely awkward practical problem. How justify its existence dramatically? How get it on? How get it off again? In radio this difficulty is removed before it occurs. The commentator is an integral part of radio technique."[17]

Only one of the scripts from the Regional Series—Joseph Liss's "Rebirth in Barrows Inlet"—actually resulted in a broadcast. CBS included that show on their *Columbia Workshop* series, but ultimately declined to take the other scripts because, according to MacLeish, "they were swamped with national and international broadcasts which they, themselves, were preparing." In July 1941, John Marshall suggested to British documentarist John Grierson that the series might have "film possibilities" and that Grierson might want to talk to MacLeish about it. Grierson's response is not known, but in any case, in September 1941, MacLeish appealed to the Rockefeller Foundation for $6,000 to produce recordings of the shows. The foundation by this time was reluctant to continue to support the actual production of broadcasts. The project's subsequent series, however, was heard in its entirety over national network radio.[18]

Hidden History

Twenty-six *Hidden History* shows were broadcast live on Sundays from May 18 through November 9, 1941, on the NBC Blue Network. The first few shows were produced in Washington; one of the later shows, "After the Chicago Fire," starring Raymond Massey, was broadcast from Hollywood, while the remainder went out from New York.

The stated idea behind the series was that American history was made by the American people, and that this "people's history" might be found "in a letter, or a diary, or on the fly-leaf of an old Bible." The series would present "a personal history of people in a democracy," throwing light not only on historic events, but also on "the recorders of events." Each show would end with a call for the American people to send to the Library material pertinent to the subject matter of the program, as "the Library of Congress is the place for the American record."

The series emphasized the view that the historical record is not complete; that newfound material can augment, challenge, or change an understanding or interpretation of the past. A number of the shows dealt with the problem of ascertaining certain knowledge about the past using variant evidence that might be contradictory or uncertain in nature. In these programs, an initial interest is created through the presentation of contradictory claims regarding the origins of

■ The idea behind the *Hidden History* series came from Alexander Woollcott, popular radio commentator and critic, known since the 1920s as the "Town Crier." At the opening of the first show in the series, Archibald MacLeish described the origination of the program idea. Photo by Carl Van Vechten, 1939. *Prints and Photographs Division.*

America's treasured heritage. The first show dealt with the claims of different localities as to authorship of the first Declaration of Independence. The next week's show presented differing assertions concerning Lincoln's Gettysburg Address. A later show consisted of a monologue of Buffalo Bill trying, and for the most part failing, to recall his own past accurately. The shows generally resolved their contradictory claims by finding significance outside of the dispute. The first show made the point that ascertaining who was first to write a declaration of independence was not as important as knowing the fact that "all the people wanted independence and fought together for freedom," and that the country's Declaration was, in fact, "written by *all* the people in *all* of America." The Gettysburg show ended with Lincoln's recitation "that government of the people, by the people, for the people shall not perish from the earth."

These endings can best be understood in light of the war in Europe and the threat posed by Fascism. Coming at a time when European democracies were being crushed, the Gettysburg Address served as a call to unite the diverse people of America behind a common history and set of values.

Some of the localities featured in the "Declarations of Independence" program were chosen, seemingly, because the inhabitants spoke with accents or even in foreign languages. One *Hidden History* show, based on the diary of an exslave, ended with the freed slave vowing a sacred oath to defend the Union. Another show, entitled "The Story of an Immigrant," establishes the importance of a Polish migrant to the Jamestown Colony. A show built around "Yankee Doodle" suggests that the song may have German, Scottish, Irish, and Portuguese roots. These stories are structured around quintessential sites, symbols, and events of American history that turn out to have multicultural origins. Without didacticism, the shows good-naturedly teach the lesson that Americans, by accepting these symbols and history, partake of a variety of cultures. If—as in the case of the Declaration of Independence, what really happened at Gettysburg, and the song "Yankee Doodle"—the origins of quintessential American symbols are shown to be irretrievable, arguments for potential disuniting essentialisms concerning the American heritage are weakened. The series calls for unity in diversity.

In naming the series *Hidden History*, the creators were attempting to involve their audience in a search. Although the surface quest was a search for factual knowledge, on a deeper level, the shows attempted to involve listeners in a search for meaning. Because motifs and patterns appeared throughout the broadcasts, alert listeners might have found the series to have been about the search for the meaning of the American experience.

Many of the stories dealt with movement and mobility, the change and transformation of individuals and communities. The past was shown to resonate with present-day Depression experience. In "Coxey's Army," an unemployed working man and a skeptical drifter join a group on their way, in 1894, from Ohio to Washington, D.C., to petition Congress for a bill so that the unemployed could be hired to build roads. Although the protest ends in failure, the drifter joins the Populists and considers becoming a working man, while the working man learns "that a man's got to feel he's wanted someplace," a message relevant, no doubt, to those displaced by the current Depression.

"The Erie Canal" presents an elegiac lament looking back to the days of the early Republic from a time in the late 1800s when the railroad's success had made the canal obsolete. It nostalgically presents a vibrant earlier time before the railroad came of towpath boys driving mules, marriages made on the canal, fights on boats for the right of first passage through the canal, and exuberant goings on at tavern stops along the canal. The reminiscence ends, however, with a look to the future: "Country's gettin' bigger. Places gettin' farther apart. Maybe speed is just what we need." The sentimental look to the past ends with a promise of new technology, a promise consistent with the current mood as evidenced by such paeans to progress as the 1939 New York World's Fair.

In "New Ghost Towns," the town of Goforth, Texas, becomes a ghost town after too many trees are cleared leaving none for windbreakers. The show ends with the establishment of a soil conservation association to build a watershed reservoir to control water so that soil is not washed

As Broadcast

The Library of Congress
Radio Research Project

NATIONAL BROADCASTING COMPANY
SUNDAY, MAY 18th, 1941
1:00-1:15 P.M.(EST) Blue Network

HIDDEN HISTORY
The Declarations of
Independence (REVISED)
Program I, p.1

CUE: (NATIONAL BROADCASTING) Company
. . . . . .30 seconds . . . . .

ANNOUNCER: HIDDEN HISTORY . . . presented by the Library of Congress in collaboration with the National Broadcasting Company. This program is the first in a new series. Archibald MacLeish, The Librarian of Congress, will tell you about HIDDEN HISTORY.

MACLEISH: One day several months ago three or four people from our staff were sitting around a table with Alexander Woollcott talking about a program in which we would bring information to the people. Woollcott, who will appear later in this series, said - "Why don't you ask the people to bring information to you?" And this, in a word, is what we want to do in this new series and so we come to the people - we come to you, for the people of America are the makers

note

devised by mess Hamell, ... of our staff

MORE NEXT PAGE

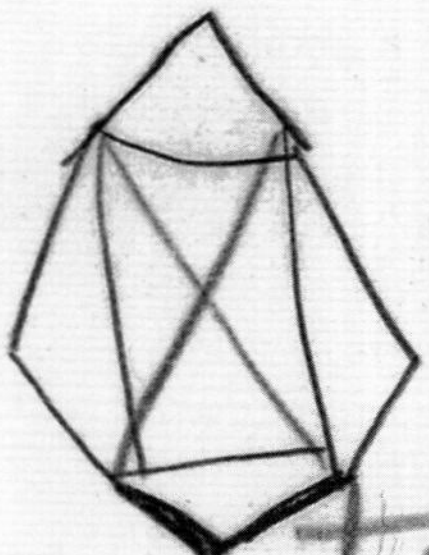

Many *Hidden History* shows resonated with analogies to present-day events and people. The show "My Day with Dolly Madison" portrayed the busy life of the fourth First Lady, but also presented an homage to the current First Lady, Eleanor Roosevelt (shown here in January 1937 in her inaugural gown), whose daily newspaper column was titled simply, "My Day." Portrait of Dolley Madison by Gilbert Stuart, Courtesy Pennsylvania Academy of Fine Arts. *Prints and Photographs Division.*

away. A former citizen of Goforth is invited to "grab a shovel," and with dreams that his town will bloom once more after land and grasses return, the citizen joins the new conservation community.

Some of the stories deflated legendary Americans, such as Buffalo Bill and Mike Fink. In "Buffalo Bill Disremembers," by Arthur Miller, the seventy-year-old showman tries to reminisce, but finds he cannot account for his life. "Nothin' seems real," he laments. "It's like I started play-acting and I lived a whole life trying to find my way out of the theatre. . . . Am I Bill Cody or Buffalo Bill? A cowboy or an actor? And when did I become which?"

As with the Regional Series, in the *Hidden History* programs, the meaning of the American experience is in question. It is shown to be something to work for, something to find in the future of the country, not necessarily something that is hidden in the past. The series attempted to form a community of listeners by appealing to them to send materials so that a new meaning could be found from Americans searching and interpreting together.

Mobility, transformations, uncertain origins, uncertain future, deflated heroes: the America heard in these "Hidden Histories" matched the unstable, insecurities of the Depression era. The success of the show was that it could celebrate just these otherwise disturbing qualities because it

had at its heart the theme that the country's hidden history could be used to guide the future. The dark side of the American history never dominates.

Documentary Series

After the Regional Series was prepared and while the *Hidden History* broadcasts were airing, the project's most ambitious series began. In his report on the documentary activities of the project, Alan Lomax criticized "the domination of regional culture by metropolitan culture" and envisioned a series out of which would "emerge a new function for radio; that of letting the people explain themselves and their lives to the entire nation."

With the new programs, the Library was about to embark on a series of radio broadcasts to document the sounds and speech of present-day American life, a project that was not envisioned when the resolution to fund the project was passed. This new direction ultimately became the most valuable for posterity, as the project's writers, researchers,

■ Large group of "Coxey's Army" listen to a speaker during their trek to Washington, D.C., in 1894 to petition Congress to pass legislation for a federal road construction project so that those left unemployed by the previous year's stock market crash could be hired as laborers to build roads. The *Hidden History* program on the protest drew on unacknowledged, but nevertheless present, echoes between the earlier push for federal employment projects and the Depression-era Works Progress Administration, and on similarities between the Coxey's Army protest and the 1932 Bonus March on Washington, when World War I veterans suffering from the Depression traveled to the Capitol to petition Congress to give them a bonus that was originally scheduled to be dispersed in 1945. Both protests were forcibly dispersed by unsympathetic presidents. Photo by Ray Stannard Baker. *Prints and Photographs Division.*

and engineers went out to selected communities and returned with discs filled with the talk, songs, opinion, and mood of "America in the Summer of 1941," as the series originally was called. The hundreds of hours of recordings made and subsequently preserved mark this series as the first extensive group of oral histories captured on record.

A documentary approach to recording and presenting to the public the country's ways of life, including its social ills, had been evidenced during the Depression in such diverse phenomena as journalism, literature, photography, film, theater, and art. As literary critic and social commentator Alfred Kazin wrote in 1942, as the era was passing, "Never before did a nation seem so hungry for news of itself."

Charting this "new nationalism," Kazin portrayed the recent search for identity in regional and folk cultures: "Chanting America, loving it, celebrating it, there was suddenly a whole world of marvels on the continent to possess—a world of rivers and scenes, of folklore and regional culture, of a heroic tradition to reclaim and of forgotten heroes to follow. America was here, now, a continent to be surveyed . . . an inheritance to rejoice in and to find strength in."[19]

These concerns came to life in Depression culture in a particular style of flaunting tradition. Author Harvey Swados, looking back in 1966, wrote that the mood of despair had given way to experimentation, "a genuine stirring, a readiness to break with the past, a receptivity to new ideas." In the case of documentary radio, the new idea that allowed a break with the past was so simple that it is easy to overlook the radical break from past practice of radio presentation that occurred.[20]

The technique—one which allowed the project's creators to put together documentary shows using segments of recorded sound juxtaposed next to one another and mixed with background noise or music—was simply to transfer the gathered recorded sound to celluloid tape, then edit the tape using film editing techniques, and finally rerecord the finished product onto discs for broadcast.

This technique changed the nature of the creation of the documentary broadcasts. With the scripted style of the Regional Series and *Hidden History*, the researcher and writer controlled the material that was heard in the program. Researchers had been responsible for choosing appropriate material; writers (who often also functioned as researchers) composed the material into coherent forms to accomplish the purposes of the particular broadcasts and wrote new material, usually narration, to further guide the programs. While the actual broadcasts, in which actors and directors worked, gave life to the written words and stage directions of the script, the meaning of the shows had already been determined by the writer.

The new documentary broadcasts shifted the responsibility for the show to those conducting interviews and recording music, those giving interviews and making music, and finally, those editing the field material. The new editing technique made it possible to easily manipulate the recorded material. Editors could cut out both extraneous and potentially controversial material. The technique gave the editor control of the juxtaposition of bits of speech. Additionally, editing made it possible to cut material while making it seem to listeners that no cuts had been made.

The reason that this editing technique had not been used previously in radio can be attributed to the preference of live, as opposed to recorded, material in most radio broadcasting. At the time of the Radio Research Project, NBC and CBS had issued regulations prohibiting the use of recorded material except for sound effects. In part because of the poor quality of recordings, even independent stations generally preferred live broadcasts, which conveyed the feel of immediacy that was missing from recordings. As a result of the dominance of live recording in radio, editing remained a crude technique.

In a report on the documentary operations of the Radio Research Project, Alan Lomax explained how the development of the project's editing technique came about. They had considered doing a series of live programs remote from various locales "utilizing local talent and authentic people as participating actors." Lomax reported, however, that they soon realized they could not effectively organize such a complicated undertaking and began to consider using field recordings. Recording engineer Jerome Wiesner, Lomax wrote, "assured us that it would be possible to edit field recordings in the Laboratory in such a way so as to eliminate material that would not be pertinent to any story we might wish to tell and to tie smoothly together speeches, interviews and conversations, so that the listener would never be aware

that the editing had been done." The technique that Wiesner devised, though effective, presented some problems in loss of audio quality: "Mr. Wiesner rented a machine that recorded on transparent celluloid tape. We dubbed from the original records onto this tape and did our cutting with scissors in the Laboratory splicing the end of the film together with Scotch Tape. It seemed for a while that this would solve all of the editing problems in sight but . . . we discovered that there was a distinct loss in quality between the original and the tape duplicate." Finally, the editing material was "put on a reel of tape and then dubbed back into the final master record." Most of the radio station program managers who returned questionnaires to the Library after playing the recordings did not complain about the sound quality.

The program entitled "Okie Festival," recorded in the summer of 1941 at "Okie" and "Arkie" migrant camps in California, exemplifies a standard intent of the broadcasts. As in the Regional Series shows, this program studied a community undergoing transformative change. "Okie Festival" stresses the survival and creative transformation of community values and traditions in a transplanted group. It begins with two adolescent Okie girls singing a song they wrote, "Government Camp Song," which spoofs migrant camp life to the tune of Woody Guthrie's "Oklahoma Hills." Commentator Charles Todd, who with his partner, Robert Sonkin, produced the program, next speaks of the migrants forming new patterns out of shattered fragments of the old ways of living. The camps had been established by the Farm Security Administration, but were governed, administered, and policed, according to the commentary, by the migrants themselves. The show presents two community settings: the camp council, modeled on the traditional New England town meeting; and the folk festival. The council meeting at Visalia, California, begins with the administering of an oath: refugees agree to uphold the Constitution of the United States and the constitution and by-laws of the camp. A former Arkansas farmer tells the assembled group that the council is not going to tell the people what to do, but "you will tell the council what you want." He promises that they will carry the concerns of the people to Washington, D.C., and will go to the limit to get a "yes" or "no" answer to their concerns, "but we won't have to take no for an answer when we are all together." The council makes plans for the first Okie festival in California for Labor Day.

Todd introduces this festival as not just a celebration of Labor Day, but "Goin' to Meeting Day in the Ozarks, hog killing time in Arkansas, Okie Day in the San Joaquin Valley." He characterizes the migrants' "old jalopies" as the "covered wagons of 1941." At night, Todd takes us to a "play party"—a dance with singing, but no music. A participant describes the origins of this transplanted tradition: "Pesky old folks" wouldn't let the younger folk have music for a "dance," so they decided to change the name of their gathering to "play party" and hold the event without music. The show ends with Todd extolling the migrants for conquering a "new frontier" with the help of their government; while there are "no Indians this time," they will need to deal with hunger, prejudice, and rats.

Lomax's concept of "letting the people explain them-

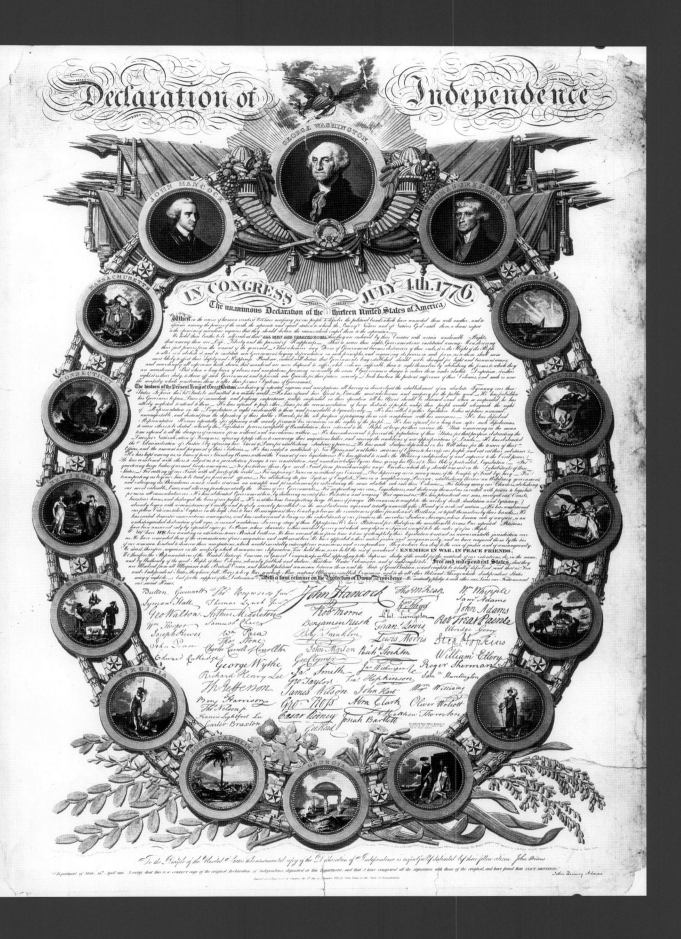

TITLE	DATE
THE IRON HORSE	September 21, 1941.
GREAT AMERICAN FALL GUY	September 28, 1941.
SCOOPS AT FORT SUMTER	October 5, 1941
BUFFALO BILL AND THE BUFFALO	October 12, 1941.
DR. WATERHOUSE	October 19, 1941.
THE ERIE CANAL	October 26, 1941.
YANKEE DOODLE	November 2, 1941.
GREAT AMERICAN HERO	November 9, 1941.

Here are a few excerpts from letters received by the Radio Research Project in response to the HIDDEN HISTORY series. Manuscripts have also been contributed to add to the collection in the Division of Manuscripts of the Library of Congress:

(From Swamscott, Mass.) ..."These letters have been precious family possessions and as I am the last in line and now over seventy I should be glad if the letters could serve any purpose in rounding out the historic record of the Civil War Period."

(From Rochester, Penna.) ..."Having heard the program presented on the radio by the Library of Congress on which you asked for the stories or fables of American characters or events, I decided to write to you the story of Daniel Boone."

(From Martinez, Calif.) ..."I have such a diary which I would be pleased to loan to you. It was written by my father who during 1864-5 was a patient in an Army Hospital in Washington, D. C., recovering from a wound."

(From Evanston, Ill.) ..."In your broadcast I noticed that you asked for letters, documents, and facts concerning the Civil War. I have in my possession letters written by a soldier; my father's brother, George Washington C....from Vicksburg, Mississippi. I have been told by stamp collectors that these letters, envelopes in tack, are quite valuable. They are written in a droll, funny way - by the common soldier."

■ Robert Sonkin (second on left) and Charles L. Todd (second on right) recording a fiddler at an Okie festival in California. Photo by Robert Hemmig. *American Folklife Center.*

■ A vote is taken at a council meeting in an Okie camp. Practices of democracy in action often were featured in the project's programs. Farm Security Administration. Photo by Dorothea Lange. *American Folklife Center.*

selves and their lives to the entire nation" developed further in the show "Ledford and His Friends" (also known as "Paul Ledford and His Neighbors"). In this broadcast, Lomax lets a resident of Union County, Georgia, Paul Ledford, conduct interviews with people in his own community, which was being evacuated due to flooding as the result of a Tennessee Valley Authority (TVA) dam project built to create electricity to produce aluminum for the defense effort. As was the case with the Okies, this community, stable for generations, was about to be uprooted. At the show's beginning, a neighbor, Barrett, who is renting a farm in the valley, visits Ledford. They sit on a swing and after languidly discussing a "rising" on Barrett's leg, Ledford interviews Barrett about the TVA. Barrett does not know much about it and complains that the TVA people have never stopped at his place. Ledford, who, like the rest of the community, is waiting for "Uncle Sam" to reimburse him for his flooded farm before he can buy a new place, sighs, "All the good times are past and gone," then sings a few bars of that song.

After dinner, Ledford takes Lomax to the cabin of the man he considers the most interesting person in the county, Uncle Joe Kirby, who, at eighty, compares old times with the present. While he likes some of the old ways "powerful well," Kirby admits the advantages of the present, saying he does not see how he could live if his wife had to make clothing the way his mother did. He relates the difficulties he and his wife went through when they first purchased the cabin, and how they eventually got by and gradually furnished it. He suddenly gets angry about the government and complains that it is unjust for them to tell him he has to get out. Uncle Joe invites Ledford to stay the night, but Ledford declines the invitation, promising to return before long.

As Ledford and Lomax leave, they see two of Ledford's friends putting up hay in the distance and drive over to them. At the mention of the TVA, the men get heated but Ledford tells them he believes they will be treated fairly. He says he thinks the government will try to put people into decent houses, but realizes that the new ones will not be "home."

His friends relate some stories of playing jokes on TVA men. At the conclusion, Ledford invites Lomax to return to show him speckled trout, virgin timber, and cold spring water bubbling out of the ground. He movingly says that some of the best people in the United States live there, all of whom are genuine Americans, who would "take up their old hog rifles" if they could shoot "old Hitler" and fight "to their last drop of blood" to defend America.

For a later program, an urban community was chosen as a subject, as the project leaders "decided that our [previous] programs overemphasized the rural life of the country." This show, "Wilmington, North Carolina," portrays a community that had increased, due to the defense industry, from 30,000 to 70,000 inhabitants in one year, and was to grow to 100,000 in the next. In the broadcast, written and narrated by Arthur Miller, nine residents are interviewed: a gas station owner outside the city; the city manager; new residents of a trailer camp; a city bus driver; an old established resident; a striker at a shirt factory; and a worker at a shipyard. Although there is some disquietude expressed, most of the people speak positively about the changes they have witnessed. Miller narrates the show heavily, a contrast to the "Ledford" show in which the residents seem to control the interviews.

These documentary broadcasts reveal an America in the process of change. Individuals, families, and whole groups who have been uprooted, try to maintain their ways of life. Yet a positive spin is placed on change, and the people interviewed persevere, strengthened by their traditions and determination. By comparing the material that was used for the final broadcast with the unedited interviews, however, it soon becomes evident that certain topics—those that touched on the most troubling things these "neighbors say" were not included in the broadcasts.

Tens of hours of recordings were produced to make each quarter-hour show. To understand the intent of these shows, the principles of selection of material have to be taken into consideration.

The discs Miller recorded in Wilmington include both a discussion at an employment center, in which disgruntled laid-off workers rail against the shipyard, and the analysis of the shirt factory strike by a union organizer. The project editors chose not to include labor dissatisfaction in the broadcast, although they did include a song by African-American female strikers, who had written new words about the strike to go with an old spiritual. Miller, in his commentary, offers warm appreciation for the music, but the reasons for the strike are never voiced. Although the project may have been trying to present strikers positively—no doubt a courageous stance for a radio show of the time to take—and to honor the music of the women, by avoiding discussion about the strike they also may have been trying to avoid controversy.

Similarly, the TVA recordings that were not included in the broadcast reveal a concern on the part of the interviewers, and on some of those interviewed, with questions of politics and ideological belief. During an interview with a group of farmers, Alan Lomax asks, "Do you think we have a democracy in this country?" When they answer affirmatively, Lomax continues, "Do you think we might make it more democratic than it already is? . . . How do you think we can get more freedom?" Lomax prods and the farmers ramble on until one of them discusses a cooperative setup they have begun: "That gives us a lot of freedom. If I've got 50 sacks of potatoes to sell, if I don't want to take 'em to Atlanta, I c'n take 'em to Blairsville. Turn 'em over to the county agent. Well that county agent—that county agent will dispose of those potatoes for me at the market price. My worries are over. It turns me loose. It gives me freedom to go back and do something else."

The absence of the words "socialism" and "communism" in the shows will, perhaps, not be surprising. In a broadcast entitled "Delaware and the Eastern Shore of Maryland," people are questioned about their lives and concerns, about rising food prices, about their families, and about Hitler. In the unedited material, Joseph Liss asks a grocer about his political ideas. After the grocer complains of corruption due to payoffs of politicians and suggests that the government should implement an upper limit on wealth to alleviate the need for payoffs, Liss contends that some might call his idea "communism." The grocer says he doesn't like labels, but says that nevertheless, some of the things he believes in

■ Fiddlin' Bill Hensley and Asa Helton, rivals in an old time fid-
dlers' championship at the Asheville Folk Festival, performed in the "Mountain Festival" program of the
Documentary Series. Following the performance, Alan
Lomax interviewed the musicians about mountain life and
their views on the war in Europe. *Alan Lomax Collection.
Prints and Photographs Division.*

might, in fact, be termed "communism" or "socialism." He
rhetorically asks, why should a person who has nothing
under the present system fight to preserve the status quo,
when that person would not be any worse off under Hitler?
This questioning of economic inequalities in America was
not heard by the audience.

Racial tensions and discrimination are issues that do not
appear in the broadcasts. In the interview with the grocer
that was not aired, Liss contends that for certain groups,
there is no democracy in the U. S. He asks the grocer if he
feels that Negroes have the real freedom of action considered essential in a democracy. The grocer agrees they do not
have it, but quickly adds that a lot of white people do not
have it either. In another interview, an African-American
man contends that England and the large countries of
Europe, including Russia, should have fought Hitler much
earlier when he began to persecute the Jews. Liss then asks
if there is racial persecution in the United States, and the
man says he has read about plenty in the South, but never
has come up against it himself. He says he read about a case
of slavery still in existence in which blacks were "paroled
out" of jail to work on a farm in which they were held as
slaves and killed if they tried to escape. This account never
made it to the air.

In the broadcast, an African-American woman in the low
country of Delaware, the wife of a church sexton, tells Liss
the long names of her children, some of whom, she says
were named after the white people for whom she works. She
describes her small family farm and what they raise, then
says she also works for cash as a paper hanger. Liss mentions
that Hitler had been a paper hanger also, and asks if she
knows that the country is very close to war. The woman says
"Oh Lord," and Liss ends the conversation by asking how
we could stop the war and make the world a better place to
live in. She suggests we kneel down and pray.

The extended interview reveals that the woman told Liss
she received five dollars from each person for whom her
children was named; thus, if a child was given ten separate
names, she was given fifty dollars. This explanation was not
in the broadcast, in which it appears that the woman had
such deep affection for her white employers that she named
her children after them. While this may have been the case,
the fact that they gave her money adds a complication to the
story, which the interviewer did not pursue in his questions
or include in the broadcast.

More importantly, in the unedited material, when Liss
asks if we should go to war, the woman responds, "I don't
think folks should have to go out there." Her husband, upon
entering into the conversation, agrees with her. These state-
ments of isolationism were not included in the broadcast. In
fact, although isolationist attitudes were common during
1941, no one in any of the documentary broadcasts takes an
isolationist stand. Nowhere is that subject broached.

Despite these hidden omitted topics—of isolationism,
racial tensions, radical political beliefs, and labor unrest—
the Documentary Series did present issues of serious import
in a manner uncommon to most radio of its time. In addition to the Ledford program, the project produced a special
half-hour CBS broadcast for the series *Report to the Nation*
from the extensive material recorded concerning the impact
of the TVA dam on mountain folk. In the broadcast, county farm agent Don Hulsey speaks to the people of the valley
at their courthouse about a dam that is to be built that will
ultimately force them to move. Like Ledford's friends, a
farmer protests: "We know you're going to give us a fair price
for our land. But what is a fair price for breakin' up a home.
I don't know how you can figure it. How do we know what
kind of new farms we're going to get? When you been farm-
ing a place as long as I have, you know what the soil tastes
like. You can't take up on a new place overnight." Hulsey
assures them that TVA men will give them assistance in getting new land at good prices: "If you use our help and all
work together, we can beat out the land sharks that are
beginning to come around looking for easy marks."

Speaking to the radio listeners, Hulsey ends the program
with a tribute to the democratic manner of solving problems: "This new way of life was worked out by the people
themselves. It wasn't handed down to them. They planned
it. The mountain people are stubborn. They are individuals.
They won't adopt a new idea unless they have convinced
themselves that it is sound and will help them. I think these
changes are a means of these people helping themselves." A
commentator then sums up the broadcast, describing the
role that the Radio Research Project would have liked to

continue to play: "What you have just heard is a segment of our history as it is actually being lived by people like your own neighbors—1941 Americans. This record does not purport to photograph the entire countryside or cover all the persons in the neighborhood. Nor is it a Gallup poll, trying to collect scientifically weighted samples. But it does dip into current life and come up with a brimming bucket of human ideas and activity. To make such records in every part of the country, to preserve the sounds and voices of America in this crisis time-that is the job of the Library of Congress Radio Research Project. This will be not only a record that men of the future may study. It is a record from which men of the present may have much to learn."

The End of the Project

John Marshall of the Rockefeller Foundation was concerned when he visited the Library in July 1941 and learned about the documentary series. In a letter to documentary filmmaker John Grierson, he suggested that Grierson visit MacLeish, who, Marshall wrote, "has given the boys rather too free a hand." He explained: "the project was supposed pretty much to draw on materials in the Library. Now the boys are getting more engaged by the possibilities of outside recording. I guess that is all right, but I would like to be surer than I am that they aren't neglecting what is right at hand in the Library."[21]

In September 1941, MacLeish met with Marshall to ask for nearly $40,000 for the project for an additional year. In a letter, he listed the programs he would have liked to continue or to begin. He wanted the project to attempt fifteen more documentaries; to assign five additional ones to outsiders; to continue the *Hidden History* series; to produce recordings for radio broadcast of the six Regional Series scripts that were completed; to prepare and distribute at least thirty more *Books in the News* programs; and to produce two "definitive programs" on the Declaration of Independence and the Constitution for schools, with information books included. He characterized the documentary series as an illustration of "how radio can explore the thinking, the origins, the folk traditions and folk songs of the people of this country," and predicted, "When these programs are ready for distribution, we feel sure that the listeners will have a better idea of the way in which their neighbors live," noting that the universities and contemporary literature had failed "in this important work of showing this country to itself." The Radio Research Project, if continued, would "explore and translate into radio terms those phases of American life, culture and history which give to the American people a sense of the importance of their democracy." He also planned to broadcast the programs through short-wave radio to show the "American way of life" to other peoples of the world.[22]

Marshall balked at the request. When he asked that the Library make financial contributions to the project, MacLeish responded that Congress would not support an experimental effort "to extend the usefulness of a national library to the people of the nation." MacLeish quoted Marshall himself on the principal value of the project—"to interpret American cultural traditions, particularly the tradi-

tion which both lives today and has roots back into the past"—and in response, Marshall agreed to recommend further support of $35,000 for two years.[23]

Meanwhile, in the preceding week, Roosevelt had established the Office of Facts and Figures (OFF) and had appointed as its director MacLeish, who continued his position as Librarian of Congress as he took on his new duties. With the American entry into the war becoming increasingly inevitable, Roosevelt established OFF to communicate information effectively to the nation concerning the defense effort.

When the Radio Research Project staff was assigned to do research for a program on the Bill of Rights that would be produced by OFF, Marshall worried that if such joint projects continued, it would "appear to many that the RF [Rockefeller Foundation] funds were being used to pay for the work of the OFF." Ultimately, because of this conflict and the uncertainty of a role for the project during wartime, the Rockefeller Foundation approved a grant only to fund the project for two months past the end of the first grant, until the end of February 1942, so that the staff could complete projects in progress.[24]

Following the Japanese attack on Pearl Harbor, the project received permission to use Archive of American Folk Song funds to document reactions of Americans to the bombing and to the president's declaration of war. On December 8, they sent telegrams to contacts in ten localities to have them record people's reactions. Late in the month broadcasts using these interviews played on stations associated with the Mutual Broadcasting System, and local stations supplied their own announcers.

The interviewers asked people about their reactions upon learning about the attack; who they thought would win the war; whether Germany was behind the attack; their opinions on Roosevelt's handling of the situation; whether the United States should accept anything other than unconditional surrender before peace was declared; their opinion of the policy that the United States had followed up to that time; their feelings about sending a son abroad to fight; how long they thought the war would last; and the reasons they thought the war began. Opinion was nearly unanimous on a number of topics. Nearly everyone was shocked at the sneak attack and bitterly condemned Japan for not declaring war beforehand; many people thought Germany was behind the attack; Roosevelt's handling of the situation was almost unanimously hailed; all who were asked said that they would send a son abroad to fight; nearly all thought that the war would last a long time. Immigrants with accents made a point of emphasizing that they would fight for the United States if they were allowed. Much anti-Japanese racist talk was spoken. In a billiard hall in an African-American section of Washington, D.C., nearly all the patrons queried responded positively when they were asked if blacks would be patriotic.

The last program produced by the project was by far their most polished. This was a live broadcast on Lincoln's birthday entitled, "Mr. Lincoln Speaks to the People and to the Soldiers," starring Walter Huston as Lincoln and Douglas Fairbanks, Jr., as the narrator. The show consists of excerpts from Lincoln's speeches arranged to seem like he is talking

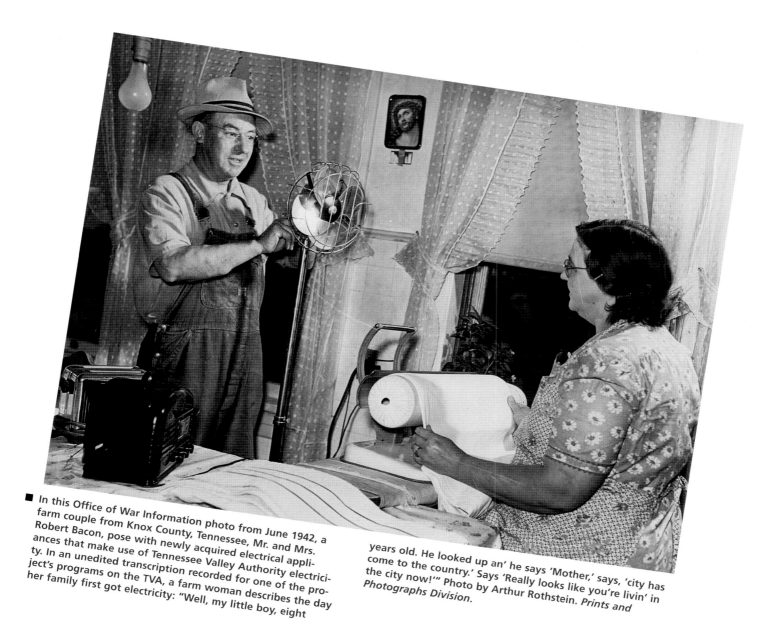

In this Office of War Information photo from June 1942, a farm couple from Knox County, Tennessee, Mr. and Mrs. Robert Bacon, pose with newly acquired electrical appliances that make use of Tennessee Valley Authority electricity. In an unedited transcription recorded for one of the project's programs on the TVA, a farm woman describes the day her family first got electricity: "Well, my little boy, eight years old. He looked up an' he says 'Mother,' says, 'city has come to the country.' Says 'Really looks like you're livin' in the city now!'" Photo by Arthur Rothstein. Prints and Photographs Division.

directly to Americans of 1942. Regarding the end of the war, Lincoln states that he does not wish to name the day, but that he hopes it will not end until their objective is accomplished. He wams against paying attention to rumors in warfare. In a poignant moment, a mother whose five sons died in the war, reads a letter from Lincoln in which he avows that they were sacrificed upon the altar of freedom and that he hopes she can take consolation in the republic they died to save. A reviewer of the broadcast noted, "Abraham Lincoln spoke during the dark times of the Civil War, but the words of hope and inspiration that he uttered were just as applicable today."[25]

After the project folded on February 28, 1942, Cohen followed MacLeish to the OFF. When the Office of War Information (OWI) was formed later in 1942, both MacLeish and Cohen joined the new organization. During the war, Liss, Lomax, Harrell, and Miller also worked for OWI on radio broadcasts.

The Documentary Series had been held up from release, most probably due to the American entry into the war. Recordings of the shows were sent to independent stations in May 1942 under a new title, *Americans Talk Back*. After

the war, the introduction of reel-to-reel audio tape into radio production made field recording and editing easier. With more superior sound quality than was possible with the Radio Research Project, documentary radio in the late 1940s continued to explore the social life and problems of America.

The Radio Research Project was animated by two strong urges: to educate the public about the value of the American democratic way of life, and to facilitate a way for Americans from different communities to listen to one another. Radio was used to accomplish both tasks by portraying, in one instance, and investigating, in the other, life in communities that made up the country. Since an important goal of both endeavors was persuasion—that the democratic way of life was worth preserving, that the fight against Fascism was just, that the communities of America were worth reviving—propaganda became integral to the project, and the speech of individuals became of less importance to transmit than the hopes of communities.

Documentary radio emerged from document-based dramatizations during this experimental project. The Regional Series, relying on documentary evidence, but

■ The Project's final program, "Mr. Lincoln Speaks to the People and to the Soldiers," was broadcast live on February 11, 1942, the eve of Lincoln's Birthday, over some ninety stations of the NBC Blue Network. Top talent for the broadcast included Walter Huston as Lincoln, Douglas Fairbanks, Jr., then a lieutenant in the U.S. Navy, as the narrator, and composer Earl Robinson. NBC provided studio facilities, an orchestra, the director, and a technical crew. In this show, as in many of the project's earlier broadcasts, a historical subject parallels a contemporary situation. Lincoln speaking through letters and speeches during wartime echoes Roosevelt's similar consoling addresses to the nation. Photo of Lincoln by Mathew B. Brady, February 9, 1864; photo of Roosevelt, 1933. *Prints and Photographs Division.*

scripted and meant to be presented by actors, inspired the Documentary Series in that both centered on American communities in flux, struggling to find ways to combine the "new and indigenous." Alan Lomax, with his field recording experience, knew the appeal and the importance that actual voices and sounds would have for presenting American communities. The experimental nature of the project with its trial-and-error ethos provided an atmosphere that allowed Jerome Wiesner to work out his ideas about editing the field recordings. Philip Cohen's background knowledge of the documentary work of the BBC provided a direction. And Archibald MacLeish's propagandistic goal, to educate the populace so that they would not willingly accept Fascism, provided a strong purpose. Documentary radio and the documentary genre as we now know it emerged as the result of the interaction of these forces and situations. Documentaries for the most part have remained in the intervening years rooted in experimentation, education, and persuasion.

Notes

1. The name of the project is misleading. While social science "radio research projects," first at Princeton and later at Columbia University (which were similarly funded by the Rockefeller Foundation), studied radio's uses, potentialities, and place in society, the Library's project, which had no ties to the social science community, centered more on the creation of radio broadcasting than on research about radio.

2. The genre term "documentary" is slippery in that historically it has been applied to a number of different types of works. In this essay, I distinguish works that do not rely on dramatized reconstructions, calling them "documentaries," from those based on historical documents that do use dramatized reconstructions to tell their tale. The latter I call "document-based" works, with the realization that the ambiguity of the term "documentary" may, in fact, relate to the slippery boundary that sometimes separates fact from fiction.

3. Unless otherwise identified, all quotations come from the Papers of the Radio Research Project, Recorded Sound Reference Center, Motion Picture, Broadcasting, and Recorded Sound Division, Library of Congress.

4. Erik Bamouw, *ed., Radio Drama in Action: Twenty-five Plays of a Changing World* (New York: Farrar & Rinehart, 1945), p. 49.

5. Archibald MacLeish, "Libraries and the Contemporary Crisis," quoted in *Congressional Record-Appendix,* October 23, 1939, p. 1256.

6. Archibald MacLeish, "When America Goes to War," *Modern Monthly* 9 (June 1935): 201; quoted in Scott Donaldson, *Archibald MacLeish: An*

American Life (Boston: Houghton Mifflin, 1992), p.333. Archibald MacLeish, *Archibald MaLeish: Reflections,* ed. Bernard A. Drabeck and Helen E. Ellis (Amherst: University of Massachusetts Press, 1986), p.107.

7. Archibald MacLeish, "Press Release: Sound Laboratory in Library of Congress," April 19, 1940, Library of Congress Central Files, box 900, Manuscript Division.

8. "Application for a Subvention from the Rockefeller Foundation to Permit the Library of Congress to Carry Out a Program of Popular Education in the United States," submitted by Archibald MacLeish, Librarian of Congress, October 27, 1939, folder 2890, box 242, series 200R, Record Group 1.1, Rockefeller Foundation Archives, Rockefeller Archive Center, North Tarrytown, New York (hereafter designated RAC); MacLeish, "Libraries in the Contemporary Crisis," p. 1257.

9. John Marshall, Memorandum to David Stevens January 22, 1936, folder 5, box 5, series 911, RG 1.1, Rockefeller Foundation Archives, RAC; quoted in Brett Joseph Gary, "American Liberalism and the Problem of Propaganda: Scholars, Lawyers, and the War on Words, 1919-1945" (Ph.D. diss., University of Pennsylvania, 1992), p. 97; Gary, pp. 99-100; Marshall, "Next Jobs in Radio and Film," September 13, 1938, folder 60, box 5, series 911, RG 1.1, Rockefeller Foundation Archives, RAC; quoted in Gary, p. 100.

10. Charles A. Siepmann, *Radio, Television and Society* (New York: Oxford University Press, 1950), pp. 176, 198. Max Wylie, ed., *Best Broadcasts of 1938/39* (New York: McGraw-Hill, Whittlesey House, 1939), p. 449; William N. Robson, "Future of Radio Drama," Third American Writers Congress, June 3, 1939, quoted in *Educational Radio & Recording,* vol. 1, no. 6 (February 15, 1940): 2.

11. Resolution RF 40133, December 3-4, 1940, folder 2892, box 242, series 200R, RG 1.1, Rockerfeller Foundation Archives, RAC.

23. Marshall to MacLeish, September 24, 1941; MacLeish to Marshall, October 6, 1941, folder 2893, box 242, series 200R, RG 1.1, Rockefeller Foundation Archive, RAC.

24. Marshall interview notes from meetings with MacLeish, November 6-14, 1941; MacLeish to Marshall, November 28, 1941, folder 2893, box 242, series 200R, RG 1.1, Rockefeller Foundation Archives, RAC; Extension of Appropriation RF 40133, December 24, 1941, folder 2890, box 242, series 200R, RG 1.1, Rockefeller Foundation Archives, RAC. The program on the Bill of Rights, written by Norman Corwin, celebrated its 150th anniversary on December 15, 1941. Entitled *We Hold These Truths*, it was, according to Erik Barnouw, broadcast simultaneously over NBC-red, NBC-blue, CBS and the Mutual Broadcasting System "to the largest audience ever to hear a dramatic performance." Erik Barnouw, *The Golden Web: A History of Broadcasting in the United States, Volume II—1933 to 1953* (New York: Oxford University Press, 1968), p. 153.

25. "Mr. Lincoln Speaks to the People and to the Soldiers," Radio Research Project, Library of Congress (M/B/RS); *New York Daily News*, February 12, I 942.

This essay was developed in a Cultural Studies research seminar at George Mason University. The author wishes to thank Lawrence W. Levine and all the students for their valued readings, criticisms, and comments. Thanks also to Sam Brylawski of M/B/RS for suggesting the topic and for his expert guidance, and Nancy Seeger, also of M/B/RS, for her reading of the manuscript and her encouragement.

ALAN GEVINSON is working on a doctorate at Johns Hopkins University in the Department of History. Formerly, he was the associate editor of the *American Film Institute Catalog of Feature Films* and the project director and editor for the AFI volume *Within Our Gates: Ethnicity in American Feature Films, 1911-1960*. Gevinson has contributed numerous essays on aspects of film history to various reference works, including *The International Film Industry: A Historical Dictionary*, *The American Film Industry: A Historical Dictionary*, *Magill's Survey of Cinema: Foreign Language Films*, *The International Dictionary of Films and Filmmakers*, *International Film, Radio, and Television Journals*, *Prima dei codici 2. Alle porte di Hays* (Before Codes 2. The Gateway to Hays), and *Sulla via di Hollywood, 1911-1920* (The Path to Hollywood, 1911-1920). He was coeditor of *Meet Frank Capra: A Catalog of His Work* and additional author of the revised edition of *The Big V: A History of the Vitagraph Company*. Gevinson is a former employee of the Library of Congress Prints and Photographs Division and Motion Picture, Broadcasting, and Recorded Sound Division. A graduate af Kalamazoo College, he also attended New York University's Institute of Graduate Film and Television and received a master's degree in History at George Mason University.

12. Philip H. Cohen to Marshall, December 17, 1940, folder 2892, box 242, series 200R, RG 1.1, Rockefeller Foundation Archives, RAC.

13. MacLeish, *Archibald MacLeish*, p 107.

14. Archibald MacLeish, "The Affirmation," in *A Time to Speak: The Selected Prose of Archibald MacLeish* (Boston: Houghton Mifflin, 1941), p. 14; quoted in Allan M. Winkler, *The Politics of Propaganda: The Office of War Information, 1942-1945* (New Haven: Yale University Press 1978), p. 11; Archibald MacLeish, "Look to the Spirit Within You," *The Reader's Digest* (February 1941): 21; quoted in Winkler, p. 12.

15. Waldo Frank, *The Re-Discovery of America: An Introduction to a Philosophy of American Life* (New York: Charles Scribner's Sons, 1929), pp. 57, 64-65; quoted in Robert L. Dorman, *Revolt of the Provinces: The Regionalist Movement in America, 1920-1945* (Chapel Hill: University of North Carolina Press, 1993), p. 85; Lewis Mumford, *The Golden Day:A Study in American Experience and Culture* (New York: Boni and Liveright, 1926); quoted in Dorman, pp. 6, 8-9.

16. Archibald MacLeish, *The Fall of the City*, in *Radio's Best Plays* (New York: Greenberg, 1947), p. 30.

17. Archibald MacLeish, *The Fall of the City*, in *Radio's Best Plays*, p. 7.

18. MacLeish to Marshall, September 22, 1941; Marshall to John Grierson, July 15, 1941; Marshall to MacLeish September 24, 1941, folder 2893, box 242, series 200R, RG 1.1, Rockefeller Foundation Archives, RAC.

19. Alfred Kazin, *On Native Grounds: An Interpretation of Modern American Prose* (New York: Harcourt, Brace & World, Inc., 1942), pp. 486, 503, 504.

20. Harvey Swados, ed., *The American Writer and the Great Depression* (Indianapolis: The Bobbs-Merrill Company, Inc., 1966), p. xiv.

21. Marshall to Grierson, July 15, 1941, folder 2893, box 242, series 200R, RG 1.1, Rockefeller Foundation Archive, RAC.

22. MacLeish to Marshall, September 22, 1941, folder 2893, box 242, series 200R, RG 1.1, Rockefeller Foundation Archives, RAC.

RADIO IN WORLD WAR II

■ Edward R. Murrow (left) was the CBS European Director during World War II, and his nightly live radio broadcasts from London described the blitz as German bombs rained down on the English capital. Shirer (right) was hired by Murrow to broadcast from Berlin for CBS in the early part of the war when America was still neutral.

1939 TO 1945

NEWS AND ENTERTAINMENT

BY
PETER T. ROHRBACH

During the 1930s the home radio had become a major part of the American culture, so that by the end of the decade there were sixty million sets in use at a time when the total population of the country was about one hundred and thirty million people. The radio offered home entertainment to American families which gathered in living rooms across the country to listen to programs which featured music, comedy and drama, with occasional live broadcasts of important news stories such as the Bruno Hauptmann trial in the Lindbergh baby killing, the explosion of the Hindenburg zeppelin, and the demagogic speeches by Adolf Hitler frcm Germany.

But in 1939 radio was to enter a new epoch with the outbreak of World War II. It became the medium which communicated directly to American homes what British historian John Keegan called "the largest single event in human history." Unlike World War I twenty years earlier, which was conveyed to the American people by cable and print, this war was fed immediately into American homes. It has been called "war in the living room." But in addition to this extensive war reportage, radio continued its extensive entertainment programs which helped sustain morale and provide diversion in that somber time when some 16 million men and women would be called to serve in the mili-

tary, many of them shipped overseas where they lost their lives in combat.

World War II broke out on September 3, 1939, and that became the biggest news day in the history of radio. Wthin the eighteen hours between 6 a.m. and midnight listeners heard live transmissions of several historical events:

> The declarations of war issued by the British and French governments.
>
> An address to the British empire by King George VI of England.
>
> A speech by British Prime minister Neville Chamberlain.
>
> A speech by President Roosevelt,

It would be twenty-seven months between the outbreak of World War II and the United States entry into it, but the American people during that interim period were kept vividly aware of the conflict in Europe via live broadcasting from overseas. These were direct on-the-spot news broadcasts without any significant commentary, just factual reporting.

The premier radio foreign correspondent of World War II was Edward R. Murrow, a former speech major from Washington State College, who had been sent to Europe in the 1930s by the National Student Federation of America to organize student conferences for exchange students. CBS then hired him as a European Director, a job which involved little more than being a booking agent for cultural European events which could be transmitted back to the United States, such as operas and the Viennese choir and folk music from Scotland. But as war became imminent the network instructed him to set up a team of news correspomdents which would broadcast direct live reports back to America on the historic events which were transpiring in Europe. The team he assembled was called "Murrow's boys," and they became legendary in broadcast journalism. They included a group of extremely talented young men: William Shirer, Howard K. Smith, Winston Burdett, Charles Collingwood, Larry Lesueur, Gene Ryder, Charles Shaw, Richard C. Hottelet, and Eric Sevareid.

Murrow himself broadcast from London each evening beginning his report in his sonorous voice with his signature introduction: "This . . . is London." CBS demanded at that time that all coverage of events in the war be live. which was an amoyance to Murrow because he thought there were things happening where he did not have the time or facilities to set up a live transmission and he would have liked to record it and broadcast it later. But CBS executives in New York insisted on live transmissions, which actually made for some astonishing broadcasts. For instance during the blitz when German bombers rained explosives on London, Murrow would broadcast from a rooftop with the sounds of exploding bombs from German aircraft and British antiaircraft fire in the background. He would broadcast about midnight London time and with the five-hour time difference these live broadcasts of aerial bombardments came on the air about seven o'clock in the evening in the U.S. Eastern Time Zone. They were riveting broadcasts, certainly war in the living room.

Although CBS was first in assembling a team of radio war correspondents, NBC soon put together a fine group of reporters to cover the tragic events of the six years of World War II. The NBC team included: Francis McCall, Wright Bryan, David Anderson, Tom Traynor, and W. W. Chaplin.

One of the most outstanding news broadcasts in the whole history of broadcast journalism occurred on June 22, 1940, the day France signed its surrender to Germany, following the breathtaking German blitzkreig through the Lowlands and France. The Germans demanded that the French sign the surrender at Compiègne, about twenty-five miles north of Paris, using the railroad car which was on display there and which was the railroad car the French had used to exact the German surrender in 1918. There were no journalists allowed inside the railroad car while German officers laid down the harsh terms of surrender to French officers, but William Shirer of CBS was outside in a clearing in the woods observing the proceedings. Murrow had recruited Shirer, a former young European correspondent for the *Chicago Tribune*, to be the CBS correspondent in Berlin where he made nightly broadcasts at that time when America was still neutral. (Shirer would later recount his experiences as a radio correspondent in Berlin in his best-selling book *Berlin Dairy*.)

Shirer had left Berlin to follow the German troops in

■ William Shirer in a clearing in the woods at Compiègne in France on June 22, 1940. As a CBS correspondent he had followed the German troops in their blitzkrieg through the Lowlands and France. At Compiègne the Germans were exacting the terms of surrender from French officials in a railroad car, the same one in which the Germans had surrendered in 1918. In this picture Shirer is sitting outside the car listening to the proceedings inside the car over a loudspeaker the Gemans had set up. (He spoke fluent French and German.) He is listening and making notes, and later in the day he made an historic radio broadcast back to the United States. He scooped the world with the details of the surrender.

their rapid advance through France and now at Compiègne he was a witness at the final act in the fall of France. He had another advantage: he spoke fluent German from his years in Berlin and fluent French from earlier years in Paris. That day in the clearing outside the railroad car he was able to listen to what was going on inside the car over a loudspeaker the Germans had set up. He took notes of the terms of surrender, and then dashed back to Paris to broadcast the story over a CBS and NBC feed he had arranged. He scooped the world, and this historic broadcast was indicative of what was happening in mass communications: electronic media—first radio, then television—would deliver the news more quickly and more directly than the traditional print journalisim. The world of communications had changed radically.

While those foreign radio correspondents were able to report factually what they saw during those first twenty-seven months of the war, the news commentators at home found themselves in a delicate position. The mood of the nation at large was still one of isolation with no wish to send American soldiers abroad as had been done in 1917 which resulted in the fierce and deadly trench warfare in France. What the network executives wanted from their radio broadcasters was a posture of neutrality. This was difficult for perspicacious people like the noted CBS news commentator

H. V. Kaltenborn, whose anti-Fascist commentaries on the news were stifled by the network. The executives told him to assess the facts but offer no opinions, and they began calling him a news analyst. Kaltenborn then moved over to NBC, but he found the same restrictions there.

Kaltenborn was a deliberate, thoughtful commentator, but Walter Winchell was another case entirely. Winchell was a jingoistic journalist and gossip columnist for the *New York Daily Mirror* who had a Sunday night radio program on NBC which aired at nine o'clock Eastern Time. His radio program of commentary, opinion, and gossip reached an audience of some twenty million people, making him America's most influential journalist. His opening salutation as he came on the air in his staccato, breathless delivery was: "Good evening Mr. and Mrs. North America and all the ships at sea." He was an ardent anti-Fascist and he missed no opportunity to lash out against this evil in his own tabloid style. He called Fritz Kuhn, head of the American Nazi Bund, a "ratzi." He referred to Hitler's foreign minister Joachim von Ribbentrop as "von Ribbentripe." And he called Hitler a "madman." That last remark was too much for NBC programming manager John Royal who sent a memo to Niles Trammell, NBC president, saying that Winchell "has been gradually going off the deep end, and going quite controversial on international affairs, under the guise of speaking on Americanism." Extant NBC memos from the period show that NBC executives seriously considered taking Winchell off the air, but in the end they concluded he was too powerful with too large an audience to touch, and they had to endure him.

But not for long. The whole question of neutrality came to an abrupt end, of course, on December 7, 1941. That Sunday afternoon regular broadcasting was interrupted by news reports of the shocking attack by Japanese aircraft of the American fleet docked at Pearl Harbor. For the next three and a half years American radio went to war.

The next day, December 8, radio carried President Roosevelt's thirteen-minute stirring address to a joint session of Congress asking that a state of war be declared. He said, in that immortal phrase: "Yesterday, December 7, 1941—a date which will live in infamy."

The following evening, December 9, Roosevelt went on the airwaves, speaking to the American people in one of his "Fireside Chats." He gave twenty-eight of these Fireside Chats over the radio during his time as president, and these radio addresses, usually about thirty minutes and given in prime time evening broadcasting, became an important part of his presidency. He had a staff of writers work on these addresses, but the final version was his and most important of all the tone was his. The language was clear and simple and direct, and Roosevelt in his resonant voice was taking the American people into his confidence. He had an enormous audience, and he opened each Fireside Chat by addressing his listeners either "My Friends," or "My Fellow Americans." And often during the talk he would mention some position held by the bankers or politicians and the businessmen and then say to his 'audience: "But *you* and *I* know." He was talking as a friend. These radio talks provided reassurance and courage and unity for the American people during difficult years. He gave his first Fireside on

■ **President Franklin D. Roosevelt delivering one of his Fireside Chats from the first floor of the White House. He did eleven of these Fireside Chats during the war, and they were an important factor in unifying the nation and assuring the people of the ultimate Allied victory.**

March 12, 1933, just a week after his inauguration, and he spoke about the crisis of the failing banks and how he was going to resolve it as a first step out of the Depression. He ended his address by saying: "Together we cannot fail."

The Fireside Chat of December 9, 1941, was the first of eleven he was to give throughout, the war, he told the American people: "We are going to win the war and we are going to win the peace that follows." The wartime Fireside Chats were given at critical times during the war and they created national unity and confidence in the outcome. On February 23, 1942, he gave a Chat during the darkest days of the war for the United States, a time when the Japanese were achieving victory after victory in the Pacific. He said: "We must keep on striking our enemies wherever and whenever we can meet them. Never before have we we been called on for such a prodigious effort. Never before have we had so little time in which to do so much." Then on July 28, 1943, when the tide of war had changed in the Allies' favor, he said in a confident Chat: "The massed angered forces of common humanity are on the march. The first crack in the Axis has come. The criminal, corrupt Fascist regime in Italy is going to pieces." On June 5, 1944, he gave an exultant Chat on the fall of Rome: "The first of the Axis capitals is now in our hands. One up and two to go." The following day, D-day, he gave an eight-minute radio address which was not a Chat but rather a reading of a prayer composed for that memorable day in history, saying in part: "Give us faith in Thee; faith in our sons; faith in each other; faith in our united crusade."

During the three and a half years of Americans, involvement in World War II news of the war dominated the airwaves, but there were also major entertainment programs being aired. Some of the principal radio programs during the war years were: *Fibber McGee and Molly, Eddie Cantor, Rudy Vallee Variety Program, Amos and Andy, Abbott and Costello Program, Red Skelton Program, Truth or Consequences, National Barn Dance, Your Hit Parade, Metropolitan Opera*, and *Information Please*.

In addition to these variety programs, there were specific wartime programs, such as *The Man Behind the Gun*, which dramatized the battles of the war; and *Stage Door Canteen*, an all-star review for servicemen hosted by Bette Davis and other personalities. But the war also infiltrated the variety programs themselves. Bing Crosby, host of the *Kraft Music Hall*, urged his audience to buy war bonds in order to "clip the Nips." And programs as diverse as *Lum and Abner* and the *Quiz Kids* made intense pitches about buying war bonds to support the American troops fighting overseas. Mary Margaret McBride was the preeminent talk show hostess of the time, and with her warm and friendly voice she drew immense audiences for her daily afternoon show. Each Wednesday her show was dedicated exclusively to the war, and she would interview generals, discuss rationing, offer meatless recipes, and talk about the war on the home front.

The war even influenced children's programing, those dramatic serials which were presented each afternoon between the end of school and dinner. For instance, there was the children's program *Don Winslow of the Navy*, which featured a Navy pilot who bombed enemy ships and professed his hatred of the Japanese. *Hop Harrigan* was about "America's Ace of the Airways" in Europe, an aviator who flew bombing runs, had dogfights with enemy planes, and rescued his wounded pal while dodging German bullets.

Before America's entry into the war, the problem for the networks was the isolationist mood of the nation, but after Pearl Harbor a new problem surfaced: censorship. Just a few weeks into the war the federal government issued its Code of Wartime Practices for American Broadcasters, asking for voluntary censorship of programs which would remove references to the weather, fortifications, troop or materiel movements, casualty lists, and anything which might provide information helpful to internal spies and saboteurs or external military or naval commanders.

Of particlar concern to the American military was broadcast weather information. Throughout the war, particularly in the early years, there was great fear of Japanese bombing on the West Coast and German bombing on the East Coast. Following the example of the British during the bombing of London, all weather reports and forecasts were removed from the air. This was particularly difficult in describing scheduled sporting events. One baseball announcer had a hard time of breaking his longtime habit of beginning a game by saying: "It's a beautiful day at the ball park." And the engineer had to cut him off when he started to make that statement. When a game was cancelled because of inclement weather all the announcer could say was that the game would not be played that day. Even more awkward was the situation of a game in progress which had to be halted because of a sudden rainstom and all the announcer could say, was that they were going to stop playing for a while.

Despite these inconveniences, American broadcasters behaved admirably during the war. With patriotism and intelligence they carefully removed from the airways items which would could help the enemy and there was no conflict with the government. Raymond Gran Swing, one of the major radio commentators of the time, wrote in his memoirs about his wartime experience:

> During World War II, none of my broadcasts was censored, though at the Blue network they were read prior to delivery by someone on the staff . . . I find it not only unobjectionable, but proper.

Early in 1942 the government developed the Armed Forces Radio Service, an operation which used both transcription discs and shortwave to deliver radio progams to service personnel around the world. Some of these programs were original productions of the AFRS and others were commercial broadcasts with the advertising removed.

By 1945, when the operation was in full gear, they were shipping 83,000 discs a month from the States to AFRS transmitters around the world. Each week they would deliver forty three programs, comprising fourteen hours of material produced by AFRS and thirty-six hours of commercial programs. The programs included dance music, comedy, sports, news, variety programs, classical music, and daytime serials.

On June 13, 1942, President Roosevelt created by Executive Order the Office of War Information, modeling it on the British Mnistry of Infomation. He appointed as its Director Elmer Davis, a veteran journalist and CBS broadcaster who set up offices in the Social Security Building near the Capitol in Washington. There were two branches of the OWI: the Domestic operations Branch, and the Overseas Operations Branch.

The Domestic Branch was the coordinating agency for wartime news and information, and it disseminated all official news and announcements pertaining to the war. The Overseas Branch was a propaganda operation, which engaged in psychological warfare by transmitting thousands of radio broadcasts to enemy and occupied countries in Europe and the Far East. It created radio programs in all the European languages and many Far Eastern languages.

In the early years of the war the OWI broadcasts attempted to convince its listeners of the evils of Fascism, the benefits of democracy, and the Allies' unrelenting success in defeating the Axis powers. But after the surrender of Italy in September of 1943 the OWI in its broadcasts began to take an active role in the actual prosecution of the war. For instance, working with British intelligence they developed programs aimed at Hitler's Balkan allies, attemping to create dissensions and defections. The OWI broadcast radio programs which attempted to pressure rulers to get out of the war, or if that did not work they urged the people to over-

■ May of 1944. Some members of the CBS D-Day team gather on a London sidewalk waiting to follow the troops into France with the invasion. From left, Richard C. Hottelet, Gene Ryder, Bill Downs, Charles Collingwood, and Charles Shaw.

■ NBC war correspondents in France after the D-Day invasion. From left, Francis McCall, Wright Bryan, David Anderson, Tom Traynor, and W. W. Chaplin. American war correspondents wore U. S. Army uniforms with no insignia of rank.

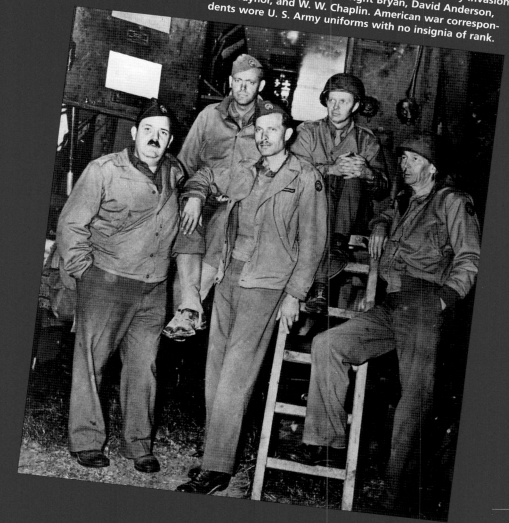

■ Radio continued to cover major news events on the home front during the war. Here on February 9, 1942, NBC reporters were on the scene of a New York City pier when the French ocean liner *Normandie* burned and capsized while in port. Sabotage by Axis agents was suspected, but this strange event remains a mystery to this day.

■ Radio also reported on domestic politics on the home front during the war. Here NBC correspondent Richard Harkness broadcasts from the floor of the Democratic National Convention in Chicago in July of 1944. It was at this convention that Franklin Roosevelt was nominated for an unprecedented fourth term.

throw the government. This Balkan operation worked, creating unrest and forcing Hitler to keep troops there which could otherwise have been used on the eastern and western fronts.

During the war the OWI carried out a massive program of broadcasting information and propaganda in both Europe and the Pacific. But on August 31, 1945, just after the actual Japanese surrender which ended the war the OWI was terminated. The Domestic Branch was completely dismantled, but the Overseas Branch was transferred into the State Department which continued its activities during the Cold War. It went through a number of mutations at the State Department until it finally became the Voice of America in 1953. The Axis powers also created radio broadcasts aimed at Allied Servicemen and civilians. The major broadcast personalities in this Axis propaganda operation were Lord Haw Haw and Axis Sally in Berlin, and Tokyo Rose from Japan.

Lord Haw Haw was William Joyce, an Irish national who lived in England during the 1930s and became part of the strong English Nazi movement. In the late thirties he departed for Germany and became the main English-speaking radio propagandist for the Third Reich. He came on the radio in his high-pitched voice and Irish brogue saying: "Germany calling." He spoke of the superiority of the Third Reich, the failure of the British government, and the inevitability of a Geman victory, all mixed with a strong dose of anti-Semitism. During the first nine months of the war—the so called "phony war"—when there was no real military activity, the British people found him mildly amusing. But when the real war started in May of 1940 with the fall of France and the evacuation at Dunkirk and the bombing of London the English no longer found Lord Haw Haw amusing, and they were determined to get him after the war, which they did. Following the German surrender in 1945 he was captured by English soldiers while he was on the run. He was taken back to London and tried as a traitor. He claimed that he was an Irish national, but the case against him was that he had traveled to Germany on an English passport therefore placing himself under the jurisdiction of the king. That made him a traitor, and he was executed in early 1946.

Axis Sally, who also broadcast from Berlin during the war, was an American citizen named Mildred Gillars who directed her radio programs mainly to the American troops. She was born in Portland, Maine, in 1901. A dropout from Ohio Wesleyan University, she went to Germany as a music student in the 1920s, and she became an enthusiast for the Nazi regime in the 1930s. During the war she broadcast programs to the American troops which urged them "to go home and forget the war." She talked about the wonderful spirit of friendship between the Germans and the Americans at the 1936 Berlin Olympics, and then blamed the outbreak of the war on the "Jewish pestilence" which set Americans against Germans. She spoke in a flat, uninteresting voice, but she played large amounts of American jazz, and thus she had a large audience among American servicemen who paid no attention to her propaganda but who liked the music. Nevertheless, she was captured by the Allies after the German surrender, tried as an American cit-

izen for treason, and sentenced to twelve years in a federal prison.

Tokyo Rose broadcast radio propaganda from Japan to American troops in the Pacific during the war. Actually, Tokyo Rose (a name given to her by the American troops) was not an individual, but a team of different women put together by the Japanese Ministry of Propaganda; they spoke good English, and they included Japanese women, Filipinos. and at least one Japanese-American. Tokyo Rose spoke in a soft, sensuous voice, and she came on the air soon after the American entrance into the war in the Pacific. She taunted the troops at Corregidor, telling them that they were being abandoned by the American goverment and that General MacArthur would soon be paraded through the streets of Tokyo. Like her counterpart in Berlin, she urged the American troops to go home, telling them that their wives and girlfriends were being dated by draft dodgers. She promised a Japanese victory and even reported Japanese military accomplishments which were pure fiction. But she, too, played a great amount of American dance music, and she was also able to attract a large audience of American servicemen in the Pacific who enjoyed the music and laughed at the propaganda. In 1945, after the Japanese surrender and occupation, the Japanese-American Tokyo Rose was captured. She was Iva Toguri Ikoku, who was born of Japanese parents in California in 1915. She later returned with them to Japan, and she joined the team of propagandists in 1942 which broadcast radio programs to the American troops. Because she was an American citizen, she was tried for treason, convicted, and sentenced to ten years in a federal prison.

By the beginning of 1945 the Allied victory in the war seemed assured, despite the fact that in the closing weeks of 1944 the Germans had launched their last great counterattack of the war in the Ardennes in Belgium. But the Allies withstood the assault and continued their march into Germany. On January 6, 1945, the president went on the radio to give a Fireside Chat which would reassure the American people once again, as he had done throughout the war, that victory would be ours. No one realized it at the time, but it would be the last Fireside Chat of his life. "The high tide of the German attack," he said, "was reached two days after Christmas. Since then we have resumed the offensive, we have rescued the isolated garrison at Bastogne, and forced a German withdrawal along most of the line of the salient." Then he went on to express his hopes for that new year: "This new year of 1945 can be the greatest year of achievement in human history. . . .We Americans of today, together with our allies, are making history—and I hope it will be a better history than ever has been made before."

Ninety days later President Roosevelt died suddenly of a massive brain hemorrhage, and four days after that, on April 16, radio carried Harry S. Truman's address to Congress in his first official appearance before that body. "With great humility," he said, "I call upon all Americans to help me keep our nation united in defense of those ideals which have been so eloquently proclaimed by Franklin Roosevelt."

After that, the end came quickly. Germany surrendered on May 7, and Japan surrendered on August 14. However, the official Japanese surrender ceremony was on September

2 aboard a U.S. battleship in Tokyo Bay. After the surrender President Truman went on the radio to address the American people. He said: "The thoughts and hopes of all America—indeed of all the civilized world—are centered tonight on the battleship *Missouri*. There on that small piece of American soil anchored in Tokyo Harbor the Japanese have just officially laid down their arms." That was the last official radio broadcast of World II.

That six-year ordeal had cost the lives of 50 million people, 290,000 of them Americans. And radio had played a vital role in America during that tragedy: it had supplied vital infomation, it had bolstered morale and provided reassurance, and it had united the country as never before—and perhaps never again.

RECORDINGS OF WORLD WAR II RADIO BROADCASTS IN THE LIBRARY OF CONGRESS

The Recorded Sound Reference Center in the Library of Congress Motion Picture, Broadcasting and Recorded Sound Division houses the largest collection of its kind in the world—over two million items of sound recordings and radio broadcasts. Included in this collection is a rich treasure of recordings of radio broadcasts during World War II. Here are some of those many World War II radio broadcasts held by the Library:

■ The National Broadcasting Company Radio Collection contains the single largest group of World War II material, some 8,000 hours of war-related radio broadcasts, including news programs, commentaries, and presidential addresses, The collection. which is recorded on instantaneous discs, also contains the popular NBC entertainment programs of the war years.

■ The Armed Forces Radio and Television Service Collection contains the AFRS radio programs broadcast to U.S. armed forces personnel beginning in 1942. The broadcast programming includes both original AFRS programs and network commercial broadcasts. These are on 16-inch and 12-inch discs.

■ The Office of War Information Collection contains about 100,000 acetate discs of the propaganda broadcasts of the OWI from 1942 to 1945. There is material in all languages of Western Eurpe and some of the Far East.

■ The British Broadcasting Corporation Sound Archive Collection contains LP discs of the BBC's most significant broadcasts. including those of World War II.

■ The Raymond Swing Collection contains several hundred radio news commentaries made during the war by one of the most influential. radio newsmen of the time. These broadcasts were first on the Mutual Broadcasting System and beginning in 1942 on the NBC-blue network (later the American Broadcasting Company).

■ There are in the Reference Center radio broadcast recordings of all the major figures of World War II. Included are the Fireside Chats of President Roosevelt; the important radio speeches of Winston Churchill, among which is his "we shall never surrender" speech during the Battle of Britain in 1940; the radio messages of Charles de Gaulle from London to the people of occupied France, telling them that their liberation would come; and the radio speeches of the German leaders, such as Hitler, Goebbels, and Goering,

■ Radio broadcasts of Edward R. Murrow from London during the blitz; and of William Shirer reporting from Berlin. The collection also includes Shirer's historic broadcast of June 22, 1940, reporting on the French surrender at Compiègne.

■ The Reference Center has recordings of the radio broadcasts from 1935 to 1955 of Mary Margaret McBride, the most popular talk show hostess of her time. Included are her wartime broadcasts, particularly her Wednesday program which she devoted to the war on the home front.

■ Recordings of the English-speaking propagandists broadcasting for Germany from Berlin: Lord Haw Haw (William Joyce) and Axis Sally (Mildred Gillars).

■ There is an extremely helpful fnding aid available in the Reference Center titled "A Selected Descripticn and Finding Aid to Recordings on World War II in the Library of Congress." This unpublished 89 page monograph was compiled by Cooper C. Graham, and it is a catalog of World War II recordings in the Reference Center including radio broadcasts. It is indexed. And there are other finding aids, such as the OWI Collection which includes shelf lists for foreign-language broadcasts and a microcomputer-based data base of the English-language recordings. But the most valuable research aid in the Reference Center is the presence of the reference librarians, competent and knowledgeable people who are ready to provide assistance.

The Manuscript Division of the Library of Congress also contains material about World War II radio broadcasts, such as:

■ The CBS radio scripts of Eric Sevareid from Europe early in the war, and then from the Far East later in the war.

■ The wartime radio scripts of Raymond Gram Swing, first for the Mutual Broadcasting System and then for the NBC-blue network.

■ Hundreds of scripts for World War II radio broadcasts by Walter Winchell on NBC. The Division also has a series of internal NBC memos which express concern about Winchell when he called Hitler a "madman" on the air when the U. S. was still neutral during the early part of the war.

The photographs are from the collections of the Library's Motion Picture, Broadcasting, and Recorded Sound Division.

PETER T. ROHRBACH is a freelance writer and editor residing in the Washington, D.C. area. He is the author of over sixteen books published in

WGAN-Saturday Night Serenade
WGY-Dinner Dance
WHAM-Hank & Herb
WHDH-Alec Templeton Time; Musical Concert
WJAR-Supper Show
WMCA-Sports
WMEX-Popular Music
WNAC-Musical Roundup
WNBC-Pappy Howard's Wagon Trail

WTRY CFCF WORC
CBS-Report to the Nation:
WABC WOKO WGAN WTAG
WABI WDRC WEEI WBRY
WPRO WLAW
MBS-American Eagle Club:
WATR WNBH WNLC WSAR
WEAN WNAC
NBC-The Day of Reckoning:
WEAF WTIC WCSH WFEA
WJAR WLBZ WHAM WGY
WBZ

CBC-Songs at Eventide: CBL
CBO CHSJ CBA CFNB CBM
CBF
CFCF-Studio Prgm.
WCSH-To be announced
WHAM-Lone Ranger
WHN-Adrienne Ames
WJAR-Eyes & Ears of the Air Force
WMCA-News
WMEX-Vocal Spotlight
WNBH-Singing Troubador

WHN-Word of Life Hour
WLAW-Advent Christian Church
★WMCA-News; Dance Party
WMEX-Musicale
WNEW-The Magic of Music
WOKO-Eyes & Ears of Air Force
WORC-Masterworks of Music
WQXR-Symphony Hall
WSAR-Dance Music
WTHT-Musicl Polish Prgm.

SATURDAY'S BEST LISTENING

See program listings for more detail and additional news programs

News and Discussion

P.M.
4:00 Elmer Davis Comments on the War, MBS
5:45 Alex Dreier, NBC
6:15 People's Platform, CBS
Lyman Bryson, moderator
7:00 Report to the Nation, CBS
8:00 Roy Porter, BN
8:30 Upton Close, MBS
9:15 Edward Tomlinson, BN
10:00 John B. Hughes, BN
10:00 News Analysis, BN
April 3 and 17, John Gunther; April 10 and 24, John W. Vandercook

Variety

A.M.
9:00 Breakfast Club, BN
Don McNeill, m.c.
P.M.
6:30 Hawaii Calls, MBS
7:30 Thanks to the Yanks, CBS
Bob Hawk, m.c.
8:00 Frank Crumit and Julia Sanderson, CBS
8:30 Truth or Consequences, NBC
Ralph Edwards, m.c.

8:30 Hobby Lobby, CBS
Dave Elman, m.c.
9:00 Alka-Seltzer Nat'l Barn Dance, NBC
Joe Kelly; Eddie Peabody; Pat Buttram; Hoosier Hot Shots; Lulu Belle & Scotty
9:00 Your Hit Parade, CBS
Frank Sinatra; Joan Edwards; Ethel Smith; Mark Warnow's Orchestra
9:30 Victory Parade of Spotlight Bands, BN
10:00 Bill Stern's Colgate Sports Newsreel, NBC
10:15 Bond Wagon, MBS
10:15 Campana Serenade, NBC
Dick Powell; Music Maids; Matty Malneck's Orchestra
10:15 Blue Ribbon Town, CBS
Groucho Marx; Virginia O'Brien; Donald Dickson; Robert Armbruster's Orchestra

Drama

A.M.
11:30 Little Blue Playhouse, BN
P.M.
12:00 Theater of Today, CBS
12:30 Stars Over Hollywood, CBS
5:00 Doctors at War, NBC
7:00 The Strange Stories of Dr. Karnac, BN
7:00 The Day of Reckoning, NBC
7:30 Ellery Queen, NBC
8:00 Abie's Irish Rose, NBC
Mercedes McCambridge; Richard Coogan; Alan Reed; Walter Kinsella

Classical Music

P.M.
2:00 Metropolitan Opera, BN
Three April broadcasts are scheduled for the Metropolitan Opera, April 3, 10 and 17
5:00 Cleveland Orchestra, CBS
Arthur Rodzinski, conductor
8:15 Boston Symphony Orchestra, BN
On April 3 a Gilbert and Sullivan operetta, starring Wilbur Evans, baritone, will be presented at this time
9:00 Chicago Theater of the Air, MBS
Marion Claire; Symphony Orchestra
9:45 Saturday Night Serenade, CBS
Jessica Dragonette, soprano; Bill Perry, tenor; The Serenaders; Gustave Haenschen's Orchestra

8:15 P.M.

BN-Boston Symphony Orchestra; Serge Koussevitzky, cond.: WJZ CBF WMFF WTRY CFCF WNBC WELI WORC WHDH
On April 3, while the Boston Symphony Orchestra is on tour, a Gilbert and Sullivan operetta, starring Wilbur Evans, baritone, will be heard at this time.
WGAN-Dance Jamboree
WHAM-American Destiny
WMEX-Popular Music
WNEW-Popular Music
WOKO-Lest We Forget
WSAR-The Latin Quarter

8:30 P.M.

★MBS-Upton Close, news: WATR WNBH WNLC WSAR WTHT WEAN WOR WNAC
★CBS-Hobby Lobby; Dave Elman, m.c.; Eric Sevareid, news: WABC WOKO WGAN WPRO WLAW WTAG
BN-Boston Symphony Orch.: WJZ WTRY CFCF WORC
NBC-Truth or Consequences; Ralph Edwards, m.c.: WEAF WTIC WCSH WTAG WHAM WGY WBZ WLBZ WFEA
CBC-Share the Wealth: CBA CBL CBO CBM CHSJ CFNB
★WABI-Waltz Time; News
WBRY-Lest We Forget
WCAX-Sports
WHN-Final Rewrite
★WMCA-News; Ralph Cooper
WMEX-Uncle Bill's Common Sense Advice
★WNEW-News

8:45 P.M.

MBS-To be announced: WATR WNBH WNLC WSAR WTHT WEAN WOR WNAC
★WABI-The Marines March; Eric Sevareid
★WBRY-Your Army Reporter; Eric Sevareid, news
★WCAX-Music; Eric Sevareid
★WHN-News

9:00 P.M.

NBC-Alka-Seltzer National Barn Dance; Joe Kelly; Eddie Peabody; Pat Buttram; Hoosier Hot Shots; Lulu Belle & Scotty; Dinning Sisters: WEAF WTIC WGY WCSH WFEA WJAR WBZ WHAM WORC
See sponsor's announcement on this page.
MBS-Chicago Theater of the Air; Marion Claire; Symph. Orch.: WATR WNBH WNLC WNAC WSAR WTHT WOR WEAN
★CBC-News; Hockey Game: CBA CBL CBO CBM CFNB CHSJ CBF
CBS-Your Hit Parade; Frank Sinatra; Ethel Smith; Martin Bloch; Joan Edwards; Mark Warnow's Orch.: WABC WOKO WCAX WABI WEEI WBRY WDRC WGAN WPRO WLAW WTAG
BN-Boston Symphony Orch.: WJZ WLBZ WTRY

party Tonight
A HALF HOUR OF FUN AND ENTERTAINMENT
The Alka-Seltzer
NATIONAL BARN DANCE
SPONSORED BY ALKA-SELTZER AND ONE-A-DAY (brand) VITAMIN TABLETS
WEAF WBZ WTIC WJAR
WGY WCSH WFEA
9:00 P.M. EWT

the United States and abroad. Some of his notable works on history include *Journey to Carith* (Doubleday); *American Issue* (Smithsonian Institution Press); *National Issue*, a sequel to *American Issue*, which was serialized in *Meekel's* magazine before the publication of the book; and *Stagecoach East* (Smithsonian Institution Press) a work on nineteenth-century American history, written in collaboration with Oliver W. Holmes. And for the Library he has written a few publications, the most recent being *The Largest Event: A Library of Congress Resource Guide for the Study of World War II*.

His many articles have been published in *Time-Life*, the *Washington Star*, *America*, *Aviation News*, and the *AIA Journal*, as well as the *Youth Encyclopedia* and the *New Catholic Encyclopedia* (McGraw-Hill).

Mr. Rohrbach's writing credits also include television and motion picture scripts for both commercial and public productions, such as the nationally syndicated television show *Wally's Workshop* and PBS's series on aging. He is a member of the Authors Guild of America and PEN, the international association of writers.

Television

From **Omnibus**

■ *Omnibus* and its host, Alistair Cooke, were dedicated to the proposition that culture and the mass American television audience are compatible. Cooke is shown here in 1956, as *Omnibus* began its fifth season. *New York World-Telegram & Sun Collection, Prints and Photographs Division.*

to NET

BY **DONALD KENT**

Are "high" culture and television incompatible? Some of America's most creative performing artists grappled with this question in the 1950s—the years that are often called the Golden Age of Television. But those years were also the adolescent stage of cultural television—full of hope, experimentation, invention, and learning. Some of the brightest lights on the American cultural firmament were searching for new and livelier ways to open up the world of opera, ballet, and theater to tens of millions of viewers who had never had the opportunity or inclination to see and hear such

In this 1953 *Omnibus* dramatization of the Hemingway short story "The Battler," the author was preoccupied with loneliness, especially with the loneliness of inarticulate people. He put his lonely punch-drunk boxer in a desolate setting that could be anywhere from the Great Lakes to the Gulf of Mexico.

things before. Commercial sponsors and foundations had to be sold on the value of sponsoring the high cost of arts programming on commercial networks in the years when National Educational Television was in its infancy and PBS was more than a decade away.

In fact, the well-remembered TV cultural program *Omnibus* was created to prove, in some sense, that culture and mass audiences not only could live together but could

actually thrive together. The Ford Foundation's Television-Radio Workshop provided start-up funds for *Omnibus* in 1951 and some financial support during its nine-and-a-half-year run. But commercial sponsors provided about three-quarters of the funds needed to keep *Omnibus* on the air, something of a triumph in light of later corporate sponsorship experiences.

Unabashed audience-building efforts were an important ingredient of many *Omnibus* shows; the more rarified the art form, the stronger the pitch, in many cases. For example, Agnes de Mille stated, "When I started dancing, the art of choreography was known to only a few, and those were probably Europeans." The year was 1956, and de Mille was introducing her *Omnibus* television program "The Art of Choreography," which can be viewed on videotape in the Motion Picture, Broadcasting, and Recorded Sound Division (MBRS) of the Library of Congress. Millions of American viewers sitting in front of their small screens in their living rooms were potential consumers of this little-known art.

It is questionable whether many of de Mille's viewers had ever seen dancers like those she was about to present—warriors, bagpipers, Watusis, dancers from the Royal Siamese Ballet and the Imperial Russian Ballet, and finally her own choreographic creation, *Rodeo*. It is possible that many viewers thought of all this as too strange, decadent, or obsolete. She played into that notion, attacked it head on, capitalized on it.

"The general American public was not even aware that dances had to be planned," de Mille uttered with a slight frown, her eyes focused inward toward those begone times. "They saw it as frivolous entertainment, suitable for women and children. The businessman, when dragged to a performance, prayed only that it would be brief, that the girls would be pretty and the boys not too silly." De Mille gave her audience encouragement, a vigorous pat on the back: "It has taken a long time for dancing to be taken on a par with the other fine arts . . . Dance grows out of living experience in hunting and fighting, in fertility and the worship of God, in the celebration of great joy and profound grief."

"These are war dances, this is a fighter from the Congo," de Mille proclaimed as the warrior's spear casts a long shadow on the wall behind her.

> He is working up steam to invoke power and protection. He has great need of courage because he is going to face his enemies naked . . . He seeks magic help from the air, from the earth . . .
>
> The true meaning of dancing and its only pure meaning is the expression of human feeling. It is not a useful nor a [de Mille cannot find the word]—it's an expressive gesture, special, patterned, stylized and rhythmic. Its purpose is to move people deeply, and in order to do this it must summon up—[the prompter's voice supplies the word *meaning*] meaning and power. In other words it is art, or as primitives would say, it is magic. But true magic is not chosen at random. It grows out of living experience. The idiom used is characteristic of the people who produced it. But the impulses behind it are basic and universal: success in hunting and fighting, in fertility and the worship of God, the celebration of great joy and profound grief.

It was a live production, as they almost all were in 1956,

■ Agnes de Mille hosted "The Art of Choreography," on *Omnibus,* in 1956.

"When I started dancing the art of choreography was known to only a few, and those were probably Europeans . . . The elements of dance are space, time, and human bodies. The choreographer or designer combines space, time, and human gesture into patterns . . . Dancing is a time-space art, and it is the only one."

■ "This girl [dancing flamenco] would never go to all that bother to suit herself. She is dependent on a paying audience, and she's getting it."

■ A dancer from the Royal Siamese Ballet appears in the foreground, and Imperial Russian Ballet dancers are seen in the background. "The kings and elite of Thailand no longer dance themselves, their proxies dance for them."

■ "This is a fighter from the Congo. He is working up steam to invoke power and protection . . . He seeks magic help from the air, from the earth."

■ Scenes from Agnes de Mille's ballet, *Rodeo.*

"This is the story of a little Texas cowgirl who was forbidden to ride with the men because she was always under foot, causing them a peck of trouble. But she persisted because she was so much in love with one of them. The cowgirl is played by Jenny Workman, and the champion roper by the man for whom the role was created, Frederick Franklin."

■ The bagpiper's "safety lies now in his quick eye, his supple wrists, and his delicate catlike feet."

■ Gene Kelly's television dancing debut in a 1958 *Omnibus* program, called "Dancing: A Man's Game," was heralded by this publicity photo. It has little to do with the *Omnibus* program, which is devoted to demonstrating macho ties between dance and sports, especially masculine spectator sports. Kelly performs sports maneuvers and dance steps with baseball player Mickey Mantle, boxer Sugar Ray Robinson, tennis star Vic Seixas, and other leading sportsmen in a blockbuster effort to destigmatize dance for male audiences. *New York World-Telegram & Sun Collection, Prints and Photographs Division.*

■ Gene Kelly with Sugar Ray Robinson in "Dancing: A Man's Game."

■ Gene Kelly and Alistair Cooke in the gymnasium where athletes and dancers are rehearsing for "Dancing: A Man's Game."

■ Gene Kelly with Mickey Mantle in "Dancing: A Man's Game."

which gave de Mille no chance to correct occasional flubs. Once or twice she relies on the voice of a human prompter off screen, which would also be heard by her audience nationwide. Those were pre-TelePrompTer days.

Gene Kelly made his first live performance on television in a now famous 1958 *Omnibus* show called "Dancing: A Man's Game." It also can be seen on videotape in MBRS. It is a scintillating television show, as engaging today as when Kelly made it. But it makes no secret of its mission of bringing mass audiences and culture together. In it, Kelly uses his great charm and persuasiveness to destigmatize the dance in the eyes of men, or change women's attitudes towards men who dance, demonstrating that dance is no less masculine than boxing, baseball, tennis, gymnastics, and fencing. In doing this he gets strong assists from Mickey Mantle, Sugar Ray Robinson, Bob Cousey, Vic Seixas, Johnny Unitas, and Vic Gnezzi.

From a balcony overlooking a gymnasium where dancers and sportsmen are warming up, Kelly intones:

> All these men, dancers and athletes alike, possess something very much in common: skill and physical movement. But more important than that, physical movement in rhythm. Just like the dancer, the athlete does not exist who doesn't move with a certain rhythm. His timing is based on the same elements as dancers'. There are just two differences: the athlete, after having trained his body to move rhythmically in whatever the demands of the sport may be, must change his rhythms to meet the spontaneous requirements of the instant. He is playing to win a game, and the ultimate thing is the competition. The dancer . . . goes even further and with the use of music tries to *express* something to the onlooker . . . In short, we could say that the athlete uses his body skills and controls in a competitive way, but the dancer must have something to say . . . Most dance movements have their counterparts in sports. The dancer takes the physical movements, exaggerates them, extends them or distorts them to say what he has to say more clearly and more strongly.
>
> Mickey Mantle throwing a ball is dancing, even though he is not doing it to music its still a beautiful rhythmic thing to watch. . . . No dancer could be more beautiful than Vic Seixas serving.

Leonard Bernstein was to become the quintessential matchmaker between music and the millions—whether the music was Beethoven, blues, jazz, or musical comedy—and it was on *Omnibus* that he made his start on this "great communicator" phase of his multifaceted career.

"We'll take the first movement of Beethoven's Fifth and take discarded sketches and find out why he rejected them . . . for a glimpse into the composer's mind, his creative process," Bernstein proposed in his famous 1954 *Omnibus* program.

"Form is not a mold for Jell-O into which we pour notes and expect the result to be a minuet, a rondo, or a sonata," Bernstein cautioned. "The real function of form is to take us on a varied and complicated journey, and to do this the composer has to have a corresponding road map. He has to know what the next destination is bound to be, what the next note is going to be, to convey to us a sense of rightness, a sense that whatever note succeeds the last is the only possible note that can possibly happen at that minute."

From *Omnibus* Bernstein moved to Carnegie Hall in 1957 for the *New York Philharmonic's Young People's Concerts* televised by CBS—conducting, performing at the piano, analyzing and illuminating the music in ways that excited his audiences.

Promotion of arts-related programming was not a major issue when American television was in its infancy. That hardly seemed necessary. In some sense the arts were right there at television's cradleside. In those first post-World War II years, television sets were very costly, and stations aired programs they believed would appeal to the small numbers of Americans who could afford to own sets. The arts were generally included in the offerings to some extent. This was partly because the stations assumed that affluent viewers were well educated and had a taste for cultural offerings. But it was also because a certain number of folk dancers, ballerinas, and opera stars were eager to accept opportunities to appear in front of the camera. (They used only one camera in those years, and there was no zoom.) Television stations welcomed opportunities to do live programming without major expenditure of effort, time, or money.[1] The technical approach was basic, with little concern for innovation in adapting television to the arts or the arts to television.

Which is not to say that there were tidal waves of art programming on earliest television. But almost always there was some. As the networks expanded their reach, ABC televised opening nights at the Metropolitan Opera, and CBS broadcast plays direct from Broadway theaters, and NBC created its own opera company, while stations in Chicago and Minneapolis showcased their local symphony orchestras.

By 1950, however, television production had become far more sophisticated and the audiences were vastly larger and much broader by any socioeconomic measure.

The 14,000 American households with television sets in 1947 had become 172,000 by 1948, then almost a million by 1949. A year later there were five million households with television sets, and then more than fifteen million in 1952. By that time the television networks had achieved coast-to-coast coverage, airing their professionally produced programs throughout the nation. From 1952 to 1960, about five million households were added each year.[2]

Propelled by such demographics, television left its silver-spoon infancy behind and became a boisterous, optimistic adolescent playing to mass audiences in the late 1940s and early 1950s.

The 1950s would become a glorious decade for popular television—Hopalong Cassidy, William Bendix in *The Life of Riley*, Lucille Ball and Desi Arnaz in *I Love Lucy*, *The Red Skelton Show*, Mickey Rooney in *The Twilight Zone*, *Dragnet*, *Perry Mason*, *Gunsmoke*, and other smash TV hits too numerous to mention.

But could high culture on the commercial networks compete and survive, especially in a real world situation where the commercial networks were in the business of reaching mass audiences for their advertisers? Indeed, the arts could and did hold onto an important place, particularly theater, even on prime-time commercial television, at least for a while. But many people were deeply concerned

■ Leonard Bernstein discusses Beethoven's Fifth Symphony on *Omnibus* in 1954.

■ Bernstein points to Beethoven's "feverish scrawls, agonized changes–there isn't room for any more notes at this point of Beethoven's manuscript," and he has to write the final version at the bottom of the page.

■ Bernstein stands on a huge score of the first movement of Beethoven's Fifth Symphony, and says: "Three g's and e-flat–everything in the first movement is based in these four notes. [It was] a gigantic struggle to achieve that rightness. It's that struggle that we would like to investigate–actually two struggles: the right notes for the themes and second the right notes to follow them . . . What is it about these four notes that is so pregnant and meaningful that a whole symphony could be based on them? . . . We take the first movement of Beethoven's Fifth and take his discarded sketches to see why he rejected them . . . for a glimpse into the composer's mind, his creative processes."

■ Bernstein conducts the Symphony of the Air in the first movement of Beethoven's Fifth Symphony.

■ Bernstein plays several rejected versions on the piano to show "how it would sound if some of the [discarded] sketches had been used."

■ Beethoven's manuscript is superimposed as Bernstein conducts. "After eight years of experimenting . . . he finally arrived at the [movement] familiar to us today."

about the future. Among them was a powerful network executive who was soon to become the president of NBC, Sylvester (Pat) Weaver, Jr.[3]

In January 1952, Weaver launched a well-publicized "Operation Frontal Lobes," aimed at bringing "enlightenment through exposure" to the fifteen million American households already plugged into television and many millions more to come. He proposed including "some element of culture or information in nearly every program in our schedule."[4]

Later, Weaver was more explicit in naming the elements and suggesting how they might be included. With what one observer called his characteristic effusiveness, Weaver explained, "We must expose all of our people to the thrilling rewards that come from an understanding of fine music, ballet, the literary classics, science, art, everything. We could, of course, present cultural events to small audiences who are already mentally attuned to them. But to program for the intellectual alone is easy and duplicates other media. To make us all into intellectuals—there is the challenge of television."[5]

In fact, NBC was already committed, without any real hope of financial remuneration, to what emerged as the 1950s decade's most ambitious television arts project, the *NBC Opera Theater*, according to Brian G. Rose of Fordham University at the Lincoln Center.[6] The NBC *Opera* broadcast up to six operas a year, in English, and many of them were American premieres or commissions. One of the most notable was Gian Carlo Menotti's *Amahl and the Night Visitors*, the story of a crippled boy and his mother who live in poverty among the shepherds but meet the Three Kings—Caspar, Melchior, and Balthaza—on their way to Bethlehem to pay homage to the newborn Christ child.

Amahl premiered in 1951, was viewed by a tremendous audience of sixty-five million, and was repeated many times "live" with different singers, particularly in the role of Amahl, which requires a boy soprano. It was the first opera ever commissioned by American network television.

Peter Pan, a 1955 television spectacular, was another triumph, hailed by *New York Times* critic Jack Gould as "a marriage of media under ideal circumstances. The advantages of 'live' television and the advantages of living theater were merged as one. Alone neither medium could have offered the miracle of Monday evening."[7]

Not everyone was pleased, however, with television's handling or mishandling of major classic works. In a letter to the *New York Times*, Arthur Miller criticized a *Hallmark Hall of Fame* production of Ibsen's *A Doll's House*, stating:

> In its original form *A Doll's House* would need close to three hours of playing time, or thereabouts. You cannot cut it in half without cutting in half its emotional, philosophical, and human value. Specifically, a profound work, the orchestration of whose themes is quite marvelous, becomes a superficial "story" at worst and a hint of something more at best, when it is told by leaping from one high point to another . . .
>
> Only one thing is lost by "digesting" great works, and it is possibly the main thing, namely, the depth of experience one might find in the originals. No matter how skillfully one

■ In 1952, a highly publicized "Operation Frontal Lobes" was launched by NBC network executive Sylvester L. (Pat) Weaver, Jr., saying, "To make us all into intellectuals–there is the challenge of television."

> "cuts to the story," eliminating the gradual development of motive and meaning, one is of necessity cutting the reason for the story to a greater or lesser extent. Literature is reduced to what E. M. Forster has called the caveman element—the "what happens next?" Why it happened, why it had to happen, what significance the happenings might have—these questions are the crucial ones for the creator and for mankind, and we are being deprived of them by digesting them out of the great works we see.
>
> However well they are played and directed, these truncated versions must inevitably confirm the opinion of those who cannot tell why they should bother with real literature or drama, for they are being given basically the plots at best, the skeletons of living organisms.[8]

Overall, theater made the transition to television with greater ease and success than the other performing arts, Brian Rose suggests,[9] owing to its naturalistic base and its appeal to audiences who already enjoyed movies and radio performances.

Theater also captured higher audience ratings than the other performing arts programs. In the Videodex ratings for December 1-7, 1954, for example, four theater anthologies rated among the top ten: *Studio One* with 31.4 percent of television homes, *Philco Television Playhouse* with 29 percent, *Kraft Television Theatre* with 28.8 percent, and *Ford Theater* with 28.3 percent. *Dragnet* was number one on the Videodex ratings that week with 43 percent of television homes, followed by *I Love Lucy* with 38.1 percent, followed in turn by *You Bet Your Life*, Jackie Gleason, and Ed Sullivan. Bob Hope came in seventh, just after *Studio One*.

The path was open for young writers to submit original

■ *Playhouse 90* presented ninety-minute original dramas, telecast live, often based on biographies or documentary material. It was one of a dozen major drama anthologies born in the 1950s.

scripts to many of the television dramatic anthology programs. The series could not rely entirely on Broadway because the major motion picture studios owned the rights to many of the plays produced in New York, where most television production was taking place during this era, and these studios steadfastly refused to permit their works to be aired over the potentially competitive television medium, according to Alex McNeil.[10]

An inspiration to new writers was Paddy Chayefsky's "Marty," broadcast on *Goodyear Television Playhouse* in 1953. Chayefsky defied Hollywood standards in his choice of hero and heroine: Marty, who calls himself "a fat little man," and his girlfriend Clara, a skinny school teacher whom his friends consider a "dog" and who does not impress Marty's mother, either. Close-ups were all-important in "Marty"—a Marty-Clara scene in an all-night cafeteria was played almost wholly in close-up, Erik Barnouw points out.[11] Like other television dramas of the period, it was a compact rather than a panoramic story, with confrontations that were psychological rather than physical, Barnouw notes.

When Broadway plays were used in the television anthology programs, however, the most common approach to adapting them for television was to prune and squeeze a three-act drama into an hour-long format. The camera was placed in a front-row auditorium situation, minus audience and footlights. However, some shows, including *Studio One* and *Philco Television Playhouse*, used more fluid camera work to combine the flexibility of the movies with the intensity of a continuous stage performance.

Starring in the drama anthology series were Helen Hayes, Paul Muni, Burgess Meredith, Edward G. Robinson, and many other notable artists. Paul Newman and Joanne Woodward got some of their first acting engagements in the television anthologies. Ronald Reagan became involved in the booming television anthology trend, as host to *General Electric Theater* in 1954. It presented what was then called "diversionary entertainment," mainly original teleplays ranging from light comedy to heavy drama.

The theater anthologies were the most thriving sector of the so-called Golden Age of Television from 1953 to 1955. But it was a Golden Age that had little in common with the classical one dear to the heart of Thomas Bulfinch, where "the earth brought forth all things necessary for man, without his labor in ploughing or sowing."

John Frankenheimer tells about his experience with television anthology dramas in New York in the 1950s, when he directed plays such as *The Rainmaker, The Turn of the Screw*, and *The Days of Wine and Roses*:

> I became a director when I was twenty-four years old, and I really didn't know any better. I think if I were to go back and try to do it now, it might be absolutely impossible I remember that I developed a terrible lower-back problem, and I shared that problem with many of my fellow directors.
>
> I remember during an air show—for instance, a *Playhouse*

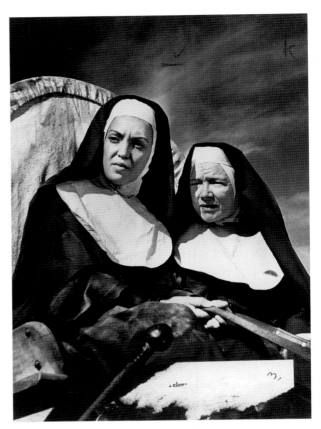

■ In a 1957 *Playhouse 90* production, "Four Women in Black," Katy Jurado and Helen Hayes play nuns who cross the desert to found a hospital in Tucson, Arizona, in 1870. *New York World-Telegram & Sun Collection, Prints and Photographs Division.*

■ Beatrice Straight and Edward G. Robinson star in "Shadows Tremble," a 1958 *Playhouse 90* production dealing with hostility to an outsider in a New England village. *New York World-Telegram & Sun Collection, Prints and Photographs Division.*

■ Van Heflin and Peter Lorre star in a Reginald Rose drama, "The Cruel Day," a story about violence in Nigeria, in a 1960 *Playhouse 90* telecast. *New York World-Telegram & Sun Collection, Prints and Photographs Division.*

■ Ricardo Montalban and Marisa Pavan hide out in a hotel room during a revolution sweeping a fictional South American country in the 1961 *Playhouse 90* production, "Target for Three." *New York World-Telegram & Sun Collection, Prints and Photographs Division.*

90—I would lose four to five pounds in perspiration. I'd have to take my shirt off and just wring it out at the end of one of those things ... I remember one show I did with Dennis O'Keefe—his first live television show. It was 1955, and he started walking behind the scenery, and he saw his leading lady there—Mary Sinclair, she was literally the queen of live television at that time. She'd done about three hundred live television shows. Dennis went up to her and said, "Mary, how do you do it?"

She said, "Well, Dennis, there's absolutely nothing to it." Whereupon she turned around and vomited.[12]

Michael Winship, a writer and coproducer of the public television series, *Television*, gives a somewhat sunnier description of the era:

Everyone was learning, almost everything was live, and anything could happen. Stage fright, flubbed lines, accidents on the set—all manner of catastrophes could befall those early days of network television—and did.

But that seemed simply to add to the spirit of adventure and discovery. The improvisational nature of those first steps could also result in moments of magic. People were allowed to do just about anything they wanted precisely because nobody really knew what they were supposed to be doing in the first place. The Golden Age was a serendipitous time, especially for television drama.[13]

Serendipitous no doubt, but Robert Saudek of *Omnibus* fame said live television was like Russian roulette. "Still, many brave souls—performers, directors, technicians—dared to expose themselves to this form of bravura, dared to pull the trigger just once more on the gamble that the next cylinder was empty; and all for the bubble reputation." Saudek, who directed the Ford Television Workshop's *Omnibus* program for nine years before becoming chief of the Library's Motion Picture, Broadcasting, and Recorded Sound Division, said that "as little as a missed cue could throw an entire cast into panic and reduce a nationwide audience to derisive guffaws."[14]

Unlike television series that reuse the same cast of characters in each successive episode, the anthology series were usually one-shot dramas of great diversity. "The anthology series said to the writer: 'Write us a play.' There were no specifications as to mood, characters, plot, style, or locale—at least, not at first," said Erik Barnouw, who founded and chaired Columbia University's Film Division and served as the first chief of MBRS.

The plays had to be producible as live programs in a gymnasium-sized studio, but except for such technical requirements the anthology series began as carte blanche invitations to writers, and writers responded, Barnouw said. Almost a dozen anthology programs were on the air, most of them weekly, by 1953. They included *Philco Television Playhouse*, *Goodyear Television Playhouse*, *Kraft Television Theater*, *Studio One*, *Robert Montgomery Presents*, the *U.S. Steel Hour*, the *General Electric Theater*, *Revlon Theater*, *Ford Theater*, and *Medallion Theater*, as well as *Omnibus*, which presented dramas on many but not all its weekly programs. These series were later joined by *Motorola Playhouse*, *The Elgin Hour*, *Matinee Theater*, and *Playhouse 90*.

By the early 1960s, however, the live drama production

■ Vivid close-ups of blood-soaked hands startled some viewers of *Hallmark Hall of Fame*'s 1954 production of Shakespeare's *Macbeth*, costarring Judith Anderson and Maurice Evans. They repeated the performance in 1960. *New York World-Telegram & Sun Collection, Prints and Photographs Division.*

■ In 1957, *Ford Theater* presented Joanna Barnes and Louis Jourdan in "The Man Who Beat Lupo," a story about a champion swordsman who fights a former friend to win the favor of the woman they both love. *New York World-Telegram & Sun Collection, Prints and Photographs Division.*

■ On the *Bell Telephone Hour*, Farley Granger played Peter Ilych Tchaikovsky, and Helen Hayes portrayed his patroness, Madame von Meck, in a 1960 drama, "The Music of Romance." *New York World-Telegram & Sun Collection, Prints and Photographs Division.*

Paddy Chayefsky picked an unglamorous, non-Hollywood hero and heroine and a butcher shop for the opening scene for his landmark 1953 drama "Marty" on *Goodyear Television Playhouse.* It inspired other writers to try to write for the burgeoning field. In a typical week's programming, seven or eight original dramas, usually written in New York and always produced there, were telecast live on the commercial networks in the 1950s. Writers usually received from $1,200 to $2,500 for a one-hour script. By 1960, most television drama production had moved to Hollywood. Chayefsky's "Marty" jumped the media fences and was made into a movie in 1955. *New York World-Telegram & Sun Collection, Prints and Photographs Division.*

■ Mary Martin and dance director Jerome Robbins take a test flight in a rehearsal of *Peter Pan.* "The advantages of 'live' television and the advantages of living theater were merged as one," wrote *New York Times* critic Jack Gould of the 1956 NBC *Producer's Showcase* program. *New York World-Telegram & Sun Collection, Prints and Photographs Division.*

■ The *NBC Opera Theater*'s production of Beethoven's *Fidelio* in 1961 was praised for its camera work, which created the illusion of spaciousness and grandeur. The principals are Chester Watson, Irene Jordan, Judith Raskin, and Fred Cushman. The opera was sung in English. *New York World-Telegram & Sun Collection, Prints and Photographs Division.*

■ In 1956, the Soviet government protested against "The Plot to Kill Stalin," before CBS *Playhouse 90* presented the hour-and-a-half-long drama in its weekly original drama series. Malenkov (who became Stalin's successor in 1953) is played by Thomas Gomez, and Beria (who was shot as an "imperialist agent" in the same year) by E. G. Marshall. Not pictured is Stalin, who was played by Melvyn Douglas. *New York World-Telegram & Sun Collection, Prints and Photographs, Division.*

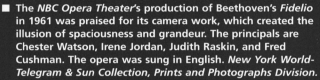

■ Francis Poulenc's *The Dialogues of the Carmelites* opened the *NBC Opera Theater*'s ninth season in 1957 with Rosemary Kuhlman and Patricia Neway. It was a moody exploration of faith and martyrdom in a convent during the French Revolution, "focusing on the nuns' faces and letting their feelings fill the screen," as Brian G. Rose commented in *Television and the Performing Arts* (1986). "The production was a triumphant example of how, with deliberately minimal resources, television could create a powerful operatic experience." *New York World- Telegram & Sun Collection, Prints and Photographs Division.*

that had been the staple of cultural television in the mid-1950s had all but disappeared from the commercial networks. Much of the production of dramatic shows had shifted from New York to Hollywood, where the formulas used to make popular films for mass audiences were being applied to television production.

Coming up from behind these golden years of cultural television programming on the commercial networks were the actions that would result in America's first noncommercial network, National Educational Television (NET). In 1952, the Federal Communications Commission lifted a four-year freeze on new channels and set aside 242 channels for educational television stations. Soon thereafter, the first television station devoted entirely to education program went on the air at the University of Houston.[15]

The Ford Foundation, which had already been supporting some individual stations, made a grant to establish a program production center which would become known as NET. It started out as a "bicycle" network system used to circulate kinescopes produced by one of the education stations to other stations around the country.[16] But it soon expanded its mission and began to produce programs of its own, with continued infusions of funds from the Ford Foundation.

NET programs stayed "much closer to the classroom than the living room," one critic noted. They were not trying to compete with mainstream commercial television for mass audiences. However, NET became the core of the Corporation for Public Broadcasting in 1967 by an act of Congress signed by Pres. Lyndon Johnson. The Public Broadcasting System set up shop in Washington to prepare for its first national season to open in October 1970.

Notes

1. Brian G. Rose, *Television and the Performing Arts: A Handbook and Reference Guide to American Cultural Programming* (New York: Greenwood Press, 1985), p. 1.

2. *Historical Abstracts of the United States* (U.S. Department of Commerce, Bureau of Labor Statistics, 1975), p. 796.

3. Weaver became NBC president in December 1953.

4. Sylvester L. Weaver, Jr., "Enlightenment Through Exposure," *Television Magazine*, January 1952, p. 31.

5. Weaver, "Enlightenment Through Exposure Is NBC Technique," *Musical America* (February 1956): 25.

6. Rose, *Television and the Performing Arts*, pp. 2 and 129- 130.

7. Jack Gould, "Delightful 'Peter Pan'," *New York Times*, March 15, 1955, sect. 2, p. 15.

8. "Mailbag—Arthur Miller on Adaptations," *New York Times*, November 29, 1959, sect. 2, p. 12.

9. Rose, *Television and the Performing Arts*, p. 189 ff.

10. Alex McNeil, *Total Television*, Penguin Books, New York, 1991, p. 418.

11. Erik Barnouw, *Tube of Plenty: The Evolution of American Television*, 2nd rev. ed. (New York: Oxford University Press, 1990), p. 160.

12. Michael Winship, *Television* (New York: Random House, 1988), p. 28.

13. Ibid., p. 24.

14. *Performing Arts Annual 1987*, (Washington, D.C.: Library of Congress, 1987), p. 28.

15. Frederic A. Leigh, "Educational and Cultural Programming," in *TV Genres: A Handbook and Reference Guide*, ed. Brian G. Rose (New York: Greenwood Press, 1985), p. 366.

16. A kinescope film is one that was photographed from an image on a picture tube, usually during a live telecast. Videotaping began to supplant kinescope in the late 1950s.

The television images were photographed by the author from kinescopes in the Motion Picture, Broadcasting, and Recorded Sound Division.

DONALD KENT writes on psychology, cultural affairs, and the information media for several professional social science publications. For his Master's degree in Russian history from the University of Maryland in 1993, he wrote on the origins of the Cold War as seen through the eyes of Russian diplomats in Washington as the U.S.-Soviet alliance of World War II turned sour and hostile. In 1995, the American Psychological Society published his three-part series on psychological research and practice in Russia since the collapse of the Soviet Union.

In earlier phases of his career, Mr. Kent was a cultural affairs officer with the Centre Cultural Américain in France for ten years and was First Secretary of the American Embassy in Paris. He has been a press officer with the Department of State and a speech writer with the Department of Health and Human Resources. He also served as Public Affairs Director of the American Psychological Association in the mid-1980s.

PRODUCTION

IN

GOLDEN

An Overview

BY **PAUL MANDELL**

MUSIC

TELEVISION'S

AGE

Back when the earth was young in 1947, television arrived after years of tinkering and promise. By 1952, it had become an inextricable part of our lives. Sights and sounds that emanated from this black-and-white universe etched the imaginations of young minds. For the sake of this narrative, a bit of regression cannot hurt.

The evening lineup was palpable. Ralph Bellamy marched through giant doors of Camel cigarette packs in Man Against Crime. A sweaty hand forged the Mark VII Dragnet logo with a blacksmith's hammer. A nightmarish glove threw an electric switch at the start of Tales of Tomorrow. Inner Sanctum was introduced by a disembodied head, and a police car lurched into frame as Racket Squad was announced through gritted teeth.

These graven images had one thing in common: ominous background music. Dragnet had a composer name on the end credits; for some reason, the others did not.

Stranger still was the sharing of interior themes from how to show. To young ears, this was a puzzlement. How could fight music from *The Adventures of Superman* play under a shootout with George Raft in *I'm the Law*, or a comical trill from *The Abbott & Costello Show* migrate to an episode of *Leave It to Beaver?* Was there some secret alliance between these shows, or was one pirating the other's sound track? The notion of background music libraries did not quite register but, as we grew up, for some of us the quirkiness of "shared music" (and ultimately the music itself) became a focal point of the video experience.

From 1950 to 1965, television relied heavily on huge libraries of recorded music. Mood pieces (called "cues") were used to enhance a dramatic moment, a romantic interlude, or provide a substantial underscore.

The best libraries came from England and burst on the American scene with brilliant quality. The jingle-jangle opener of *Captain Kangaroo*, for example, which played weekly on CBS for almost thirty years, came off a ten-inch shellac 78 rpm record of Edward White's "Puffin' Billy" from the Chappell library (disc C-433A). *Password* used Kurt Refeld's "Holiday Jaunt" from the J. W. Weinberger library. The yearning melody for chimes and strings that closed *The David Susskind Show* on Sunday nights was actually Robert Farnon's ode to Canada, "Gateway to the West" (Chappell disc C-364A).

The illusion, of course, was that these themes were written for the shows, which was hardly ever the case. The libraries functioned anonymously, serviced programs with bright musical trademarks, and saved producers a bundle in original scoring. In 1953, WNBC music director Margaret Snyder beamed: "We've just ordered our third dozen of King Palmer's 'The Film Opens' [from Paxton]. This is the popular theme of *Eleventh Hour Theater* and is played five times a day for station breaks, besides being played on the program. What a windfall for the composer."[1]

Ken Hughes, who directed *Casino Royale* and *Cromwell*, recalled his salad days as a television music editor: "With a sharp blade and a keen ear, you could bring in that cinematic chord, throw out music that didn't work, and call all the shots. If you didn't like the cloth or the cut of the material, the libraries supplied a dozen alternatives. You had tremendous orchestras at your fingertips you just couldn't afford any other way."[2]

Some of the best film composers in the world wrote for the libraries. Bernard Herrmann, Jerry Goldsmith, Fred Steiner, Arthur Honegger, Hugo Friedhofer, Victor Young, Ernest Gold, Laurie Johnson, David Rose, and Maurice Jarre all wrote for them at some point in their careers. It was fertile soil for some of their best inventions, but it never made them famous. For Jerry Goldsmith, its existence is an affront to his cinema ego: music should be written for the screen image, and anything else is a cheat. (Bartók and Stravinsky, on the other hand, were not writing to click tracks.) Goldsmith will talk passionately about his television scores, but not about his CBS library cues. A shame, because they were hauntingly original. "It's a time that's long gone, one that was not particularly a milestone in my career. I tried to make the music interesting, and you tried to stay awake! It was a lonely time for me, but it was an education you couldn't get in college."

A less sensitive John Cacavas, who wrote volumes of library music before scoring *Kojak*, and still does, points out that "it's just another market for a composer. It's *work*. There's more care taken in the recordings. With television scores, you just rattle it out and add sound effects. Library people are very fussy. Writing the material is a lot of fun. And it's a living."

A clear definition of what "library music" means as it applied to early television is imperative. There were cataloged libraries of commissioned production music—"music for possible productions." There were network libraries, CBS being the most prominent. And there were "wild track" libraries—music cribbed from motion picture sound tracks. The television cue sheets supplied to ASCAP and BMI were rife with bogus composer credits and apocryphal information. Untangling those webs spun fifty years ago entailed a decade of interviews with veterans of the era, screenings at the Library of Congress, access to original cue sheets, and a bit of cryptography.

Little Caesar

James Caesar Petrillo, the son of a Chicago sewer worker, rose through the ranks of the American Federation of Musicians to become its czar in June 1940. Petrillo was germphobic, rode in a bulletproof limo with six bodyguards, and kept a revolver in his desk. Almost immediately, he began an unrelenting series of bans on mechanically produced music which he deemed a menace to live musicians as a result of its use. This included phonograph records, jukeboxes, canned music on radio, and his final target, television.

In 1949, Petrillo issued a thirty-two-point edict to agencies and networks that threw them into a tailspin. He demanded that a reuse fee of twenty-five dollars per musician (fifty dollars to conductors) be paid whenever a post-1948 motion picture played on television, banned the use of prerecorded music for new shows, and outlawed the use of foreign sound tracks.

What crippled the industry was his ordering television producers to cough up 5 percent of the cost of an entire show that used union musicians, made payable to the Music Performance Trust Fund he created "to alleviate the distress and loss of employment attributed to the inroads of canned music product." In 1955, a television score using ten musicians averaged $3,500. The same music, if foreign recorded, might have cost $300. Thus, Petrillo priced his union members out of the business. Music contractors either scrambled for sessions in Europe and Mexico, or found more devious ways to achieve the same end.

Albert Glasser recalled seizing the moment when he was hired to write the underscore for the 1950 series *Big Town*. "I called my buddy Serge Glykson in Paris and told him I would orchestrate a ton of music and send him a bundle. There he would get the music copied and recorded on the new Ampex tape machine. The shows hadn't even been *made* yet. I had to visualize the scenes from the scripts."

I Love Lucy, with a budget of $35,000 per episode, could afford union-rate musicians to perform the title theme and

Mood Music.

bridges by Elliot Daniel and Wilbur Hatch. *Dragnet*, filmed at Disney, was sufficiently bankrolled to cover proprietary scoring by Walter Schumann. *Medic* boasted original scoring by Victor Young. But producers of filmed series for the first-run syndication market, with lean-cow budgets of $15,000 or less per episode, were forced to turn to a new breed of entrepreneur: the television music packager.

David Chudnow, Raoul Kraushaar, Bert Shefter, and David Gordon were major players, with backgrounds as composers' agents, orchestrators, and music contractors at minor studios. They amassed fortunes by laundering extant motion picture tracks and collecting on them as publishers, and very often as composers. The unmixed music elements on film rolls and discs were wrangled from studio music departments in backroom deals. The harvest was transferred to magnetic tape, cataloged with new cue titles and numbers, and shopped around town as TV tracking libraries.

The testimony lies with the music editors. Erma Levin (1920–1998) tracked *The Gene Autry Show*, *Annie Oakley*, and *Death Valley Days*, and became the first female editor to receive a supervisory music credit on a television series: "Analytically speaking, any time [the packagers] could get their hands on a feature with participating composers, the music was used. I would cut out principal melodies and motifs that were dangerous to play games with. But the tracks were *liberated*. A lot of it was very good and would otherwise have never been heard."

Irving Friedman was a clarinet player in the Paul Whiteman orchestra before getting a foothold in Hollywood. According to music editor Graham Mahin, "Friedman was a politician and did all the contracting for Screen Gems [Columbia Pictures' television outlet]. He got 500 dollars a reel when everyone else was getting less. I suspect there was a big kickback thing going on." When Don Ferris was hired to write the *Captain Midnight* theme, Friedman's name appeared on the cue sheets as the cowriter. Thus began the "split-copyright" deal of television music contractors raking in royalties with composers. Often these were "take-it-or-leave-it" propositions.

Dick Berris was a music editor on *Ben Casey*. The underscores, including David Raksin's main title theme, were recorded in Brussels and rerecorded domestically when the union ruckus blew over. Berris cut track at Sunset Editorial, which was strictly legitimate. But he remembered the darker days. "A lot of stuff was taken out of editing bins. It was pirated right out of pictures. We once used a cue for temp purposes to sell a show to the network. I borrowed it from someone but qualified it to the producer. It had a big sound. I said it couldn't be used if the show went to series. I didn't stay after the pilot. Then the show sold and I heard this *big* cue! I couldn't say anything because it put me in a funny spot. But I'm sure this happened intentionally a hundred times over."

Independent Music Suppliers

The first music library for a series was packaged by George Trendle for *The Lone Ranger* (1949–1957). Trendle, who owned the character, had it recorded in Chicago using clas-

■ Gale Storm with cameraman Walter Strenge on the set of *My Little Margie* at Hal Roach Studio in 1953. The series used Alexander Laszlo's "Bows and Strings in Teasing" as the title theme, which he wrote generically for his Structural Music Library.

sical works plus music written for the *Lone Ranger* serials rerecorded in Mexico. The library consisted of twenty-five single-sided discs. In 1955, it was supplanted by the C-B library written by Emil Cadkin and Harry Bluestone. The title theme, of course, was Rossini's *William Tell* overture. One wonders if Rossini would have smiled or revolved in his grave as the Masked Man and Tonto rode the range to his masterwork.

The Guild-Universal "Program Aids" library was used by the Hal Roach television unit in 1950. The composer was Alexander Laszlo (1895-1970). Guild consisted of 100 disc transcriptions of Laszlo's old film scores masquerading as European-performed recordings. The first programs to use it were *Mystery Theatre* and *Burns & Allen*.

From 1950 to 1953, Laszlo supplanted Guild with his Structural Music library, a whopping thirty-eight volumes of sheet music. The Roland Reed-produced shows *My Little*

BOWS AND STRINGS IN TEASING

by ALEXANDER LASZLO (ASCAP)

Theme of the Television Series "My Little Margie"
from Structural Music Volume VI. p.15.07
(Copyright by GUILD PUBLICATIONS of Calif. Inc.
Ep 55026, May 23, 1951

■ Production Music Labels (center, then clockwise from upper left). Capitol Q Transcriptions was the Mutel Library on disc, which was licensed for radio broadcasts. "The World of Tomorrow" was used for *Superman*. Various KP Music cues were written by Maurice Jarre, who composed the film score for *Dr. Zhivago*. "Puffin' Billy" was the title music for *Captain Kangaroo*. "Tumult and Commotion" was written by Miklos Rosza, who composed the film score for *Ben-Hur*. "Grip of the Law" was used in the series *Decoy*.

Margie, Racket Squad, Rocky Jones, Space Ranger, and *Waterfront* used Structural Music for main and end titles. Laszlo's "Bows and Strings in Teasing," for example, based on a 1946 film cue, was fleshed out as Structural Music sketch No. 15, Volume VI, and copyrighted on May 23, 1951, as the *My Little Margie* theme. Laszlo often used a theremin for an otherworldly effect. As music editor Robert Raff recalled, "I'd describe things I wanted, and Alex would compose them and go to Mexico, I think, or record them in his garage."

Manuel and Alec Compinsky, a cellist and violinist, wrote minimalist scores for the 1954 films *Killers from Space* and *The Snow Creature*. They started a bootleg tracking service by dubbing acetate discs of old film scores onto tape. According to Graham Mahin, "The Compinskys hired an Oriental slate boy to voice-slate the cues, to create the illusions that they were done overseas. We called them the Compinsky Trio." Manuel Compinsky became a dean of music at a California university.

Lee Zahler composed action music for the low-budget Mascot serials of the thirties. When he died, his son, Gordon Zahler, used his father's cues for the *Wild Bill Hickok* television series. The main title was actually Lee Zahler's "Wild Bill No. 2" from the serials. It was not uncommon to hear 1933 film cues from *Tarzan the Fearless* in the *Gangbusters* television series tracked by Gordon Zahler in 1951.

An empire was created by David Gordon (1907-1983), a Beverly Hills music publisher. Gordon became music supervisor Stanley Wilson's key supplier of background music for the *MCA-Revue* television shows. He routinely bought the publishing rights to motion picture scores, accessed the recordings, and turned them into television cues. Family members were listed as composers on his cue sheets, usually that of his wife Ruth Layne or his son Melvyn Lenard. Gordon operated as Marlen Music (ASCAP) and Gordon Music (BMI). *Lassie, Wagon Train, Death Valley Days*, and *Alfred Hitchcock Presents* were a few shows that used his bounty of track. The series *Federal Men in Action* and *Police Call* actually bore the end credit "Music by Melvyn Lenard." According to film composer Paul Dunlap, "Some of my scores are supposedly by Gordon's *sons*. He got a couple from me when I neeeded money badly. But he didn't buy them; he said he wanted to 'publish' them. I think he paid me $200 per score. There was a series of cues I wrote for *The San Francisco Story*, which I used to hear *constantly* on television. I always wondered why I didn't get credit for it from ASCAP." Gordon claimed that his *sons* wrote those!

The Mutel Music Service

In 1953, a groundswell of "new" music burst on the scene with ballistic force. It was used as title themes and underscoring for *The Adventures of Superman, Captain Midnight, Terry and the Pirates, Ramar of the Jungle, I'm The Law, Annie Oakley, Buffalo Bill Jr., Stories of the Century, Burns & Allen, The Life of Riley, Space Patrol*, and many others. The program list was encyclopedic. The supplier was David

■ **Emil Cadkin created the C-B Library with Harry Bluestone in 1954. His cues were packaged by Capitol and tracked into** *The Lone Ranger* **and** *Jungle Jim.*

Chudnow (born 1902), a feisty packager of low-rent film scores in the forties. In 1949, he formed Mutel (Music for Television). His first client was *Lucky Strike Theater*. It went on from there.

From 1952 to 1956, Mutel was the dominant television tracking library. The brew included big orchestra fights and chases, suspense themes, Western and love themes, dance numbers, and slashing action themes. This rogue music became so famous that much of what was legitimately scored later paled by comparison.

The library was culled primarily from sound tracks of independently made B pictures released through Monogram, PRC, Eagle-Lion Pictures and other studios from 1946 to 1949, either as direct lifts or as new orchestrations recorded overseas to circumvent the union stranglehold on domestic performance.

According to Chudnow, his partner Serge Glykson, a flutist with the NBC orchestra, had ties with George Tzipine, the music director of Gaumont Newsreel in Paris. Tzipine assembled orchestras in France and conducted selected cues from these motion picture scores. Since these scores had no publisher attachments, Chudnow listed himself as Byron Music with BMI to collect whenever Mutel-licensed programs were televised. Tzipine served as a foreign composer front to shield the writers from the wrath of the union. His name routinely appeared on cue sheets but he wrote nothing for Mutel. Fictitious names with odd European bents also appeared. Thus, on a given episode that tracked the library, the background music was credited to "Serge Dupre," "Josef Lpizive," "Sigfried Sawatski,"

Jack Shaindlin conducts a New York session of dramatic newsreel underscore for Fox Movietone in 1947. One of the first suppliers of library music for television, his Langlois Filmusic company tracked such fifties shows as *Mr. and Mrs. North, Man Against Crime, Science Fiction Theater,* and *Father Knows Best.* He went independent as Cinemusic in the sixties.

At his desk as music director for Four Star Television in 1960, Herschel Burke Gilbert cowrote the first music package for Mutel in 1949. Gilbert was one of the first composer-orchestrators to maintain a music publishing company. At Four Star, he wrote title themes for *The Rifleman* and *Burke's Law* and used his own library of film scores to track numerous television series.

"Pierre Domat," "Joseph Solon," and other concocted monikers. The actual composers were Herschel Burke Gilbert, Joseph Mullendore, Rudy Schrager, Paul Sawtell, Mahlon Merrick, and others. Chudnow indexed the tracks by mood and number and created cue titles to make them appear generic: LM 22 "Western Love Theme," MYS 35 "A Nightmare," CH 56 "Children's Chase," and so on.

The film *Open Secret* (PRC 1948), about a gang of white-supremacist hoodlums and the murder of a Jewish store owner, had a score by Herschel Burke Gilbert. *The Guilty* (Monogram 1947), about the murder of the wrong twin sister, had a score by Rudy Schrager. Thirty compositions from these scores—themes of high drama, horror, suspense, and romance—formed the backbone of the Mutel 100 Series, the first package sold to television. Joseph Mullendore and Herb Taylor reorchestrated them in 1950 to make them more marketable to producers.

The Mutel 400 Series (MYS 401-FI 416) were serial-style fight cues and misteriosos that almost defy description, with pounding rhythms, thick battle chords, morbid bassoon entrances, and vertiginous string lines. The first year of *Superman* made the most of them. The composer and the source film remain a mystery.

The 600 Series was a symphonic set of tracks written in the style of Wagnerian tragedy. The composer is believed to have been Paul Sawtell, and the music is keenly associated with the *Ramar of the Jungle* series starring Jon Hall. The music helped transform *Ramar's* scant jungle sets into a dark, foreboding milieu. The 700 Series featured tracks with wailing oboes and trumpet stingers. Cue 710, "Animal Snarls," was discreetly used by CBS in the *Gunsmoke* pilot for scenes of oppresssive heat.

Mahlon Merrick wrote bright, bouncy show themes for the Mutel library. His cues "Soft Shoe Dance," "Toy March," "Burlesque," and others were used to open and close *Burns & Allen, The Abbott & Costello Show, Private Secretary, The Life of Riley,* and the *Jack Benny* program.

Chudnow also made deals with legendary composers Hans J. Salter and Max Steiner. It was not uncommon to hear a Salter fight cue from the 1943 *Frankenstein Meets the Wolfman* score in an episode of *Sky King!*

By the mid 1950s, the Mutel numbers had spiraled to 29,000, via the pirating of foreign sound tracks. "My partner Serge Glykson used to pull music out of French and Italian pictures," Chudnow unflinchingly admitted. "Nobody knew who wrote them so we broke them down into cues and gave them names." It is not known if this contraband ever received television play.

In 1957, the library was brought to Warners Television by supervising music editor Erma Levin. The classic Mutel suspense cues of years gone by were tracked into *Maverick.* Chudnow had recorded dramatic music with big-band artist Billy May in Mexico; some of May's cues surfaced in the first year of *Maverick.*

David Chudnow could not have imagined the impact his rogue music would make on entire generations of baby boomers. To them, it is an awesome sound track that taps into childhood memories of early-evening "video noir." To

■ Joseph Mullendore, circa 1946. Starting as an orchestrator on minor films, he cowrote music for the Mutel Library in 1951 with Herschel Gilbert and Herb Taylor. His cues were tracked into *The Adventures of Superman.* His march for Mutel, "Parade of the Chessmen," became the end title for *Racket Squad.* Mullendore moved to Four Star Television, where he wrote the themes for *Zane Grey Theatre* and *Honey West* and later scored *Star Trek* and *Mannix.*

■ Herb Taylor circa 1950. A trombonist and arranger, Taylor wrote the Mutel Library theme used to open *Death Valley Days* and *Annie Oakley.*

his peers, he proved that great coin could be made by thumbing his nose at the union and recycling motion picture music as he saw fit. At age 100, he continues to collect royalties from BMI.

Langlois Filmusic Inc.

Jack Shaindlin (1909-1983) began scoring the *March of Time* newsreels in 1942 and served as music director of Fox Movietone News in New York. Around 1950, Shaindlin and his composer-partner Robert McBride organized their newsreel and documentary tracks and started Filmusic, "the largest sound-on-film library in the U.S. with over 2,000 moods for dramatic, news, and comedy films." In 1954, Shaindlin joined forces with Cy Langlois of the Lang-Worth radio transcription service, and Filmusic became Langlois Filmusic Inc. The fanfare for the "torch lady" logo at the end of every Screen Gems television show was a celebrated piece from this collection.

What made the library famous were the sneak-alongs with spooky clarinets and brass stingers used in *Mr. And Mrs. North, Boston Blackie, Science Fiction Theatre,* and the final year of *Superman.* "In Cold Blood," "Closing In," "Crime Lab," "Manhunt," and "Sweating It Out" were typical cue titles. McBride wrote most of them and Shaindlin orchestrated them. These were shrewdly crafted works, remarkable for their economy, with repeated pauses and

■ One of the unsung heroes of showbiz television music, Mahlon Merrick was a mainstay composer for David Chudnow's Mutel Library. His bright, bouncy cues became the title themes for *The Jack Benny Show, Burns and Allen, The Life of Riley,* and *Private Secretary.*

abrupt hits to facilitate the seamless editing of one with the other.

As Shaindlin's key tracker Frank Lewin observed, "Jack never wrote anything himself. He always had a stable of writers working for him." Among them were Louis Applebaum, Rick DuPage, George Chase, Lan Adomian, and German composer Richard Mohaupt. Charles Strouse of *Annie* and *Bye Bye Birdie* fame ghostwrote much of Shaindlin's show music. Even Morton Gould lent a helping hand with the light comedy cue "Toboggan Run."

Langlois Filmusic disbanded in 1960. In the mid-sixties, Shaindlin went independent as Cinemusic, a genreorama servicing news shows, sporting events, and educational films.

The World Broadcasting System

Cincinatti's Frederick W. Ziv (born 1905) pioneered the marketing of packaged radio shows and first-run syndicated television. In 1948, he moved to Hollywood to produce *The Cisco Kid* series. He did this for under 11,000 dollars per episode and filmed it in color when color television was still a pipe dream. The call letters of ZIV Television Programs intriguingly resembled Roman numerals. In all, he produced twenty-seven series from 1948 to 1960 including *I Led Three Lives*, *Highway Patrol*, *Sea Hunt*, *Science Fiction Theatre*, and *Bat Masterson*. In 1960, he sold his television empire to United Artists and Wall Street investors for thirty-four million dollars.

One of *Ziv's* canny acquisitions was the World Broadcasting System radio library which he bought from Decca Records in 1948. These were wide-range transcriptions of popular songs, jazz and big band numbers, dramatic recitations, and mood music.

Of special import to Ziv were the WBS discs containing generically written program themes. These were compiled on later issues called the D series. From this came the famous title themes for *Mr.District Attorney* (disc D568, Documentary Theme No. 2), the *Science Fiction Theatre* theme by Ray Bloch, the *Times Square Playhouse* theme by Peter Yorke, and the *Favorite Story* theme by Jack Shaindlin.

Since the American Federation of Musicians had banned the television use of radio music libraries, the cover name "Ray Llewellyn" was reported on cue sheets that used those themes. The name was a composite of the most popular World Broadcasting artists: bandleader *Ray* Bloch, drummer *Lou* Belson, Duke *Ell*ington, and *Lyn* Murray. Since he had bought the WBS library "rights free," Ziv collected composer royalties under this phantom name and publisher shares as Esteem Music.

In 1957, Fred Ziv began producing several network series and commissioned the scoring of original titles for them. Included were the *Bat Masterson* theme by David Rose, *The Man and the Challenge* theme by Warren Barker, and the *Stoney Burke* theme by Dominic Frontiere.

The "bumper" music used for commercial breaks in the thirty-nine filmed episodes of *The Honeymooners* were actually recordings of Ray Bloch's themes in the WBS music library tracked in for syndication. Bloch's music for *The Ed Sullivan Show* was also in the WBS library, including the

■ Rudy Schrager wrote numerous film scores contracted by David Chudnow in the forties. Parts of his score for *The Guilty (1947)* can be heard in the earliest *Superman* episodes. Schrager served as music director for *Lux Radio* and *Lux Video Theatre* and wrote cues for the CBS Music Library and themes for Four Star Television, including *Wanted Dead or Alive* and *Target: The Corruptors.*

show tunes "Ridin' High," "Guess Who! Guess What!," and "Music from Coast to Coast," which played relentlessly under jugglers, magicians, and high wire acts.

And Who, Disguised as Clark Kent

The Adventures of Superman, starring George Reeves as the Man of Steel, was a rare bird. During its six seasons from 1953 to 1958, it used five music libraries for its underscores. This music became so closely identified with the series, historians believed for a time that it had all been written for it. For the first year, the producers chose the Mutel 100 and 400 Series of action and suspense themes. Of the thirty-five-plus programs that tracked this music, only in *Superman* did it sound rarefied and truly functional.

Leon Klatzkin (1914-1992) was the first year's music director. His job was to select Mutel tracks and tell the editors under what scenes to place them. He is also the credited composer of the *Superman* theme, a bristling 6/8 march which to Eisenhower kids was the equivalent of "The Star Spangled Banner." Klatzkin's authorship of the theme, however, is questionable, based on the testimony of his contemporaries.

In 1953, Klatzkin was replaced by Irving Gertz, a first-

Dramatic Suspense # 2   R. Schram

■ British composer Jack Beaver in 1932. Beaver wrote many cues for the production music catalogs. The best ones were immortalized in America as underscore for *The Adventures of Superman* in 1953. He cowrote the film score for Alfred Hitchcock's *The 39 Steps* and created a style which fomented such works as "The Warsaw Concerto" and "The Cornish Rhapsody."

■ Leon Klatzkin, the credited composer of the *Superman* theme.

■ Ronald Hanmer was a prolific mood music composer who, along with Jack Beaver, wrote many of the dramatic themes for the Francis, Day, and Hunter library used in *Superman*. The photograph was taken in 1992 when he was conductor of the St. Lucia Orchestra in Brisbane, Australia.

rate composer at Universal, who decided to utilize two English mood libraries for *Superman*. One was the Francis, Day & Hunter "Mood Music" recorded at EMI's Abbey Road Studios under the direction of Sidney Torch. The other was Paxton "Records of Distinction" conducted by Walter Collins. From hundreds of ten-inch discs, Gertz chose thirty-one FDH recordings and twenty-four Paxtons and had them transferred to tape for tracking.

Jack Beaver (1900-1963) and Ronald Hanmer (1917-1994) were the British composers whose recordings inadvertently shaped the series. Beaver had cowritten the score for Alfred Hitchcock's *The Thirty-Nine Steps*. Hanmer wrote voluminously for the BBC. Both men were influenced by the film scores of Max Steiner and Miklos Rosza.

Beaver's crashing themes "The Sword of Damocles," "Atlantic Rollers," and "Crime Doesn't Pay" from the FDH library hammered alarm into establishing metropolis scenes. His "World of Tomorrow" had a romantic motif inspired by Max Steiner's score for *The Big Sleep* and ended with strident trumpets and harp arpeggios. It closed episodes of *Superman* on a warm triumphant note.

On the Paxton label, Frederick Charossin's "Eerie Night" curled viewers' toes with nerveracking tremolos. John Foulds's "Tell-Tale Heart" imbued scenes with great stealth. Miklos Rozsa's frightening "Tumult and Commotion" was actually Variation No. 7 of his "Theme, Variations, and Finale" written in 1933. The Paxton version was arranged by Walter Collins. Rozsa claimed no knowledge of how his first international success had become a British library cue.

In 1955, the series switched to the Emil Ascher Video Moods library in New York. Sixty tension builds and releases by George Chase and Wladmir Selinsky were used. "Dark of the Moon," "Hypertension," "Confused Vision," "and "Hour Glass" were the most ubiquitous of the bunch.

For *The Adventures of Superman's* final season, producer Whitney Ellsworth turned to Jack Shaindlin and leased a budget package of Langlois Filmusic cues. "Emotional Underscore," "Stealthily," "Manhunt," and "Excitement under Dialogue," were used throughout until production ended in November 1957.

Lassie and the Martians

The original *Lassie* show—starring Tommy Rettig, Jan Clayton, and George Cleveland—aired from 1954 to 1957 and won a family values Emmy for Robert Maxwell, who two years earlier had produced the most violent *Superman* episodes. *Lassie* was one of the first filmed series to have an extensive mood library written directly for it, but it had a rough start.

Raoul Kraushaar (born 1908) served as a music supervisor at Republic Pictures in the 1940s. In 1954, he was hired to package music for *Lassie*. He could orchestrate and conduct his own sessions, but he mostly took credit for other people's work. He operated a music-for-cash business and demanded the surrender of all composer rights to him.

Earlier, Kraushaar supplied scores to a number of exploitation pictures. The most famous was *Invaders from*

Tommy Rettig and the star collie Lassie in 1954. For its first season, *Lassie* used underscore from such unlikely features as *Invaders from Mars* and *Bride of the Gorilla* via music contractor Raoul Kraushaar. It was replaced with uncredited music by David Rose written for the Omar Library in 1955.

Mars (1952), ghostwritten by Mort Glickman. He also took solo composer credit on *Untamed Women*, 80 percent of which consisted of cues from the Paxton record library.

Lassie needed a signature theme, so Kraushaar turned to William Lava, who had written a sentimental main title and score for *The Courageous Dr. Christian* in 1940. The music was "unpublished" and Lava had kept his acetates. In 1953, the acetates were used as title and interior music for director Edward D. Wood's transvestite film *Glen or Glenda?* In 1954, Kraushaar took the same theme, rearranged it with an accelerated tempo, and transformed it into the *Lassie* theme. Thus collie and transvestite shared the same music. Somehow it made sense, as Lassie was supposed to be a she but was really a he.

For *Lassie's* underscores, Raoul Kraushaar tapped into films he had music-supervised. Dramatic slugs from *Invaders from Mars*, *Bride of the Gorilla*, and Elmer Bernstein's *Robot Monster* became part of *Lassie's* sound track. Since most of these scores had been published by David Gordon, Kraushaar worked a deal with him. As a result, 1954 cue sheets for *Lassie* credit Gordon's wife Ruth Layne as the primary composer.

The patch-quilt motion picture sound was often harrowing. In one segment, young Tommy nearly suffocated in a cave; in another, his grandfather was bitten by a rattlesnake, all to music lifted from *Bride of the Gorilla* and *Invaders from Mars!*

Peter Frank inherited Omar Music when the other partners divested their interests. Capitol Records distributed it. In its day, it serviced such shows as *Alfred Hitchcock Presents*, *Father Knows Best*, *Leave It to Beaver*, *The Untouchables*, and the MGM series *The Thin Man* and *Northwest Passage*. Frank was often given as little as 5,000 dollars to score thirty-nine episodes, but he made his money back several times over in BMI royalties. By 1962, Omar had peaked and started to fall into disuse.

The Capitol Hi-Q Library

Long before Capitol Records moved to its spaceage tower off Hollywood and Vine, it serviced radio stations through its broadcast division with transcriptions of rights-free music recorded in Europe. The service went out of business in 1951.

In 1952, production chief Ken Nelson and library manager John Seely created the Capitol Q Series by leasing the Mutel library from David Chudnow and distributing it on 175 double-sided 78 rpm vinyl records. Q supplied music for the radio shows *Yours Truly*, *Johnny Dollar*, *True Detectives*, and bumper music for television station breaks. Contractually, however, Capitol was forbidden to track Q as background music for television.

■ Hayden Rourke and George Reeves in the 1953 *Adventures of Superman* episode "The Face and the Voice," which used Ronald Hanmer's eerie cue, "Lost in a Fog," from the Francis, Day, and Hunter mood music library. *Courtesy of DC Comics.*

In 1955, the makers of *Lassie* decided to replace the shopworn track with a new library written anonymously and brilliantly by David Rose. They called it Omar Music, an acronym of the surnames of assistant producer Dan Ocko, Robert Maxwell, production manager Rudy Abel, and Raoul Kraushaar. The sessions were recorded in England. David Rose's bright, rustic melodics and heavy tension cues became the classic *Lassie* underscores of 1955 to 1957. His sentimental themes were of crystalline beauty, his danger cues dark and threatening.

Peter Frank, an ad executive for the show's sponsor Campbell's soup, was instrumental in organizing Omar: "I didn't like the canned music from the first year, so I hired Raoul to contract new music for us. The first Omar music was recorded in London. A lot was done in Baden-Baden. Dave Rose was our biggest writer. He just wanted to pick up a fee, so we didn't use his name on cue sheets. We used Raoul's instead. We made a deal with an orchestra at Rank Studios in London. He'd be doing a major session and slip our music in. That way we had a full orchestra sound."

■ Before he scored *Bonanza*, David Rose supplied more anonymously written music packages for television than any other individual. His music became underscore for *Lassie*, *Sea Hunt*, and *Hitchcock Presents*. The Capitol Library paid Rose top dollar for his music.

■ Bill Loose composed the initial package for the Capitol Hi-Q Library in 1956. He supplied large quantities of cues for the Theme Craft, Omar, and OK libraries distributed by Capitol.

From this came the title themes to *Dennis the Menace, The Donna Reed* Show, and *Real People*.

In 1955, Capitol decided to create its own music library and approached Nelson Riddle to write it. Riddle was busy with his groundbreaking arrangements for Frank Sinatra, so Capitol hired Bill Loose, a pop composer-arranger with a good melodic sense. In January 1956, Loose turned in an astounding 5,500 pages of sheet music. The sessions were recorded by Phil Green's orchestra in London and brought back to Hollywood.

John Seely cataloged it by mood and packaged it on 110 reels of quarter-inch tape and fifty-five corresponding audition discs. The twenty-two-hour package was christened Capitol Hi-Q, a reference to the new buzz on high fidelity. The entire library was made licensable to film and television producers for as little as 350 dollars.

A major part of Hi-Q was Theme Craft, a name invented by Seely to house powerful mood music by David Rose. "Bill Loose and I paid Rose a bunch of cash," said Seely. "He had to sell it rights-free and composer-free. It was all on reels of quarter-inch tape. We spent 100 dollars a minute for it. Everybody thought we were crazy, but I insisted that it was worth it. Then Bill agreed to write as much as David did and we put our names on the entire package."

Rose's music packed a wallop. TC 2 ("Heavy Chase") was an ear-splitting horror theme with cascading trombones and sizzling clusters. His "Dreaming Ghost" and "Sparkling Ghost" cues (TC 16-24) with ethereal strings, gossamer harps, and otherworldly woodwinds were used for underwater tension in *Sea Hunt*.

Theme Craft cues by Bill Loose caught on as signature themes. A light comedy piece with a xylophone "nose twitch" became the theme for *Dennis the Menace*. TC 430 ("Happy Day") became the theme for *The Donna Reed* Show. Loose's cowriter Jack Cookerly recalled: "We wrote a bunch of cues we jokingly called 'Music to Wash Windows By.' We called them 'domestics' and the industry really ate them up! The *Donna Reed* people picked that particular theme; it wasn't written for the series at all! Irving Friedman of Screen Gems made the deal to restrict its use. It could be tracked into an industrial film, but not for broadcast."

Capitol became the largest distributor of canned television music in America. A 1965 memo to Hi-Q subscribers listed twenty-two supplementary libraries with over two hundred hours of music. There were packages by Fred Steiner, Mahlon Merrick, Jack Meakin, Phil Green, Nick Carras, and outer space music by Ib Glindemann. Also distributed were the KPM, TRF, Synchro, and Omar libraries, Les Baxter's pop themes and Latin rhythms, and the C-B library written by Emil Cadkin and Harry Bluestone. Producers no longer had to woo independent packagers—they got their music from Capitol and reported the usage on forms supplied with the tape reels.

Some hotshots at Capitol were able to grab performance royalties by bankrolling music packages. George Hormel, a pianist related to the Hormel meatpacking empire, laid claim to Hi-Q music which he financed but did not write. Spencer Moore was another. Composer Nick Carras recalled the scene: "Moore made his money by bringing his investors to Capitol and putting his name on our music. It got to be kind of a joke! We were young and green. I didn't even know what a cue sheet was! Often you'd see cues list-

■ Composer Fred Steiner conducting the National Philharmonic Orchestra in London in 1976. Steiner wrote the title theme for *Perry Mason* and scored numerous *Gunsmoke* and *Twilight Zone* episodes at CBS.

ing Spencer Moore and George Hormel as authors in the Hi-Q catalog. Some people in the business might say 'That looks legitimate.' It all depended what side of the fence you were on."

CBS Enters *The Twilight Zone*

Anyone who watched a segment of *Perry Mason, Have Gun Will Travel,* or *The Twilight Zone* has heard music by such giants as Bernard Herrmann and Jerry Goldsmith from the Rolls Royce of network libraries. CBS had twelve which serviced its radio and television input from 1948 to 1963.

The architect of the library was Lud Gluskin, a former drummer and bandleader. In 1937, he was appointed music director of CBS Radio and was given automony on all music matters by the network's founder, William S. Paley.

Gluskin routinely made trips to Europe to record music for the library, which ultimately cost him his union card. "When Petrillo demanded the 5 percent surcharge," said CBS library manger Don B. Ray, "that changed everything. Good writers didn't know what to do. Academy Award-winning writers were begging Lud for work."

At first, two small radio libraries were in use. CBS-A had twenty-two minutes of music by Alexander Semmler plus Lyn Murray's radio score for "The Devil and Daniel Webster" broadcast on June 19, 1948. CBS-B had twenty-five minutes written for the *Gunsmoke* radio show plus two reels of music by CBS conductor Alfredo Antonini dated October 9, 1953.

CBS Library One consisted of ninety minutes of music for *Hallmark Playhouse* and *Jergen's Theatre.* In 1955, music director Eugene Cines of CBS-New York secured two hours of Inter-Art Music from J .J. Lynx in London. This was the first of many British disc libraries CBS stockpiled as needle-drops for live broadcasts. Library Two, the first indicated for radio and television, had two hours of music recorded in Italy. Library Three had thirty-two minutes written by Paul Baron.

CBS Library Four, by Wilbur Hatch, was recorded in Paris for use in *Our Miss Brooks, December Bride,* and *My Favorite Husband.* CBS Library Five consisted of Rex Khoury's *Gunsmoke* themes adapted for television by Fred Steiner, Rene Garriguenc, and Lucien Morawek. Library Six had a hundred minutes written by Morawek plus twenty-two minutes of music by John Strauss for *The Phil Silvers Show.*

Library Seven was the first big one with 26 hours, 38 minutes of music by Jerry Goldsmith, Fred Steiner, and others recorded in London, Paris, Rome, and Mexico in 1956. Library Eight's 25 hours, 22 minutes of music cost 127,000 dollars in 1957. It included a mini-library of *Perry Mason* themes by Fred Steiner, avant-garde cues by Marius Constant, Faustin Jeanjean, Jacques Lasry, and Rene Challan, and music by British composers Trevor Duncan, Bruce Campbell, and Wilfred Josephs. Library Nine stockpiled 22 hours, 51 minutes of music by Lyn Murray, Nathan Van Cleave, Leonard Rosenman, Jerome Moross, Nathan Scott, Laurence Rosenthal, and William Lava in 1958. Library Nine was recorded in Stuttgart, Germany.

■ Seen here conducting for a CBS radio play with Charles Laughton, the uncompromising Bernard Herrmann virtually put the CBS Music Library on the map. His unnerving suites and celestial cues were tracked into *Have Gun, Will Travel, Twilight Zone,* and *Perry Mason.* Much of it was recorded in London, Paris, and Mexico. Herrmann was often commissioned to compose scores for special scripts.

■ CBS Music Library organizer Don B. Ray conducting a recording session for the 1975-1976 season. He wrote numerous scores for *Hawaii Five-O* and won an Emmy for his work.

During this period, William Grant Still was hired to write "The Laredo Suite." This and works by Bernard Herrmann were commissioned expressly for the CBS library. Herrmann's "Western Suite" was recorded in Mexico. Herrmann griped over the boxiness of the acoustic, but the cues "Ambush," "Tranquil Landscape," and "Rain Clouds" came out of it, which had more to do with his fantasy-desolation motifs than music for Westerns. "Rain

■ Film composer Jerry Goldsmith began his career writing imaginative cues for the CBS Music Library in 1956, which were used profusely in *The Twilight Zone.* When live scoring was requested, Goldsmith composed for *Climax, GE Theatre, Front Row Center,* and *Playhouse 90.* He often scored three shows a week.

Clouds," for example, was built entirely on growling contrabassoon-bass clarinet chords ascending chromatically, evoking great tension and dread. These cues were routinely tracked into *Have Gun Will Travel, The Twilight Zone,* and others series.

In 1957, Jerry Goldsmith was given $2,000 to write the CBS-RID Radio Library. With a small ensemble of winds, vibraphone, a few horns and strings, and a novachord, the results were the stuff of dreams. Goldsmith's cue "Strange Return" mimicked an otherworldly female voice. "Silent Flight" was a skin-crawling piece with habanera-rhythm bass thumps, bumblebee tremelos, and muted trumpet beeps. Other Goldsmith cues in this genre were "The Secret Room," "Departure in a Fog," "Ran Afoul," and "Mysterious Storm.'"

The Twilight Zone had watershed scores, but the importance of the cue libraries to the series cannot be overstated. Classic episodes make this clear. "Mirror Image," about a woman haunted by her evil twin in a bus depot, used Goldsmith's "Silent Flight" throughout for high anxiety. "The Hitchhiker" used parts of Bernard Herrmann's original radio score and Jerry Goldsmith's "Knife Chord" and "The Secret Circle" cues repeatedly. "Judgment Night," about a Nazi commandant doomed to ride the ghost of the ship he torpedoed, used Herrmann's "Rain Clouds" and Rene Garriguenc's "Shock Therapy #3" for the character's psychotic breakdown. The offbeat "It's A Good Life," about

a boy who mindcontrols a town, used Marius Constant's demented waltz "Bergson #1" and "Mistral."

Don B. Ray organized the CBS Music Library. "I told Lud, 'We have to catalog this.' He said it was unnecessary. But we had no choice, since most CBS shows were being tracked, and music indexing was essential to the editors. I created reel numbers, band numbers, take numbers, and country codes: A for London, B for Munich, C for Mexico, through E. Library numbers were indicated by Roman numerals." Thus Jerry Goldsmith's cue "Silent Flight" became VII:23A-1, Herrmann's "Ambush" was indexed as VII:56C-2, and so on.

Apparently Lud Gluskin was playing a shell game. To avoid the union surcharge and reuse fees, he often arranged dummy sessions in Europe, went through the recording motions, but actually used Hollywood orchestras to meet broadcast schedules. According to Fred Steiner, "This became evident when my *Twilight Zone* scores were released on LPs. That was clearly me conducting the Hollywood orchestra; it was not a foreign version as one was led to believe. If the union wanted to look at a cue sheet, Lud would say 'It was recorded in Rome' and he'd have the paperwork to back it up. He had to cover himself."

■ *Hawaii Five-O* theme composer Morton Stevens with his wife Annie, circa 1975.

The quarter of a million dollars Gluskin ultimately spent on these libraries did not exactly endear him to CBS or to his nemesis, the AFM. On May 1956, Congressional hearings were held to determine if a union tympanist was actually a Communist drumbeater. Gluskin tried to explain to the Committee what "canned music" was and why it was recorded abroad. He shrugged off his expulsion from the union with the remark, "I got it in the end with both feet."[3] "Lud was always pushing that damned library," said Jerry Goldsmith. "He had a fiduciary relationship to it that wasn't all that legitimate. You couldn't quite fire Lud. He was getting a piece of the action and hated to see live music come in."

The CBS Music Library had its own clearing units, April Music (ASCAP) and Blackwood Music (BMI). In the 1960s, the CBS E-Z Cue catalog was created and the entire library was made licensable. Producer Quinn Martin leased chunks of it for *The Fugitive* on ABC (1963-1967) to supplement original music by Pete Rugolo, and added music packages from other sources. Of the fifty-five composer names attached to *The Fugitive*, thirty-eight were CBS-affiliated.

Chaos and Resolutions

Lud Gluskin was not the only one in the Congressional hot seat on May 20, 1956. In an atmosphere that smacked of the Joseph McCarthy witch hunts, James Petrillo and his men faced off with targeted dissenters. Thirty-five subpoenas had been handed out, based on Petrillo's claim that the revolt against him was "Communist-inspired."

The hearings were precipitated by a massive strike. On February 26, 1956, 2,000 members of Local 47 stormed into the Hollywood Palladium. On March 13, the Local's president John te Groen was ousted and replaced by trumpet player Cecil Reed, who organized the Musician's Guild of America to blast Petrillo out of office.

At the House subcommittee hearings, Dean Johnston, an attorney for producers, pointed out that "90 percent of television films are being made with canned music" as a result of Petrillo's edicts. Marshall Cramm, a member of the *Dragnet* radio orchestra, tried to explain to the Committee how he failed to get reuse payments because the coin had been turned over to Petrillo. Ozzie Nelson's band manager Holly Humphries, under pressure from ABC, tried to outline a plan to use live musicians for *Ozzie and Harriet*. The show had been tracking the Harmonic library. Nelson griped that "Petrillo's years of unquestioned authority are bound to warp anyone."[4] When he offered to pay a flat fee of 400 dollars to the AFM for twenty musicians in place of the 5 percent surcharge, Petrillo shot him down.

Meanwhile, music editors were usurping production music on a scale that seemed to escalate with the political unrest. The only way a composer knew for certain if his or her music was being misused was to stay glued to the tube. Jack Cookerly happened to spot an episode of *Death Valley Days* one evening on NBC. "Raoul Kraushaar was putting the music together. I had been writing cues for Capitol. I called the ad agency and said, 'The show that aired last night used my music, which was unauthorized.' Then NBC called. 'We'll be in your office with the film and a projector. We want you to identify your music.' When I heard my cue, I said 'Stop the film!' and played it on my tape recorder, which was proof enough. Raoul was whitefaced. The cue sheet showed a phony composer name and cue number. He claimed that he found the roll of music on the floor. The cue sheet was corrected the next day."

■ **British library composer Trevor Duncan, 1956. Duncan's library cues highlighted many catalogs, including those of Boosey and Hawkes, Parry, and Impress. A sound engineer and orchestrator for the BBC, he wrote the film score for *Intimate Strangers* and music for the CBS library. Duncan's Impress cue, "Grip of the Law," was used as the main title of the cult film *Plan 9 from Outer Space* and the television series *Decoy*.**

A major blowup occurred at CBS when it was discovered that music editor Martin Klein had been systematically doctoring *Gunsmoke* cue sheets to his benefit. Klein was suspended. The incident rocked the industry.

The larceny seemed to recede when the political climate stabilized. When it was determined that James Petrillo had misappropriated over thirteen million Trust Fund dollars during his reign, he knew his days were numbered. In June of 1958, he simply gave up, declining to run again. His successor, Herman Kenin, vowed to reverse Petrillo's policies. In a three-page letter written to Musicians Guild president Cecil Reed on September 5, 1961, Kenin outlined a plan to reinstate expelled union members and insure their participation in the collective bargaining process. It marked the end of fifteen years of strife and heralded the legitimate contracting of television scoring on a regular basis.

■ CBS Music Library chief Lou Teischer and CBS music coordinator Victor Quan, circa 1975. Composer Bruce Broughton can be seen in the background.

Newscasts and Urban Moods

In the 1950s, sounds of immediacy for news shows were culled from music libraries and commercial discs. A gallant section of "Jupiter" from Gustav Holst's *The Planets* was often used as a news opener. In 1953, the Mutual Network in New York was the first to popularize the "Communications" theme in the Capitol Q library.

Around 1960, CBS News began to use Ronald Hanmer's "City Desk" [FDH 009]. The cue contained a staccato phrase of trumpet attacks and wood block hits played in unison which mimicked a telegraph sound. By putting those notes on a loop, the music editor created an "urgency" call to open the network's news programs.

In 1970, ABC in New York made a maverick decision to use part of Lalo Schifrin's score for the film *Cool Hand Luke* as the "Eyewitness News" theme. That passage, which in the film played under a prison work sequence, conveyed a strong sense of teletype machinery and charged office movement.

The whole scene changed in the mid-1970s with the library themes of Keith Mansfield. KPM Music asked Mansfield to write "power cues" described in their catalog as "strident documentary" and "purposeful mechanical movement." Mansfield's "Olympiad 2000" [KPM 1200] and John Scott's "Gathering Crowds' [KPM 1138] became aural icons of news and televised sporting events and paved the way for ABC's *Nightline* theme by Gary Anderson.

Urban themes (called metropole) were rife in the fifties and sixties. Two personalities are keenly associated with them. Robert Farnon (born 1917) could convey sweeping city images with a few musical brush strokes. His "Portrait of a Flirt" in Chappell, with its bustling vision of a fashion model's dress taken by the the wind during a romp on Fifth Avenue, was one of the few library cuts to make it big as a commercial release. An international society is devoted to the man and his music.

Roger Roger (1911-1995), pronounced rozhay rozhay, was double-named by his father as a whim. His was a rollicking world of Parisian street scenes, traffic, and machinery. His work was embraced by the Chappell and Major Valentino libraries. "Le Moustique," "Eccentric Walk," "TeleSki," and "Tipsy Mockingbird," with their rakish xylophones and snickering trumpets, are the "scores" of Toulouse-Lautrec and Norman Rockwell. His animation music was the embodient of Saturday morning TV nostalgia.

Rite of Passage

Today, television music is a clean but vapid world of whole-note synthesizer chords, seamless and functional, but utterly formulaic and unmemorable. The old clichés disappeared, but much was lost in the process. Gone are the gripping suspense themes slugged into *Superman*, the sledgehammer crescendos that riveted *Dragnet* and *The Untouchables*, the icy tension themes in *The Twilight Zone*, and the yearning strings in *Bonanza* and *Little House on the Prairie*. The music was an entity. It was the sound track of our lives.

No one is more sensitive to this than baby boomers who now hold high rent positions at production music libraries. They cater to corporate bigwigs seeking to promote the right image with such trendy music packages as "Race to Achievement," "Workforce," "Industrial Panorama," and "Look on the Bright Side." But that lost world beckons. It echoes with a quality that goes beyond nostalgia for its own sake but cannot be marketed otherwise.

Music libraries now turn to buyouts of "vintage analog" and digitally transform them into spanking new archival CDs. Chunks of Chappell, Conroy, FDH, Impress, and Paxton have been depopped, declicked, and otherwise made pristine by Associated Production Music, BMG Production Music, Carlin Music, and Killer Tracks.

Send-ups of *The Donna Reed Show* sell kitchen appliances using those plucky "domestics." Laurie Johnson's cue "Man About Town" puts a fifties sheen on supermarket spots. An ad campaign for Franklin's Power Book computer is set up as a spy drama using Ronald Hanmer's classic suspense cue "Menace." The power, of course, is the music, which strikes psychological chords. One wonders if the product being hawked is remembered at all.

The Nickelodeon channel uses vintage library themes to promote their evening lineup, a mecca for what television used to be. Ironically, as the old shows play on, none of the actors or the original creative forces collect residuals. The money goes to the estate of the crafty entrepreneur who walked away with the music publishing rights in 1953, and to the credited composer, who may not have written a single note, or even existed in the first place.

Notes

1. Roger Bowman, "Television Notes," *Film Music Notes*, vol. 12, no. 4 (1953).

2. Ken Hughes, "Ready to Wear," *Music from the Movies* (spring 1995).

3. *Variety* (May 21, 1956).

4. Willard Carpenter, "Rebellion in Local 47," *Frontier* (April 1956).

PAUL MANDELL is regarded by many Hollywood composers as an authority on the subject of television background music. A graduate of the Brooklyn College film department, he returned there in 1976 to preside over film history classes. He worked for Armed Forces Radio overseas in 1968 and played transcriptions of television broadcasts nightly. In 1973, he was awarded a grant from the Louis B. Mayer Foundation of the American Film Institute and coanimated a series of stop-motion short subjects for the Children's Television Workshop on PBS. His articles on film music and visual effects have appeared in *American Cinematographer, Cinefex, Filmscore Monthly, Cinefantastique,* and *Scarlet Street.* He coauthored *Adventure, Romance, and Terror* for the ASC Press in 1990 and wrote the revealing work "How DeMille Parted the Red Sea" for the American Society of Cinematographers.

Mr. Mandell created the sleeve notes for the Cinemusic series of archival CDs released by Associated Production Music in 1998. He is a member of the Robert Farnon Society in England, plays keyboard, and produces sound tracks for Varése Sarabande and Retrosonic Records.

AT THE LIBRARY

BY KRIN GABBARD

The Motion Picture, Broadcasting, and Recorded Sound Division (MBRS) at the Library of Congress documents the entire history of American television. During the medium's early years, jazz artists were regularly captured doing what they do best. Curiously, the relative dearth of good jazz on network television today may be related to how the music was presented in the early years. In spite of its shady origins, jazz was regularly described as serious art by the talking heads on television in the 1950s and 1960s. This tradition has borne fruit in recent years; the music is now considered the equal of the ballet, the opera, and the symphony. A jazz musician has even won the crusty old Pulitzer Prize. Perhaps as a result, jazz has been increasingly removed from the popular sphere. The voice of Louis Armstrong or the clarinet of Benny Goodman can be heard in the occasional television commercial today, but any full-scale presentation of the music seldom, if ever, makes its way to network prime time.

The Library's collection reveals, however, that jazz was once a regular presence throughout the broadcast day. Virtually all of the jazz videos available in stores today can be found in the Library, including classic programs such as *Jazz on a Summer's Day, The Sound of Jazz, Jivin' in Bebop, Jammin' the Blues, Texas Tenor—The Illinois Jacquet Story,* and *Thelonious Monk—Straight, No Chaser.* But most of the Library's jazz videos have never been available commercially in spite of the extraordinary interest they hold for jazz enthusiasts. The Library has, for example, a copy of the only known film of Clifford Brown, the trumpet genius who died at the age of twenty-six in 1956. It also has rare footage of the revered jazz singer Johnny Hartman, who recorded so memorably with John Coltrane in 1964. The great jazz drummer Jo Jones can be seen in a duet with Chatur Lal, a virtuoso percussionist from India. The Count Basie Orchestra is in full cry at Birdland on a live broadcast of *The Steve Allen Show* from 1956. Duke Ellington is exhaustively represented in the collections of Jerry Valburn, who indefatigably assembled a wealth of Ellington material which the Library of Congress acquired in 1991. Even Cecil Taylor, long ignored by all but the most devoted jazz fans, can be seen not only playing but even reciting poetry in a 1965 broadcast.

What has been called The Golden Age of Television was also a defining moment in the history of jazz. In the 1950s, talented writers, directors, and musicians were given huge blocks of time to broadcast just about anything they could create. A nation fascinated by the new medium was eager to consume the exciting new images. A simultaneous phenomenon that may or may not have been related to the explosion of interest in television was the growing belief that jazz was a valid art form, separate from the dance music of the 1940s or the kiddie pop of the 1950s. Even though there was still a large popular audience for jazz, the music could still be presented as a topic worthy of serious study, complete

with an evolutionary history and a canon of genius composers and instrumentalists. For a television industry hungry for programming to fill up its broadcast day, jazz was the ideal commodity: it could both delight and instruct. National Educational Television, later to become the Public Broadcasting System, was especially invested in celebrating all types of jazz performance. In the first decades of television, however, drily intellectual commentary was the almost inevitable companion of jazz performance.

Some earlier jazz videos in the Library's collection reveal how differently jazz was treated before it became a regular fixture on early television. A 1937 Vitaphone short featuring Jimmie Lunceford and his Orchestra begins with an actor dressed as a road-show Satan emerging from a fiery pit singing about "sin-copation." Lunceford's extravagantly dressed orchestra is first superimposed over the image of the devil before the stage is given over completely to the band and several vaudeville-type performers, including the tap-dancing Three Brown Jacks. Lunceford himself introduces the performers but says nothing about how the audience will be intellectually enriched by listening to Myra Johnson singing "You Can't Pull the Wool Over My Eyes" or Eddie Tompkins scatting through "Nagasaki." The band swings heartily, the soloists play with artistry and abandon, but the presentation is all for fun.

Let's Make Rhythm, a 1947 RKO short also transferred to video, is even more surprising for its lack of pretense, especially because it features the large "progressive" jazz orchestra led by Stan Kenton. The plot of the twenty-minute film involves the romance between a sailor and a telephone operator but manages to find moments for several impressive performances by Kenton's band, including a version of Duke Ellington's "Just a-Settin' and a-Rockin'" with an appealing vocal by June Christy. And even though the orchestra plays a composition ostentatiously titled "A Concerto to End All Concertos," no one suggests that the music is anything more than a pleasant diversion.

As I have argued elsewhere,[1] the notion that jazz was not just a simple entertainment without a history began to appear regularly in the American cinema of the late 1940s. In *A Song Is Born* (1948), for example, Danny Kaye plays a professor writing a history of jazz with the help of Louis Armstrong, Benny Goodman, Tommy Dorsey, and several other revered jazz musicians. By 1950, Kirk Douglas was starring in *Young Man with a Horn*, based loosely on the life of Bix Beiderbecke, the legendary jazz trumpeter who died young because a philistine music industry could not appreciate his art.

The idea of jazz as serious art was very much in the air as television was becoming omnipresent in American life. Although much of what was *said* about jazz in the 1950s and 1960s has not aged well, the music has kept its vitality. Consider the program *Omnibus*, a triumph of live television throughout most of the 1950s. Audiences could watch an exciting reunion of the Benny Goodman Trio (1953), or the extraordinary encounter between Jo Jones and Chatur Lal (1956), but always with Alistair Cooke solemnly giving them permission to enjoy it. Or consider an NBC program from 1958 called "The Subject Is Jazz—Cool." Gilbert Seldes, the author of *The Seven Lively Arts* and one of early television's official intellectuals, introduces a group of jazz musicians as if they were members of the Budapest String Quartet. Led by Lee Konitz (also sax) and featuring Don Elliott (trumpet and mellophone), Mundell Lowe (guitar), Warne Marsh (tenor), Billy Taylor (piano), Ed Thigpen (drums), and Eddie Safranski (bass), the band plays lively versions of "Godchild," "Half Nelson," "Move," and "Subconscious Lee" while the camera pans over photographs of Miles Davis, Lennie Tristano, and Lester Young. At one point, when Seldes asks Billy Taylor if jazz can be cool and still swing, Taylor obligingly demonstrates at the piano while the camera zooms in on the sheet music to "Lady Bird." Jazz as a written text has seldom been taken so seriously by a television camera. Toward the end of the program Seldes quotes the French critic André Hodeir on the nature of "cool jazz" and then asks Konitz to explain what Hodeir means. Not entirely comfortable with Seldes's (or Hodeir's) approach to jazz, Konitz says he does not know.

Then, shrugging a bit, Konitz says that he always thought that Louis Armstrong's Hot Five recordings were cool.

The intellectual approach to jazz served many purposes, even if musicians such as Konitz seemed amused by it. In 1962, when the Bossa Nova was gaining in popularity throughout the United States, a CBS News program "Eyewitness: The New Beat" paid special attention to the emotionless faces in a coffee house, where João Gilberto performed "Desafinado," and at the White House, where Paul Winter played for Jacqueline Kennedy. Charles Collingwood and Charles Kuralt, the two earnest reporters for the program, both assure the viewer that audiences are actually involved with the music in spite of their blank faces. Kuralt hopefully suggests that the new Brazilian beat will replace rock and roll, thus soothing teenagers rather than whipping them into a frenzy. When Antonio Carlos Jobim is interviewed alongside Gerry Mulligan, both speak again about the lack of emotion exhibited by listeners, but these two are much more concerned with making music. In what is clearly an unrehearsed performance, Jobim plays piano and sings "One Note Samba" while Mulligan, without his usual baritone saxophone, plays lovely fills on a clarinet. The camera continues to roll while Mulligan and Jobim discuss how best to phrase a Bossa Nova tune before playing again with even more sympathetic interaction. The sequence ends with Jobim exclaiming, "Good, Gerry, perfect!" Jazz may have been promoted as serious art by those who would condemn rock and roll, but the intellectual approach could also produce moments of exciting television like this encounter between Mulligan and Jobim.

The intellectual approach also made room for the great novelist and critic Ralph Ellison to comment at length on jazz and its history. Ellison is especially articulate in programs broadcast in 1965 from the Village Gate, for many years a premiere showcase for jazz in New York's Greenwich Village. As part of the NET series *USA: Music*, Ellison put the performances of several groups into a larger cultural context than the music was usually allowed. In an episode devoted to "The Experimenters," Ellison tells us that jazz "attempts to humanize the world in terms of sound" and to "impose an American Negro sense of time upon the larger society and upon the world of nature." He even acknowledges the value of jazz's new legitimacy as serious art, referring to "a musical route to social respectability and to a wide acceptance among the cult of jazz intellectuals." He adds that the jazz musician must strive to absorb Western traditions without losing touch with the origins of the music. He then introduces the Charles Mingus group, with Charles McPherson (alto sax), Danny Richmond (drums), Jimmy Owens (trumpet), Hobart Dotson (trumpet), and Howard Johnson (tuba), playing some of its most ambitious music. Later in the same program, Ellison introduces Cecil Taylor, who also makes no compromises for the television audience. Taylor prefaces his music with a typically allusive prose poem that deserves to be quoted in full:

> The philosophical premise that this music is based on is that man begins a transliteration of the mean fact toward symbolic representation when mind and body move, recog-

■ Thelonious Monk (1917-1982) appears in three of the most famous jazz videos: *The Sound of Jazz* (1957), *Jazz on a Summer's Day* (1960), and *Straight, No Chaser* (1989). *Jerry Ohlinger's Movie Material Store, Inc.*

■ Dizzy Gillespie (1917-1993), in full bebop regalia, photographed at roughly the same time that he appeared in the film *Jivin' in Bebop* (1947). *Photo by William P. Gottlieb.*

■ Pianist Bill Evans (1929-1980) is one of several jazz artists who performed in a CBS memorial for Robert Kennedy after his death in 1968. *Jerry Ohlinger's Music Material Store, Inc.*

■ Illinois Jacquet (born 1922) as he appears in *Texas Tenor–The Illinois Jacquet Story* (1992). *Jerry Ohlinger's Movie Material Store, Inc.*

nizing their singularity, therefore their unity, and therefore their sanity. The question is, where the economic and social factor determining an artist exist, those which permit the expression of time through time to one whose consumption is unlimited or were they the producers for others? The name of the piece will be "octagonal skirt and fancy pants."

Taylor and his group (Jimmy Lyons on sax, Sunny Murray on drums, and Henry Grimes on bass) play an intensely dissonant composition during which Taylor leans deep into the piano and plucks the strings by hand.

The program from the Village Gate continues with a reappearance by Mingus's group playing an elaborately orchestrated version of "Peggy's Blue Skylight." Ellison speaks briefly about how the meeting of European and Black American experience helped make jazz unique and then reintroduces Mingus, who reads his own highly political prose poem, "Don't Let It Happen Here." Mingus's text is about a world in which Communists, Jews, Unionists, and then Catholics are each taken away by an oppressive government. In each case, Mingus says, "I said nothing

because I was not a member." At the end of the poem, when the narrator himself is taken away, Mingus says, "Again I said nothing because I was as guilty of genocide as those who killed the eighteen million people along with me." The recitation ends with Mingus urging the viewer to "speak out and don't let it happen here." It is difficult to imagine a major network broadcasting this kind of politically charged material today.

Even when network television was most timid about presenting the more experimental jazz, the music still carried an aura of art. For example, when Johnny Hartman appeared on the short-lived *Sammy Davis Junior Show* (NBC) in 1966, he was kept separate from the rest of the program. The other guests that evening were the Andrews Sisters and the Supremes. As host, Davis interacted with both groups and then asked them to sing each other's hits. The two sets of singers were called upon to "act," responding to Davis's requests and then to each other as if nothing had been rehearsed. Hartman, however, who two years earlier had made the Impulse album with John Coltrane that at least one critic has called "The Greatest Record Ever Made,"[2] is introduced reverentially by Davis and then displays his deep, romantic voice on Rodgers and Hart's "It Never Entered My Mind." Accompanied by Milt Hinton on bass and Hank Jones at the piano, the tuxedoed Hartman carries himself very much in the style established by Nat King Cole, the last black entertainer before Davis to have his own network program. Hartman's records have sold substantially more since his death in 1982 than they did in the 1960s, perhaps because the man we see in this video does not *look* like the man we seem to be hearing on the records. A short man with an unflattering haircut and awkward gestures, Hartman possesses little charisma as a performer. When his number is over, Davis embraces Hartman warmly, but there is no conversation between the two men. Scarcely resembling a popular performer, Hartman seems to be there only to create art. The earnestness of the Hartman segment—not to mention the beauty of his performance—starkly contrasts with the jokiness of the Andrews Sisters singing "Stop in the Name of Love," and "Baby Love" and the Supremes performing "Bei Mir Bist Du Schoen," and "Roll Out the Barrel."

One of the names that appears regularly in the Library of Congress's registry of jazz on television is Ralph Gleason. In addition to narrating a number of programs for NET, Gleason hosted *Jazz Casual* on KQED in San Francisco in 1963 and 1964. Although Gleason brought a certain dignity to the programs, he was seldom interested in promoting the music as great art in spite of the fact that most of the canonized jazz artists from that era appeared on his half-hour show: John Coltrane, Dizzy Gillespie, Ben Webster, Sonny Rollins, Cannonball Adderley, Woody Herman, Art Farmer, Dave Brubeck, and many others. In one of the most memorable episodes, Jimmy Rushing sits at the piano, playing, singing, and chatting with Gleason in a single, unbroken camera shot for thirty minutes. Nothing could be more "casual" than a sustained gaze at the great blues singer, but the music and the stories he tells are often exciting, even when he is reminiscing about playing piano in 1923 with Jelly Roll Morton as his drummer.

■ Count Basie (1904-1984) and his orchestra are captured live in an extraordinary broadcast from Birdland on *The Steve Allen Show* (1956).

■ Stan Kenton (1911-1979) was regularly filmed with his "progressive" jazz orchestra. *Photo by William P. Gottlieb.*

Although more than one camera was in use when Lambert, Hendricks, and Bavan appeared on *Jazz Casual* in 1963, the program did not stint on the amount of extraordinary jazz singing it presented. As always, the vocal trio is impeccable as it works its way through the fiendishly difficult close harmonies it first began performing in 1957 when Annie Ross was the female singer. Ross's replacement during the last two years of the group's existence was Yolande Bavan. Dressed in her native Ceylonese gowns and wearing dramatic eye makeup, Bavan has no difficulty keeping up with the veteran vocalists Jon Hendricks and Dave Lambert. Accompanied by Gildo Mahones (piano), Jimmie Smith (drums), George Tucker (bass), and Pony Poindexter (sopra-no saxophone), the group sings "This Could Be the Start of Something Big," "Melba's Blues," and "Cloudburst." On "Shiny Stockings," Bavan successfully puts words to the great trumpet solo that Thad Jones played on the original recording with the Count Basie band. "Cousin Mary" features Hendricks scatting his way through the same solo that Coltrane improvises on his 1959 recording of the tune.

Just as the Golden Age of Television in the 1950s coincided with the arrival of jazz as art, the early days of live television were ideally suited to presenting jazz artists performing "in the moment." In a sense, live television adds an extra level of excitement to live jazz. This was definitely the case when Clifford Brown appeared on a Soupy Sales program when Sales only had a local show on a Detroit station. Standing before a curtain alone, Brown plays "Oh Lady Be Good" and "Memories of You." Even though the unseen musicians accompanying him were probably not members of the Brown-Roach quintet, the trumpeter plays with his usual fluidity and energy. Brown is no show-off; he displays no attention-grabbing mannerisms. He simply bears down on his horn, closes his eyes, and lets the music flow. This extremely rare glimpse of Brown can be dated to about 1954 by a bit of conversation toward the end when Sales says that Brown had recently worked with his coleader Max Roach in the film *Carmen Jones*. (Brown is the only member of the group who does not appear on camera in a brief scene in that film.) Brown is very much "Sweet Clifford" in this segment: though shy and unassuming, he radiates warmth and charm. The dignity with which he carries himself and the beauty of his improvisations transcend the limitations of the old kinescope from which the Library's video copy is taken.

Some of the most intriguing videos in the collection do not involve musicians who have since been installed in the pantheon of great jazz artists. Pianist Vince Guaraldi, best known for the music that accompanied Charles Schulz's *Peanuts* gang on the animated television programs, is the subject of three NET programs from 1964 called "Anatomy of a Hit." Narrated by Ralph Gleason, the programs take a detailed look at the career of Guaraldi when he was riding a wave of popularity with his record, "Cast Your Fate to the Wind." The tune was an original composition by Guaraldi and found its large audience almost by accident. Guaraldi had recorded an album of songs from the art house hit, *Black Orpheus*, but needed something short for the B side of a 45 issue. To everyone's surprise, Guaraldi's trio performance of "Cast Your Fate" had great financial success. The first of the three programs, titled "The Serendipity Groove," shows the Guaraldi Trio (with Jerry Granelli on drums and Fred Marshall on bass) rehearsing, recording, and discoursing on the difficulty of reaching a large public

■ June Christy (1925-1990) displays her talent as a jazz singer in the RKO short *Let's Make Rhythm* (1947), with Stan Kenton and his orchestra. *Photo by William P. Gottlieb.*

■ Benny Goodman (1909-1986) is featured in the films *Hollywood Hotel* (1937) and *Stage Door Canteen* (1943) as well as in a stirring reunion with Teddy Wilson and Gene Krupa on a 1953 *Omnibus* broadcast. *Photo by William P. Gottlieb.*

as a jazz artist. Looking very much the San Francisco Beatnik, Guaraldi works in sweatshirt and jeans with a handlebar moustache and black horn-rimmed glasses. He is not, however, an especially flamboyant personality. That role is reserved for Max Weiss of Fantasy Records, Guaraldi's record company. With a large fur hat reminiscent of the one John Phillips wore with the Mamas and the Papas in the early sixties, Weiss talks about the record business while absentmindedly waving an unloaded revolver above his head. (The announcer had prepared the audience for this mannerism with a few unironic words about Weiss's collection of guns.) Clearly having fun at the expense of the earnest interviewer, Weiss attributes much of the success of Fantasy Records to the intuitions of his brother and the company's recording engineer, Sol Weiss. According to Max, Sol is able to predict the success of a recording *only* by watching the VU meters that register sound levels in the studio. Max insists that Sol never even listens to the music; he only watches the dials.

The Library's collections include many other fascinating glimpses into the careers of relatively minor figures such as Guaraldi, but it also possesses hours and hours of footage of the most famous performers in jazz history. Louis Armstrong was almost constantly before the eyes of Americans thanks to film and television. He appeared in twenty-three feature-length American films and numerous documentaries such as *Satchmo the Great* (1957), *Jazz on a Summer's Day* (1960), and *Jazz, the Intimate Art* (1968) as well as the three-minute soundies from the early 1940s, "When It's Sleepy Time Down South," "Shine," "I'll Be Glad When You're Dead You Rascal You," and "Swingin' on Nothin'." Virtually all of this material is in the Library's collections along with numerous programs devoted entirely or in part to Louis Armstrong and his music. A great deal of fascinating material was assembled for a CBS News Special shortly after Armstrong died in 1971. The program begins with archival footage of Armstrong playing while Leonard Bernstein conducts the New York Philharmonic with an aged W. C. Handy in the audience. Bernstein throws his whole body into extracting a jazz performance from his orchestra. Still filled with exuberance after the performance, the conductor breathlessly tells the audience that Armstrong's music is "real and true and honest and simple and even noble. Every time this man puts his trumpet to his lips, even to practice three notes, he does it with his whole soul." The program continues as Charles Kuralt dourly invites a group of musicians to reminisce about the trumpeter: Tyree Glenn, Milt Hinton, Buddy Rich, Bobby Hackett, Dizzy Gillespie, Earl Hines, Budd Johnson, and Peggy Lee. Most of the artists have nothing but praise for the departed trumpeter, and some are quite eloquent in their tributes. Bobby Hackett, for example, says he learned everything from Armstrong and that the great message from the man was, "Love thy neighbor and cut out the nonsense." Seemingly unaware of the publicity that Armstrong garnered in 1957 when he denounced Arkansas governor Orval Faubus and Pres. Dwight Eisenhower over the segregation of public schools, Kuralt asks why Armstrong was never "political." Gillespie quickly corrects him, recalling the Faubus incident and assuring Kuralt that Armstrong was

■ Billy Taylor (born 1921) explains the meaning of "cool" to Gilbert Seldes in a 1958 episode of *The Subject Is Jazz*. *Photo by William P. Gottlieb.*

■ Gerry Mulligan (1927-1996) acted in films such as *I Want To Live* (1958) and *The Rat Race* (1960). He also plays clarinet in a memorable duet with Antonio Carlos Jobim in a 1962 program produced for CBS News. *Institute for Jazz Studies, Rutgers University at Newark.*

■ Charles Mingus (1922-1979) is the subject of a 1968 documentary, *Mingus*, and a featured actor in *All Night Long* (1962), an English film based on Shakespeare's *Othello*. The manuscripts of his extraordinary biography, *Beneath the Underdog*, are also in the Library's collections. *Charles Mingus Collection, Music Division.*

■ Cecil Taylor (born 1929), for four decades one of the most uncompromising performers in jazz, performs with his band on *USA: Music* (1965). *Institute for Jazz Studies, Rutgers University at Newark.*

■ Johnny Hartman (1923-1983), who made the great album with John Coltrane in 1963, appears in a 1966 episode of *The Sammy Davis, Jr. Show. Institute for Jazz Studies, Rutgers University at Newark.*

Jimmy Rushing (1903-1972), who sang the blues with Count Basie in the 1930s, reminisces with Ralph Gleason in a 1964 broadcast of *Jazz Casual. Photo by William P. Gottlieb.*

■ Clifford Brown (1930-1956), one of the most inspiring soloists in jazz history, can be seen in a rare kinescope of *The Soupy Sales Show* (1954). *Institute for Jazz Studies, Rutgers University at Newark.*

■ Louis Armstrong (1901-1971), who perfected the art of the jazz solo, was filmed regularly throughout his life. The Library of Congress has many hours of film and video documenting forty years of the trumpeter's career. *Photo by William P. Gottlieb.*

■ Louis Armstrong in a publicity photo taken in 1931, when he began appearing in films. *Jerry Ohlinger's Movie Material Store, Inc.*

capable of "calling everybody everything." The segment concludes with Peggy Lee slowly singing "I Can't Give You Anything But Love, Baby" while Glenn, Hackett, Gillespie, and Johnson play a historically eclectic range of accompanying figures. This musical tribute is still moving today.

The career of Ella Fitzgerald is also well documented in the collection. Although not as ubiquitous as Armstrong, Fitzgerald appeared in a number of films, including *Pete Kelly's Blues* (1955) and *St. Louis Blues* (1958). Playing a drug-addicted blues singer, Fitzgerald acted alongside Burl Ives, Shelley Winters, Jean Seberg, and Ricardo Montalban in an obscure film in the Library's collection, *Let No Man Write My Epitaph* (1960). She can also be seen in several television broadcasts, such as the Frank Sinatra vehicle, "A Man and His Music—Ella and Jobim" (1967), and an episode of *The Nat King Cole Show* (1957). As Ella herself points out when she appears in the "All-Star Swing Festival" in 1972, "I'm the only girl." Amidst performances by Duke Ellington, Benny Goodman, Count Basie, Dave Brubeck, Joe Williams, and Lionel Hampton, Fitzgerald sings an appealing "Oh Lady Be Good" with the Basie Orchestra and a stirring "Body and Soul" with her regular accompanist, Tommy Flanagan. Interestingly, by 1972 the need to justify jazz as an art form seemed to have dissipated. The host of the "All-Star Swing Festival" is Doc Severinson, who wastes no time talking about André Hodeir or the need to listen to jazz instead of rock and roll. He simply introduces the artists and gets out of the way.

Perhaps the most exciting video performances by Ella Fitzgerald *and* by Duke Ellington are contained in a *Bell Telephone Hour* broadcast from 1959. Accompanied by Jim Hall (guitar), Gus Johnson (drums), and Wilfred Middlebrooks (bass), Ella and Duke appeared here for the first time together on television. Ellington is especially energetic in this broadcast, perhaps trying hard to impress the person just off camera, at whom he seems to be casting frequent gazes. Nevertheless, Ellington finds time to interact joyously with Fitzgerald, who rises to the occasion as she sings several of the great Ellington songs she had recorded a few years earlier when she made *The Duke Ellington Song Book* for Verve Records.

Of course, no artist was able to embody the idea that jazz was serious business more effectively than Duke Ellington. From the beginning he was portrayed as a devoted composer rather than as a mere entertainer. The Library owns a copy of *Black and Tan*, a short film from 1929 in which Ellington plays himself as a composer-bandleader with principles and courage. The film begins with Ellington at the piano, teaching a new piece to his trumpeter with a sheet of written music. By the end of *Black and Tan*, Duke has walked out of a performance because of the management's inhuman treatment of its star dancer, played memorably by Fredi Washington. No African American artist had ever been presented in this fashion in an American film. More often than not, black jazz musicians were portrayed as simple folk expressing their feelings "naturally" in music without relying upon thought, much less upon compositional skill.

Ellington continued to carry the unique distinction of being considered a serious artist throughout his career, even

■ Ella Fitzgerald (1918-1996), shown here with Dizzy Gillespie, is featured in numerous movies and television programs, including *The All-Star Swing Festival* (1972) and a remarkable *Bell Telephone Hour* program (1959) with Duke Ellington. *Photo by William P. Gottlieb.*

when the business of entertainment was least attentive to his achievements and in spite of the fact that Ellington himself was always quite modest in describing his own work. Thanks to the extraordinary collection of Jerry Valburn and the Library's other holdings, over forty years of Ellington's career can be closely studied on film and video. While Louis Armstrong regularly acted in films, beginning with his role as Henry in *Pennies from Heaven* (1936) until his moving performance thirty years later as Sweet Daddy Willie Ferguson in *A Man Called Adam* (1966), Ellington spoke lines of dialogue in precisely two films, *Black and Tan* in 1929 and *Anatomy of a Murder* in 1959. In all of his many other film roles, he was almost inevitably presented as the leader of his own orchestra. Among the many recommended appearances of the Ellington Orchestra on film, the Library has *Bundle of Blues* (1933), *Belle of the Nineties* (1934), *Symphony in Black* (1935), *Cabin in the Sky* (1943), *Reveille with Beverly* (1943), and excerpts from several other films. Ellington's music is a thrilling presence throughout *Paris Blues* (1961), a film that finds still another opportunity for the acting talents of Louis Armstrong, this time playing a character named Wild Man Moore.

Ellington was a familiar presence when television became a fixture in the American home. When Edward R.

■ **Duke Ellington (1899-1974) in the 1940s, about the time that he and George Pal made the "Puppetoon," in which animated perfume bottles danced to "The Perfume Suite," composed by Ellington and Billy Strayhorn.** *Photo by William P. Gottlieb.*

Murrow interviewed him on *Person to Person* in 1957, he looked relaxed and fit in his New York apartment. He happily shows off the portraits of his parents on the wall. He is just as proud of his real-life children, Mercer and Ruth, who sit demurely on his sofa. More self-effacing about his work, Duke refuses to characterize it in grandiose terms, insisting only that his music is an attempt "to capture the life of the people." The camera follows him around his apartment as he moves from his grand piano to a phonograph on which he plays a few minutes of his latest recording, *A Drum Is a Woman*.

Even earlier, on an episode of *Masquerade Party* from 1955, Duke is witty and dignified even though he is dressed as a camel driver. This panel show presented celebrities in disguise to a panel of lesser celebrities who tried to guess their identities. The disguises were usually justified by some aspect of the guest's career. In the case of Ellington, the vaguely Arabic get-up was motivated by his hit record of Juan Tizol's composition, "Caravan." As the panel tries to guess his identity, Ellington is consistently imaginative as he parries their questions. When asked if he works with camels, Duke says he prefers Chryslers and Cadillacs. When one of

the panelists wonders if he is a golfer and if his outfit suggests a play on "sand traps," Ellington says no but that he does some swinging. And asked if he is famous for traveling in Arab countries, Duke replies that he "doesn't get around in that region of the world much anymore."

But there are great *musical* moments from Ellington as well. Some of the most unusual include a 1972 video from Japanese television in which Duke accompanies four male singers and a female vocalist doing "Satin Doll" with perfect American enunciation. There is also a beautifully edited commercial for Craven, a brand of Australian cigarettes, that rapidly cuts back and forth between members of the band traveling and performing. And there is an especially revealing glimpse of the interactions between Ellington and his great tenor saxophonist Paul Gonsalves on a 1972 video made at a master class when the Ellington band was in residence at the University of Wisconsin. Most of the program is taken up with Ellington reminiscing at the piano. Late in the broadcast he invites Gonsalves to join him on stage. Although no mention of the incident is made in the video, the program was made one day after Gonsalves had been too intoxicated to perform at an important concert in Milwaukee. Still upset, Ellington summons Gonsalves with the words, "Stinky, you juiced again?" Very sheepishly, Gonsalves approaches the stage and suggests that the two play "Happy Reunion." He then puts the saxophone to his lips and plays the most beautiful and emotional version of the song that he had ever recorded. Ellington responds with a stirring solo of his own. After the performance, Gonsalves lovingly walks over to him and motions to his cheeks for Ellington's famous "four kisses," which Ellington delivers in regal fashion. There are few other moments on film or video that say so much about how Ellington felt about his musicians and how they felt toward him. And this is only one of many musical encounters in the Library's collection that does not require a commentator to convince us that we are watching something artistic.

The Library has many extraordinary moments on film and video featuring all but the most obscure jazz musicians. This article has only touched on a tiny percentage of the great jazz that can be found in the Library's vast collections.

Notes

1. Krin Gabbard, *Jammin' at the Margins: Jazz and the American Cinema* (Chicago: University of Chicago Press, 1996), esp. chap. 3.
2. Daniel Okrent, "The Greatest Record Ever Made," *Esquire* (June 1990): 46.

The author wishes to thank Larry Applebaum, Curator of the Library of Congress Jazz Film Series, for his assistance in recommending titles for viewing.

KRIN GABBARD is Professor and Chair of Comparative Literature at the State University of New York at Stony Brook. He grew up in the rural Midwest listening to jazz and trying to play the trumpet like Miles Davis. He spent his college years at the University of Chicago and undertook graduate study at Indiana University, where he took a Ph.D. in comparative Literature in 1978. After teaching at the University of South Dakota and

■ Duke Ellington's first appearance on film: *Black and Tan* (1929) with Arthur Whetsol (left) and Freddie Washington (center). Institute for Jazz Studies, Rutgers University at Newark.

Stephens College, he moved to Stony Brook, where he has taught since 1981.

Most of Professor Gabbard's research has been devoted to cinema studies. In 1987, he coauthored *Psychiatry and the Cinema* (University of Chicago Press) with his brother Glen O. Gabbard, a psychoanalyst at the Menninger Foundation. Krin Gabbard's articles have appeared in *Cinema Journal*, *The Psychoanalytic Review*, *American Image*, *The Journal of Popular Film and Television*, and *Comparative Literature Studies*.

In the 1990s, Professor Gabbard made his lifelong love of jazz the center of his scholarly writing. He published two jazz anthologies, *Jazz Among the Discourses* and *Representing Jazz* (both through Duke University Press), in 1995. His 1996 book, *Jammin' at the Margins: Jazz and the American Cinema* (University of Chicago Press) was nominated for the National Book Award. He is presently at work on *Playing the Male: Music, Movies, and Masculinity*.

GROUCHO MARX RUNS THROUGH

Outside of a dog, a book is man's best friend.

Inside of a dog, it's too dark to read.

GROUCHO MARX

America became aware of a very unusual partnership in the making the night of October 5, 1965. That was when Groucho Marx appeared on *The Tonight Show* and gave a letter to Johnny Carson to read to his television audience. As he handed it to him, Groucho proclaimed, "It astonished me so much that I thought the world ought to know about this."

Johnny looked into the camera and explained to his audience, "The letter is signed by L. Quincy Mumford, Librarian of Congress." He then read:

May I ask you if you have made suitable provisions for the preservation of your personal papers? If not, I invite you to consider the claims of the Library of Congress as an appropriate repository. In the Library's Manuscript Division you can find many of the nation's manuscript treasures, including the personal papers of most of the presidents.

Johnny stopped reading, looked up and said, "This is all legitimate." Then he returned to the letter:

The distinguished collection would be enhanced by the addition of your papers. I invite you to present them to the American people for inclusion in the national library. If the invitation appeals to you, and I earnestly hope that it does, I shall be happy to provide further details. Meanwhile, I enclose an explanatory brochure for your information.

THE LIBRARY OF CONGRESS

GROUCHO MARX

33 BLUE RIBBON LANE · "BLUE RIBBON TOWN"

HOLLYWOOD, CALIFORNIA

When Johnny finished, Groucho commented, "I don't know how they got wind of this, but I've been corresponding with a number of people for about twenty-five years: Bob Benchley, James Thurber, Goody Ace, Fred Allen (we wrote every week, maybe). I was so pleased when I got this thing. Having not finished public school, to find my letters sitting next to the Gettysburg Address . . . I thought it was quite an incongruity in addition to being extremely thrilling. And I am very proud of this thing."

The gift was made, and the Library of Congress received a major part of Groucho's personal papers and audiovisual memorabilia. Added to the audio and visual material already in the Library, all parts of the comedian's life and career are available to researchers.

Fitting together the many pieces of the puzzle of the life of Groucho Marx brings forth a feeling of participating in the ramshackle pace often set in the Marx Brothers movies: the action is fun, a bit wacky, and wholeheartedly satisfying. This guy had a sharp and sarcastic wit both on screen and off.

The complexity of Groucho's career is as multilayered as his humor. He was in show business just over seventy years, and he used that time to tackle successfully nearly every part of the entertainment industry: vaudeville, stage, film, radio, television, and recordrd sound. His story, and his humor, live inside the Library of Congress.

The broadcast medium played an important part in Groucho's career and life. First, it was radio that helped

■ On October 5, 1968, ...
Show and showed Johnny Carson a ...
Congress L. Quincy Mumford, in which he asked Groucho
Marx to donate his personal papers to the Library.

■ Groucho explains to Johnny, "It astonished me so much that
I thought the world ought to know about this."

■ "This is all legitimate," Johnny Carson tells his audience.

■ The Marx Brothers in the filmed version of one of their most popular Broadway plays, *Animal Crackers*.

establish and expand his career. And years later, it was television that was the sustaining factor in reviving his career because it allowed him to develop his successful radio program, *You Bet Your Life*, into one of the most popular television shows to date. The radio program ran for four years, and *You Bet Your Life* ran on television for eleven years. The Library of Congress's Motion Picture, Broadcasting, and Recorded Sound Division (MBRS) has a large selection of his radio and television appearances, recordings, films, films stills, and lobby cards. The Manuscript Division has a major collection of his personal correspondence, a dozen scripts

he kept from his film days, and drafts of two of his books. The Music Division has sheet music from his plays and films. And, of course, throughout the general stacks, a number of books can be found written by and about this man who is recognized as one of America's top comedians.

Groucho (Julius) Marx was born October 2, 1890, and started out in vaudeville in 1905 as a teenage member of the Leroy Trio. His younger brothers were also bitten by the show business bug and joined him around 1912, and the Marx Brothers act was born. Groucho, Harpo, and Chico were the act, with Gummo or Zeppo joining them at vari-

■ Groucho in *A Day at the Races* (1937), with Sig Ruman and his constant foil, Margaret Dumont, who gave a different meaning to the term *leading lady*.

ous times. Their style and individual personality traits developed quickly and stayed with them throughout their careers. In Groucho's case, some of the humor you heard from him on his stage, film, or television appearances represented the wit of the real man, although throughout his career he hired humorists such as George S, Kaufman, S. J. Perelman, Mac Benoff, and Irving Brecher to write his songs and lines. But he frequently had a hand in the development of the material he used, and after separating from his brothers he changed his image by giving up the greasepaint moustache for a real one and toning down his comic style for his classic television show, *You Bet Your Life*. This show further established his reputation as an improvisational genius, but actually it was carefully scripted and orchestrated.

The brothers continued in vaudeville until they could move to Broadway and establish themselves with early hits like *The Cinderella Girl* (1919), and *I'll Say She Is* (1924). This gave them the chance to take their biggest step, right into the world of motion pictures. The 1930s and early 1940s saw the golden era of the Marx Brothers and, as always, Groucho commanded the center of the stage. Their first movies, *The Cocoanuts* and *Animal Crackers*, were filmed versions of their Broadway hits. Then came such

films as *Monkey Business* (1931), *Duck Soup* (1934), *A Night at the Opera* (1935), *A Day at the Races* (1937), *Room Service* (1938), *A Night in Casablanca* (1946), and many others. These slapstick comedies are now considered classics. The film industry recognized their success in 1974 when Groucho received a special Oscar from the Academy of Motion Picture Arts and Sciences for the achievement of the Marx Brothers in the art of motion picture comedy.

By the midforties, their popularity had peaked, and the brothers started going their separate ways. Groucho continued to make films like *Copacabana* (1947), *Mr. Music* (1950), and *Double Dynamite* (1951), with Frank Sinatra and Jane Russell. He also became a frequent guest on a number of radio programs and took an active interest in a new format, television.

The Motion Picture, Broadcasting, and Recorded Sound Division

The Recorded Sound Reference Center in MBRS holds the Groucho Marx radio and recording materials, many of which highlight his film days; other parts cover his radio days, which formed a transitional bridge for him to cross

■ *A Day at the Races*, one of the early Marx Brothers films, is considered a classic.

from film to television. The Center has indexes to the NBC, NPR, and BBC programs. The Library does not have all the productions listed in the indexes, but researchers will be able to assemble a complete listing of Groucho's appearances for these entities.

The "NBC Radio Collection Index," in addition to being an index, provides information about the thousands of NBC programs and scripts in the main collection. It lists over seventy radio appearances by Groucho, most from the 1940s and early 1950s. A partial list of the entries indicates the breadth of Groucho's work:*The Rudy Vallee Show* (from 1941 and 1942), *Information Please* (a quiz show, 1941), *Dinah Shore's Open House* (1944 and 1945), *The Chase and Sanborn Program* (1945), *The Andrew Sisters Show* (1945), and *The Big Show* (Groucho was on several shows in 1951 and 1952).

The "National Public Radio Index" lists several interviews, appreciations, and news notes. The "BBC Sound Archive Index" identifies BBC radio programs that had Groucho as a guest, including interviews and performances. One key to reading the BBC index is that if an entry has "LP" by the number, the Library probably has a copy.

There are also a number of recordings which contain the comedy of Groucho Marx, some of which are commercial. Here are some of the materials in the Recorded Sound Reference Center that are commercially available:

■ *The Mikado*. Originally issued on Columbia Records in 1960. Presented on the *Bell Telephone Hour* on NBC-TV.

Starring Groucho Marx as Ko-Ko. Norman Luboff Choir, Bell Telephone Orchestra, Donald Voorhees, conductor.

■ *Groucho Marx and Jerry Colonna* (Ace of Hearts 103). A reissue of: *Hooray For Captain Spaulding* (Decca). Several of Groucho's favorite songs, the majority from his films.

■ *Salute to Groucho Marx*. Sound recording. Air Forces Radio and Television Service. 1977, 2 hours, 30 minutes. The recording includes an interview with Groucho, who talks about how he got started and how the brothers got their nicknames. There are also excerpts of his guest appearances on radio in the 1940s.

■ *A Tribute to Groucho Marx*. AFRTS, 1977, 25 minutes.

■ *The Marx Brothers*. The original voice tracks from their greatest movies. Decca DL 79168.

■ *An Evening with Groucho Marx*. A&M Records, 1972, two-record set. Songs and monologues recorded live at Carnegie Hall, New York.

The MBRS collections on Groucho Marx are considerably enhanced by the fact that they include far more than just his most popular works. For example, one film documentary, *Screen Snapshots* (1943) has a profile of Groucho doing a radio broadcast. A short film, *Monkey Business* (circa 1930), has the same title as their popular film, but is actually a clip of one of their vaudeville skits.

One of Groucho's top successes came late in life and is often the first thing to pop into people's minds when his name is mentioned. *You Bet Your Life* started on radio in

■ Groucho with Carmen Miranda in *Copacabana* (1947), which was one of the first movies Groucho made after the Brothers went their separate ways.

■ A scene from *Copacabana* (1947).

■ *Love Happy* (1950) gave Groucho the chance to work without his famous brothers, but the film was not a success.

■ *Double Dynamite* (1950) paired Groucho with Frank Sinatra.

■ Groucho and cigar, this time on television, in
You Bet Your Life.

1947 before it was introduced on NBC-TV in 1950 and ran until 1961. During the first few years it was on television, it continued to be broadcast on radio. It was essentially a comedy show masquerading as a quiz show; it existed to showcase Groucho's wit and sarcasm, some scripted, much ad-libbed. He interviewed the contestants before they played the quiz. Each show also had a secret word; if a contestant said the word during the program, a stuffed duck would drop down with a hundred dollar bill. The show brought Groucho an Emmy Award in 1950 as television's "Most Outstanding Personality." Groucho's personal copies of his series were donated to the Smithsonian and then transferred to the Library of Congress.

MBRS has the NBC Television Collection and its index lists over forty shows under Groucho's name, including "The Mikado" (*Bell Telephone Hour*, 1960) and *The Tonight Show* (in addition to guest appearances, he hosted the show for a week in 1962). Groucho hosted the *Kraft Music Hall* special "A Taste of Funny" (1967). The last show Groucho, Harpo, and Chico appeared in together was a *General Electric Theater* production in 1959 called "The Incredible Jewel Robbery."

Other Marx family members who can be found in the indexes are Harpo, Gummo, Chico, and Zeppo. Even Groucho's daughter and son are listed. But a listing in the index does not automatically indicate that the show they appeared on is included in the Library's collection.

Film scripts are available in two locations: MBRS and the Manuscript Division. Some of the titles included are: *A Day at the Circus*, *A Day at the Races*, *A Night at the Opera*, *A Night in Casablanca*, *Animal Crackers*, *Copacabana*, *Duck Soup*, *Go West*, *It's Only Money*, *Monkey Business*, and *Room Service*.

The Music Division

A fascinating collection of sheet music from the Marx Brothers films can be found in the Music Division. The biggest surprise is that Irving Berlin wrote the music for *The Cocoanuts* for Groucho. Another top songwriter of the era, Harry Ruby, cowrote music for *Animal Crackers*. Groucho played Captain Spaulding in the film, which contained one of Groucho's best-known songs, "Hooray for Captain Spaulding," written by Harry Ruby and Bert Kalmar. Both Irving Berlin and Harry Ruby were friends of Groucho and remained so through regular correspondence. Their letters are part of Groucho's correspondence collection.

The Manuscript Division

Aside from the film scripts mentioned above, the Manuscript Division has a valuable collection of over a thousand items from Groucho Marx's private papers covering the years from 1930 to 1966. A great part of the collection includes letters between Groucho and Fred Allen, Goodman Ace, T. S. Eliot, and others. Holding and reading the letters, you can feel the spirit of the man and his personality. The clearest picture of the personal life of Groucho Marx is presented by the man himself through his

■ Groucho corresponded with a number of famous people over the years. He is shown here holding some of those letters, which he donated to the Library's Manuscript Division.

intimate letters to friends and family over the years. He wrote in the same style as he spoke—with humor. Many of these letters appear in *The Groucho Letters*. In addition to the letters, there are a dozen film scripts and the manuscripts for two of his books: *Memories of a Mangy Lover* and *Groucho and Me*.

Particularly revealing is his correspondence with comedian Fred Allen and writers Norman Krasna and Arthur Sheekman. Norman Krasna was an Academy Award-winning screenwriter, playwright, director, and producer. A writer specializing in comedies, he cowrote a play with Groucho titled *Time for Elizabeth*, which had a short run in 1948. Groucho also collaborated with close friend Arthur Sheekman, who was a scriptwriter and a playwright. Their work together included some of Groucho's early books, and Arthur wrote the introduction to *The Groucho Letters*. He also collaborated on a number of Marx Brothers films, including *Monkey Business* and *Duck Soup*. Some of his other screen credits include *The Gladiator*, *Call Me Madam*, and *Some Came Running*.

Surfing the Internet for Groucho

The Library of Congress has established an Internet site: <http://lcweb.loc.gov>, which provides considerable information for researchers through access to its catalog and to the Copyright Office databases, which contain information about books, films, recordings, and other materials. In addition, each reading room has a location on the site that introduces its unique collection. However, be aware that the site does not provide access to everything at the Library. Many collections have not been cataloged and therefore cannot be found on the Internet.

Once you become aware of the Groucho materials

April 18, 1956

Dear Irving:

    I suppose you're still sunning yourself on the sunny shores of the Everglades, but presume your staff will see to it that this reaches you.

    First of all, thanks for the impressive parcel of songs, plus the catalogue and your invitation to "roll my own". Little did you know! While perusing it, I found some fifty-odd pieces (list attached) that I'd like to add to my repertoire.

    Next time let me have your address so that my thanks can reach you directly, rather than strained through a telephone wire from New York.

    Warmest regards,

Mr. Irving Berlin
Irving Berlin Music Corp.
1650 Broadway
New York 19, N.Y.

GM:db
encl.

■ Irving Berlin wrote music for Groucho's film and stage appearances and was a long-time personal friend.

January 14, 1964

Dear Eddie:

The two biggest laughs that I can recall (other than my three marriages) were in a vaudeville act called "Home Again."

One was when Zeppo came out from the wings and announced, "Dad, the garbage man is here." I replied, "Tell him we don't want any."

The other was when Chico shook hands with me and said, "I would like to say goodbye to your wife," and I said, "Who wouldn't?"

I'm glad you're working, for when one is laboring in the vineyards he hasn't time to get mixed up with other dames.

I've often told Harry Ruby that I would like to come to see you with him, but he always gives me curious answers.

Take care of yourself.

Regards,

Groucho Marx

GM:db

Mr. Eddie Cantor
9360 Monte Leon Lane
Beverly Hills, California

Groucho donated two of his best jokes to Eddie Cantor for his column in the Diners' Club magazine.

May 9, 1944.

Dear Mr. Sheekman,

      Enclosed find a check for $1.44 --
your share of the income on "Beds" from 7/1 to 12/31/43.
You made $1.44 clear for yourself on "Beds". I know
a girl who, last night, on Melrose Avenue made $11
clear on beds and had a lot of fun besides. The moral
is obvious: you are in the wrong racket, so throw away
that fountain pen and get a fountain syringe; throw
away that ream of paper and encase yourself in a lacy
nightie; toss out your thesaurus and don a pair of
silkie nylons. As far as income tax in concerned,
this lady on Melrose has no traffic with the revenue
department. There is no way of actually checking on
her activities except through a keyhole and Morgenthau's
manikins haven't gone that far yet.

      Please cash this check quickly for,
if Dewey is elected, I predict another bank holiday.

      Yours sincerely,

      Groucho.

His friend and occasional cowriter, Arthur Sheekman, was
a top scriptwriter in his own right.

June 19, 1961

T.S. Eliot, Esq.
Faber and Faber, Ltd.
24 Russell Square
London W.C.1, England

Dear T.S.:

Your photograph arrived in good
shape and I hope this note of thanks finds
you in the same condition.

I had no idea you were so hand-
some. Why you haven't been offered the lead
in some sexy movies I can only attribute to
the basic stupidity of the casting directors.

Should I come to London I will
certainly take advantage of your kind invitation and if you come to California I hope
you will allow me to do the same.

Cordially,

Groucho Marx

GM:db

■ This note was written at the start of a friendship between
Groucho and T. S. Eliot.

throughout the Library of Congress, you can almost feel him running about with his sloping walk, flipping the ashes from his cigar, and raising his eyebrows at the joy of being in the same archives as past presidents and many of the world's greatest writers.

The illustrations are from the collections of the Motion Picture, Broadcasting, and Recorded Sound Division and the Manuscript Division.

The following books were written by Groucho Marx and can be found in the Library of Congress: *Beds* (1930, 1977), *Many Happy Returns* (1942), *Time For Elizabeth* (1949, Norman Krasna, coauthor), *Groucho and Me* (1959), *Memories of a Mangy Lover* (1964), *The Groucho Letters* (1967, 1987, Richard J. Anobile, coauthor), *The Secret Word Is Groucho* (1976), *The Groucho Phile* (1976), and most recently *Groucho Marx and Other Short Stories and Tall Tales* (1993).

One book coauthored by Groucho has an excellent set of photos. It is *The Marx Brothers Scrapbook* by Groucho Marx and Richard J. Anobile (1973). It contains a number of photos of Groucho and his brothers early in their careers with their mother (Minnie Palmer), Groucho and Margaret Dumont, and friends Harry Ruby and Arthur Sheekman.

Groucho's children have written about their father. His daughter, Miriam Marx, wrote *Love, Groucho*, letters from Groucho Marx to her (1992). The broadest picture is presented in a series of books by his son Arthur: *Life with Groucho* (1954), *Son of Groucho* (1972), *Groucho* (1988), *My Life with Groucho: A Son's Eye View* (1991, 19992).

Copyright © Barbara Pruett, 2000.

BARBARA PRUETT is a librarian, researcher, and writer who currently resides in Washington, D.C. In the early 1970s she was head of the Information/Research Center for Caesar Chavez's United Farm Workers before taking a position as head of Catholic University of America's Social Sciences Library. Recently she retired as library director for an international trade library. Currently she writes about subjects in the entertainment industry. Scarecrow Press has published two of her books: *Marty Robbins: Fast Cars and Country Music*, and *Entertainment Research: How To Do It and How To Use It*.

She also designs and maintains Web sites for people in the entertainment industry. Actor Patrick McGoohan, Country music performer Junior Brown, and international broadcaster Judy Massa are among those who have used her services.

A TRIBUTE TO

Gerard Joseph Mulligan

Born New York City, 1927

Died Darien, Connecticut, 1996

The Library Opens a Permanent Exhibition for the Gerry Mulligan Collection

BY IRIS NEWSOM

In a career that spanned six decades, Gerry Mulligan firmly established himself as one of the great jazz innovators and saxophonists. He left an incredible legacy as a composer, arranger, instrumentalist, songwriter, and bandleader. His life and legacy were celebrated by the Library on what would have been his seventy-second birthday—April 6, 1999—by the opening of a permanent exhibition of the Gerry Mulligan Collection in the foyer of its Performing Arts Reading Room and the performance of an all-Mulligan concert in the evening in the Coolidge Auditorium.

One of the giants of jazz, Gerry Mulligan had a distinctive, personal style. Pianist-composer Dave Brubeck once said, "When you listen to Gerry Mulligan, you hear the past, the present, and the future." As a saxophone player, whose technical mastery and expressive range continued to grow throughout his career, Mulligan was an international jazz celebrity. As a composer-arranger and improviser, his extensive discography attests to his originality, versatility, and rhythmic vitality. As Jon Newsom, Chief of the Music Division, has written for the permanent exhibition, "Gerry Mulligan, composer, arranger, and instrumentalist, was a self-taught virtuoso whose elegant and original ideas changed the sound of jazz and enriched many other musical genres. As a performer, he made the baritone saxophone an eloquent vehicle for brilliant solo improvisation. As an arranger, he used the contrapuntal genius so evident in his ensemble playing, combined with his refined sense of orchestral color, to weave the rich textures that characterized his work even as a young artist. As a composer, he created pieces that are among the distinctive icons of a great era in American music.

"His youthful work shows an early mastery of the complex idiom of jazz in the 1940s and 1950s. He could spin out, with the best of his generation, a long and playful line with brilliant and unexpected turns. His classic *Young*

Blood, composed for the Stan Kenton band and recorded for the album *New Concepts of Artistry in Rhythm*, treats Kenton's large ensemble, while taking full advantage of its powerful forces, with the deftness and transparency that would later make his "Pianoless Quartet" among the most successful innovations in the history of jazz.

"Gerry Mulligan's great versatility resulted in fruitful experiments with a variety of musicians beyond the world of jazz. He worked with Anita Loos on a musical, and with Judy Holliday as lyricist. The popular music of Brazil, flourishing in a culture as richly diverse as that of North America, nourished American music through the artistic collaboration between Mulligan and Antonio Carlos Jobim. Mulligan also joined forces with Argentina's legendary composer and bandoneonist, Astor Piazzola, long before the widespread revival of interest in the tango. Mulligan was noted for his exploration of different instrumental combinations, as in his landmark recording *The Age of Steam* and in the *Birth of the Cool* album. Moreover, at the invitation of Zubin Mehta, he composed for the traditional symphony orchestra. Throughout his creative life, Gerry Mulligan achieved even greater beauty and nobility of tone in his playing."

The exhibition, mounted by the Library's Interpretive Programs Office, is the brainchild of Jon Newsom, who negotiated the donation of the collection with Gerry Mulligan before he died and afterward collaborated with his wife, Franca Rota Mulligan, who donated the centerpiece of the exhibition—Mulligan's gold-plated Conn baritone saxophone. This is the instrument that Mulligan played in all public performances during the last decade of his life. Crafted by C. G. Conn in Elkhart, Indiana, it was Mulligan's preferred instrument, capable of greater projection than his older silver-plated saxophone, also a Conn, which he used for recordings. Some of the items now on dis-

play (others will be shown in the future on a rotating basis) include the Grammy Award Mulligan received for his album *Walk on the Water*, photographs that document Mulligan's long career, music manuscripts in his hand, record covers, performance programs and posters, and a photograph of Gerry and Franca Rota Mulligan with President Clinton and Hillary Rodham Clinton at the White House, below which is a letter of condolence to Mrs. Mulligan with a handwritten note from the president which reads: "No one ever played that horn like he did, and no one *ever* will." Dominating the back wall of the exhibition is a set of eight handsome wood- block prints in various hues, showing a larger-than-life close-up of Mulligan's face. The prints, by the artist Antonio Frasconi, were his gift to Mulligan's wife, who is also the president of Mulligan Publishing Company.

The entire Mulligan Collection consists of some seven hundred items now being processed by the Music Division. They are divided into several categories reflecting Mulligan's diverse interests and accomplishments from his adolescent years until his death. Included are music for recordings, lead sheets and sketches, arrangements and parts for his Concert Jazz Band, miscellaneous arrangements for his tentet, small-band arrangements, a few symphonic arrangements, correspondence with jazz notables, and papers relating to different concerts and projects.

At the opening ceremony for the exhibition on the afternoon of April 6th, Librarian of Congress James H. Billington remarked that "Gerry Mulligan would not, could not be categorized, and he flourished through changing times, in many cultures, and with many musical voices ranging from the baritone saxophone that was his principal instrument, to the full orchestra." The Venerable Thamthog Rinpoche, abbot of monasteries in Tibet, director and master of the Center for Tibetan Studies in Milan, and a close friend of Mulligan and his wife came from Italy to bless Mulligan's saxophone and drape a ceremonial scarf, or "Kata," on it. In the evening, the Gerry Mulligan Tribute Band performed an all-Mulligan concert in the Coolidge Auditorium as part of the Library of Congress Concert Series. Featured were longtime Mulligan colleagues and former members of his various groups: trombonist Bob Brookmeyer (who also led the band), bassist Dean Johnson, pianist Ted Rosenthal, drummer Ron Vincent, baritone saxophonist Scott Robinson (who played Mulligan's instrument), alto and tenor saxophonist Dick Oatts, and trumpeter Randy Brecker.

Gerry Mulligan was a self-taught virtuoso whose elegant and original ideas changed the sound of jazz and enriched many other musical genres. He was inducted into the ASCAP Wall of Fame on September 14, 2000.

Index

Page numbers in italics indicate illustrations.